To Linden
Church
Women's Ministry Dept.
God bless,

Josh 1:1-9

Pastor [signature]

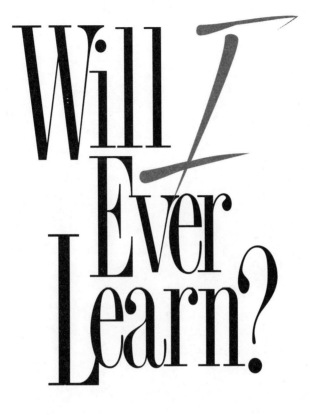

# Will I Ever Learn?

## One Woman's Life of Miracles and Ministry

## Hyveth Williams

REVIEW AND HERALD® PUBLISHING ASSOCIATION
HAGERSTOWN, MD 21740

This book was
Edited by Jeannette R. Johnson
Designed by Ron J. Pride
Cover photos by Dennis Crews
Typeset: 11/14 Utopia


PRINTED IN U.S.A.


06 05 04 03          7 6 5 4


**R&H Cataloging Service**
Williams, Hyveth
       Will I ever learn? One woman's life
of miracles and ministry.

       I. Williams, Hyveth Page.   I. Title.

                 [B]


ISBN 0-8280-1098-6

# Acknowledgments

# To God Be the Glory!

My undying gratitude goes to my son, Steven, who prefers to be called Steve; my mother, Margaret Page; my sister, Renita Taylor; my brother, Trevor Page, who is still where I once was; my friends Ella Taylor, Olive Wheeler, Ivybelle Royce, Gerry Pruitt Davis; my friends at Sligo church and members of the Boston Temple; and the multitude who have helped me through bitter and sweet experiences.

To Wendy Bahramian, without whom I could not have completed this project, I extend my heartfelt appreciation.

To the Bertram Melbourne family for their hospitality; Maysie and Alvin Wint for their care of my mother; Dr. Milton and Claudette Haynes for their generosity; Dr. William Rankin, dean and president of the Episcopal Divinity School in Boston, and the Reverend Janice Robinson of the College of Preachers, Washington National Cathedral, for the gift of learning.

To the enthusiastic, brave practitioners of our faith, who are determined to know nothing more than Jesus Christ, and Him crucified.

And to those wonderful, preaching women, who know how rocky is the road we tread, thanks for your commitment that gives me strength and encouragement.

# Contents

# Chapter One

# My Story

**M**ine was a Damascus Road conversion. My world was turned upside down by direct, divine intervention. I had no idea of the impact this would have on my son, Steven, or on my responsibilities as a single mother. My former friends are still astonished by the dramatic transformation from an atheist to a Christian. The metamorphosis began in Hartford, Connecticut, where I was a successful executive assistant to Mayor George A. Athanson.

In 1978, after nearly eight years of serving the city in this capacity, I decided to resign my post and challenge my boss in the upcoming mayoral election. This wasn't the first time I had toyed with such an idea. That seed was planted in my ambitious heart the first time I met the mayor at a political rally in the fall of 1970.

Hartford's duly elected mayor, a Republican female, was appointed by President Nixon to a post in the Department of Transportation in Washington, D.C. Her deputy, Attorney George Athanson, a Democrat, automatically became acting mayor. Athanson, a gregarious Greek whose political fortunes were made—and later lost—on his ability to ingest every kind of ethnic food, kiss multitudes of babies, and outtalk his opponents, was gaining attention for his Laguardiaesque comic relief at official gatherings.

I was women's editor at WINF radio in Manchester, Connecticut, working as an account executive during the week and cohosting a talk show on Sunday mornings. One Sunday on the show, I echoed the sentiments of the negative press reports regarding Athanson's performance by announcing that I could do a better job than the acting mayor if I were blindfolded with both hands tied behind my back.

At that very moment a police officer who was chauffeuring the mayor to an appointment in his cruiser happened across my station just as I was berating his boss. The mayor ordered the officer to drive to the station, marched into the studio, and challenged me to spend two weeks on the job with him. Then, if I found that I could do a better job than he was attempting to do, he would resign.

Well! Opportunity was not only knocking on my door, it had just been escorted into my life by a mayor and a police officer. I accepted the challenge on the spot.

On our first appointment with a university political science class, the mayor was most articulate and admirably dynamic in his presentation. I was both enchanted and alarmed—though I had great ambitions, I was illiterate when it came to American politics, having arrived from England less than a year before. I determined to read all I could on the subject so that I could be conversant and relevant on the issues affecting the city. By the end of the two weeks the enormous needs of the people who were recovering from the devastating race riots of 1969 and early 1970 led to my commitment to serve humanity.

So in April 1971, when acting mayor George Athanson became the mayor of Hartford, beginning the first of five terms, I accepted his offer of a full-time position in his office as receptionist. In January 1972 I was promoted when the mayor selected me, with the city council's approval, from among 75 applicants to serve as his executive assistant. Thus began my meteoric rise to the top of the city hall professional ladder. As time passed, I received kudos from city residents, letters of commendation in local newspapers, and citations from the Kiwanis Club and Chamber of Commerce. The Hartford City Council, the Connecticut General Assembly, and the United States Conference of Mayors added their praise. By 1978 I was convinced that I deserved to be mayor. I was running the office anyway and enjoyed the admiration of the people, both at city hall and in the community. The increasing plaudits from local and national organizations seemed to confirm this.

My job as executive assistant included representing the mayor when he was unable to attend engagements. One day as I addressed a group from the insurance industry, the audience seemed to be simply mesmerized by my presentation. After a long standing ovation, several remarked to me that I should be mayor. Blinded by ambition, I decided to challenge my boss for the job of mayor. Consequently, our working relationship became increasingly sour until I finally had no alternative but to quit.

My resignation created an unexpected feeding frenzy in the local press. Newspaper headlines shouted, *Athanson Forces Aide Out Early* and *A Mayor Without a Staff!* Editorials in Connecticut's largest newspaper bemoaned my resignation. The station manager of Channel 3 asked, "What's happened to the mayor?" As producer of the mayor's weekly half-hour TV program, I took the opportunity to present my own report on the city on WTIC radio. The telephone calls, letters of support, and subsequent job offers were astounding. Placing my political future in the hands of a small group of experienced, successful political candidate makers, I quickly became a shooting star to which everyone seemed eager to hitch his or her wagon.

With the idea of garnering as much positive notice in the press as I could, I began feeding documents to reporters who exposed some corrupt activities and ethically questionable actions in city government. I became the driving force in the creation of Organized Northeasterners, an organization that later renovated houses in the north quadrant of the city so that low-income families could own their own homes. My political fortunes were incredibly boosted when this idea took off. Other candidates, including the late Governor Ella Grasso, vigorously courted me for my endorsement.

Professionally, my life was very successful. Personally, I was falling apart. Added to the pressures of being a political candidate, I was involved in an intimate, dysfunctional relationship that was causing me excruciating emotional trauma. The stress began to manifest itself in many ways—sleeplessness, paranoia, loss of self-confidence. I began to hear an "alien" voice, mellow and comforting, yet disturbing in its persistence, whispering, "Your time has come!" What time? What did this all mean? My political advisors were convinced I was headed for a nervous breakdown. Privately, I thought I was teetering on the brink of insanity, and one adverse decision would throw me off the precipice into total madness. I had to withdraw from the mayoral campaign before it even got under way officially.

By Christmas, whether out of fear or because the Holy Spirit was wooing me, I began to think about going to church for the first time since I'd been a teenager. I quickly put the thought out of my mind, reminding myself that I was a confirmed atheist. I was simply reacting to a tough time in my life. Even when a fire started at a party, where enough alcohol flowed to fuel a lake of fire that nearly burned my house to the ground, I still laughed with my infidel friends at the idea of God intervening in my life. We concluded that Christians, unlike us, were only weak people with no inner resources to control their destinies. We would never allow ourselves to be duped like the "Jesus freaks" who roamed the city, annoying us by knocking at our doors, trying to introduce us to their God. We would not solicit their God's help; we would depend on our self-determination.

In spite of this clever declaration, the "alien" voice gave me no rest. One afternoon a TV reporter was interviewing me in front of my home regarding my response to a local issue. Just as I began to speak in my most official, concerned-candidate voice, I heard my name called, loud as a peal of thunder.

"Hyveth, your time has come!"

Surely the reporter and cameraman and all the nosy neighbors peering out of their windows heard it!

"Say what?" I shouted back. Turning my face to the sky I screamed, "Either tell me what you want from me or leave me alone!"

The startled reporter instructed the cameraman to stop rolling the film, circling a finger around his ear to indicate I was "cuckoo."

I stormed into my house, slamming the front door behind me, and leaned against the door, my heart racing, cold sweat breaking out on my forehead. I cried out for relief from this unknown invader of my psyche.

I had to get help. My psychiatrist, chosen not only for his reputation as an excellent physician but, more importantly, because he was an avowed atheist, had introduced me to the writings of Karl Jung, Elizabeth Kübler Ross, and Jean Paul Sartre. When I told him about the voice his answer angered and shocked me. "If this is the Christian God calling you, answer. Go with Him. If you obey all that He says you will never need me, or any other psychiatrist, again!"

After all the money I had invested in this therapy he was telling me to find a minister to help guide me to what he kept referring to as "a higher power"? I felt betrayed, but I knew even then that I would follow his recommendations.

In those days I had no confidence in religious people. As administrator of the mayor's ministerial alliance, I met monthly with local clergy from nearly every denomination in the city. And I made sure I was never alone with any of these men of the cloth in an elevator or a car because it was like fighting off an octopus. So I struggled alone, waiting for the worst to happen.

A few months later, when I consulted my personal astrologer, he warned me of impending doom. As he always did, he took my jade ring and began rubbing the green stone. Immediately, he went into a trance, speaking in my native Jamaican patois dialect, swaying and groaning. Finally, he spoke. "I see two roads. One leads to fame and fortune."

I was elated when he described my road to riches. His advice had been good in the past. On his recommendation, I had incorporated a business that provided young fashion designers with a public forum for presenting their creations. The first event had drawn hundreds of patrons and received excellent media coverage. I now had new investors, and my public relations company seemed poised on the brink of a major breakthrough in the local fashion world.

But now the astrologer was moaning, looking as though he were about to faint. "But I see another road—dark and foreboding . . . Don't go down that road, whatever you do!" He grabbed the table for support. "Don't go down that road!" he shouted again. "I can't see to the end of it! Danger and death await you there!" he exclaimed dramatically before fainting to the floor, overcome by the darkness he had seen on that road in my future.

I left that session more terrified of death than I had been in my entire life. Years later, I would agree that the astrologer had been right. Being an agent of the devil, the dangerous road he foresaw was my conversion. He couldn't see how "death" could bring such beautiful new life. He couldn't understand how a new creature could come out of the chrysalis of corruption.

One day shortly after this incident, I was involved in a terrible fight with the mayor over confidential files I had stolen from his personal cabinet before resigning and carefully hidden in the flue of my fireplace. Finally, the personnel director of the city was called to mediate between us. I was very angry, and used the foulest language I could think of in an effort to intimidate the mayor.

In a very calm voice, the personnel director interrupted our hot words. "Hyveth, a soft answer turneth away wrath."

I stopped, shamed into silence, as his words penetrated my darkened heart like bullets. After the meeting he invited me to his office and told me how he had been an alcoholic, destroying his marriage, alienating his children, and jeopardizing his career. Then Jesus Christ came into his life and gave him strength to turn away from the spirit in a bottle to the Spirit in the Word. He gave me a red-covered King James version of the Bible and I went home, planning to quickly leaf through it before putting it aside. Instead, I was drawn to it like a magnet. I sat down to read a text or two, but in about three days had read the whole thing, from Genesis to Revelation. It then became clear to me that the voice I had been hearing was not confusion in my head or stress in my life; it was the voice of God calling me!

As the truth of this began to sink in, I thought of the times I had attempted suicide, not because I wanted to die, but because I wanted relief from my guilt-ridden, fear-filled past. I had used drugs, alcohol, sex, partying, and every secular humanist ploy to fill the emptiness in my broken heart. Finally, I decided that no God would allow a little girl to suffer as I had. So I embraced atheism. In an effort to overcome some childhood issues, I had created an entirely new persona. For almost 10 years I became an aggressive, career-driven, self-educated, alcohol-swizzling, cigar- and three-pack-a-day-smoking, workaholic feminist who always wore pants and an Equal Rights Amendment bracelet. At a time when there was no legal recourse against sexual discrimination, I abhorred being treated like "the little woman," and became one tough, foul-mouthed cookie whose nickname at city hall was "Big H."

Not until I became a converted Christian was I was able to face my past and become reconciled with it. From the time I was 2 years old, I had been sexually violated by teenage cousins, and later by older adults until I was 16. To cope with this, I invented a little girl who had had a happy childhood. But as I grew older, the made-up child became an amoral woman, who soon began to battle for supremacy over the real little girl who had been so abused, but was now crying out for acceptance and love. As these two personalities struggled for recognition, it became almost impossible to keep the lies and fictitious stories of a happy childhood straight. Perhaps the greatest gift that salvation has brought into my personal life has been God's grace to integrate that little girl into a healthy, emotionally-healed, mature adult.

During this time I was hearing the "alien" voice, one of my political advisors was a Seventh-day Adventist. I knew he didn't smoke, use alcohol, or swear like the majority of us did, but I didn't know it was because of a particular religious affiliation. A year after my conversion and baptism into the Adventist Church in London, England, I returned to the United States and visited a church in Hartford. There was my former associate leading the song service! As I sat there that Sabbath morning, I praised the Lord for not only saving me and bringing me into this incredible message, but for also touching one of my friends. I couldn't wait to hear the story of his journey. When he recognized me, he introduced me to the congregation. I seized the opportunity to ask when and how he had become an Adventist. To my surprise, he told me he had been a Seventh-day Adventist for more than 30 years, educated in Adventist schools, graduating with a master's degree. He taught in Adventist academies and eventually landed a prestigious post in city government, where we met.

I was shocked. He had never mentioned God to me. As I remembered the turmoil I experienced when I began to hear voices during my aborted political career, and how he had never even offered me a consoling word, a pamphlet, or a prayer, I became angry. Left up to him, I would still be drowning my sorrows in the bitter waters of the world. When I confronted him, he excused his failure to share the gospel by reminding me that my lifestyle, attitude, and profanity made it seem to him that I was "unsavable." How often do we make these kinds of judgments about family, friends, and coworkers as we withhold the dynamic, life-transforming truth of God from them? We dare not analyze appearance for we cannot convert anyone; it is the work of the Holy Spirit. Our privilege is to share the gospel and let God do the rest, for our God can do anything!

As I read the Bible, my life began to change rapidly. I was reading the book of Isaiah the day the plumber arrived to repair my hot water heater. He immediately recognized the Bible and asked how long I had been a Christian. When I told him I really wasn't a Christian, he sighed. If he, a churchgoer, couldn't understand Isaiah, then surely a nonbeliever like me wouldn't.

I invited him to sit down while I read a chapter and explained it to him. He listened in rapt astonishment. I even amazed myself at my grasp of it. Memories of my years at Oberlin High School, a Christian boarding school in Jamaica, flooded my mind. Things pertaining to God that I had given no thought to in years suddenly seemed familiar, encouraging me to read further and study more.

That week, as I read through the entire Bible, the personnel director from city hall called and invited me to his church for a prayer meeting. I went. It was a small group of about six people and the minister. I don't remember any of the minister's words, but at the end he asked if anyone wanted to give his or her life to Christ. I didn't really know what that might mean, but a lady sitting near me took me by the hand and knelt with me, praying earnestly that God would come into my life. As she spoke so eloquently on my behalf, my cold, calculating, unemotional exterior began to melt away. Her words cut to my heart and I began to feel awfully corrupt and filthy, helpless and lost. Soon I was crying uncontrollably, something I would never allow myself to do in public since I regarded tears as a sign of weakness and lack of self-control. That evening, among strangers in the Baptist church, I opened my heart to Jesus Christ and, though lacking in Christian graces, invited Him into my life. I had no idea what this would mean.

The very next day the newspapers ran a big story about corruption at city hall, based on information I had leaked to my best friend, an investigative reporter. I was naive about the impact my actions would have, and thoroughly unprepared for the reaction from some of those who were exposed to federal investigations of the situation. There were threats on my life. My phone was tapped. I was followed.

One day while visiting a friend, we noticed a strange car parked in front of her home. In it sat a man with a shotgun across his lap. We were terrified and called some of the men in her family to escort me away from the danger. Even when a professor friend from the University of Connecticut kept me hidden in his secluded home for the weekend, my whereabouts were discovered because, as I learned later, I had forwarded my telephone calls to his home. He had to sneak me out at night and sequester me in a motel.

I finally became tired of running, dragging my young son from place to place, losing his toys, losing my mind. So I returned home, but I hired an armed bodyguard to travel with me and show my opponents that I was in this fight to the bitter end and would not be intimidated by their scare tactics. At one tense confrontation, some of my supporters accompanied me to the mayor's office for a showdown over actions the mayor had taken to eliminate my participation in a federally-funded program for which I was researching and writing. I suddenly blurted out the fact that my life was being threatened and that I had hired a bodyguard, who was also present at the meeting. The mayor informed my bodyguard that the people who were making threats were only trying to frighten me into giving up my foolish resistance. He cautioned me to cooperate, because both he and his wife were also being pressured as a result of my actions. If I stopped, so would the threats. But if I didn't, he warned, he couldn't be responsible for the outcome.

I was too defiant for words. But when threats came against my son's life, and messages were left on my answering machine that he would be kidnapped while walking home from school, I panicked. My life became a nightmare. Like a scene from a spy movie, I decided to whisk my son out of the country to my family in England. I bought his ticket and made what I thought were fail-safe arrangements with the airlines to have an attendant look after him during the long flight. I knew I was being followed, so I purchased an auburn wig and large sunglasses to disguise myself as I carefully left home for the airport in a rented car. Once at the airport, I realized I had rushed out without my son's passport. No matter how much I pleaded, the airline would not accept him without it.

I was at my wit's end, pacing the floor in the waiting area, chain-smoking, and swearing under my breath at my stupidity.

"Hyveth, what are you doing here dressed like that?"

There stood an Immigration and Naturalization Service official with whom I had once worked.

"You're not supposed to recognize me; I'm incognito!" I blurted. When I told him my story, he said that he was on his way to Florida to participate in a big case related to a Nazi war criminal caught in the United States. He graciously signed the papers so my son could board the plane.

Unfortunately, by that time the flight had left and all my careful arrangements had gone awry, so I had to accompany Steven to New York. I boarded the plane, unaware that God had already started to take control of my life and was protecting my every step, no matter how foolish and outrageous I was.

I sometimes look back at those days and think that I was like a fish on a hook, thrashing about to free myself. All the while, the One who had caught me was carefully reeling me in so that He could one day train me as His disciple. Just as the first disciples were fishermen, called to leave their trade of catching live fish, destined to die, to begin catching dead men and women, like myself, who were destined to live by divine grace, so I was caught, even though I did not yet understand the profoundness of eternal life.

We arrived in New York just in time to hear the first boarding call for Steven's flight. But when I checked him in, they refused to allow him on board unless he had adult supervision. What was I to do? I sank down on the steps leading to the departure lounge and wept. My little boy climbed to the step above me and hugged me tightly, wiping away my tears with his bare hands. "Please, don't cry, Mommy. I'm here to look after you. I will always look after you."

Those comforting words, unforgettably special, restored my confidence. I began to ask all who passed us if they would be willing to "look after this very adorable child" on the flight to London. Finally, a kind English couple agreed to care for him, saying Steven reminded them of their only grandson whom they were leaving behind in New York and were already missing. I watched until his plane disappeared into the night sky.

I did not have a return ticket, so I had to catch a Trailways bus back to Hartford. The long ride was filled with haunting thoughts of hastily sending my son away and of the threats to my safety. I arrived in Hartford about 4:00 a.m. and took a cab to my home. The drama of my life was about to unfold.

I inserted my key in the lock and pushed against the door. It didn't yield an inch. I rattled the knob and tried again. Then I noticed the door had been dead-bolted from inside. I knew I had locked it from the outside before I left the previous afternoon. I pressed my face against the glass panels in the door. I could make out the silhouette of a chair by the door. Yesterday's newspaper, which I had left unopened on the sofa, was lying open on the floor next to the chair.

Most people would have realized something was amiss and run away, but I didn't. Perhaps my heart was too numb from the trials of the previous day, or maybe I was just too tired to think straight. I walked around to a side door. It opened instantly when I turned the key in the lock. As I pushed the door open, I caught sight of the shadow of a man pressed against the wall. My heart stopped beating. I couldn't scream. I couldn't run. How many times had I been in this nightmare? Only this time it was real.

I don't know how I got back to the street. I often comfort myself with the thought that my guardian angel intervened, as he did so often as I made the transition from the house of darkness into the marvelous light of our Lord Jesus Christ. I ran to a public telephone down the street and called a friend, telling her I was on my way, then called a cab. I was frightened beyond reasoning. Every person I saw could be a potential assassin, and danger lurked around each corner. On the way to my friend's house I instructed the cab driver to call another cab to pull up beside us, as though the drivers were talking. Then I crawled across the floor of my cab and slipped into the other cab, lying on the floor, terrified, until I reached my friend's home.

When I returned to my house a few days later with my lawyer, we saw that it had been terribly vandalized. An expensive television set, designed in the shape of a champagne glass, had been completely destroyed. Fragments of its glass covered the living room floor, as though from a terrific explosion. Messages of hate and threats of murder were scrawled across my beautiful walls in bright red lipstick. My two cats, who had never been allowed outside, were never seen again. The police found where the intruder had entered through a basement window. They took as evidence the glass from which he drank while waiting for me to come home. They filled out the proper reports for insurance purposes, but I was never given a final report of their investigation, even though I requested one many times.

Once I was safely inside my friend's home, I immediately called my secretary. I wanted her to know where I was so that if anything happened to me she could retrieve the confidential files I had stolen from the mayor's office and hidden in the flue of my fireplace. She was then to release the material directly to the press. What I did not know was that she had told an intern in my office about these documents. The intern was having an affair with my lawyer. After my lawyer visited my home to survey the damage, the intern secured a key from him, retrieved the files, and turned them over to one of her newspaper reporter friends. This situation had become as complex and confusing as the brainless plots of the soap operas I used to watch.

My friend made me comfortable on the sofa, and I immediately fell into a strange and troubled sleep. It was almost as though I was unconscious, my limbs numb and immobile, even though I could hear the sirens and other sounds of life outside the house. In my mind, I realized I was in trouble and would not be able to come out of this deep sleep, so I cried out for help. I could hear my voice, I could feel the power of the sound of it being forced from my throat, but no one could hear me as I slipped deeper into this comatose state.

I knew I was going to die. In an instant, it seemed as though I stepped outside my body, leaving it there on the sofa. My struggles for fame and fortune seemed to mock me now. I was a total failure with nothing to show for all the trouble I had seen. I hadn't accomplished my dream of being a movie star—and there had been so many opportunities in television and theater in England. My political dream of becoming the first Black, female mayor in the United States had never materialized, even though the opportunity had seemed to be mine for the taking. I had failed in marriage, and even in motherhood, while trying to make it in a man's world. Now here I was, about to die. Alone!

I began to cry deep, wrenching moans from the depths of my hungry heart. "I don't want to die! Please, I don't want to die! Somebody, please, help me!"

Many people who report their near-death experiences describe a light that guides them through a tunnel before the details of their lives are flashed before them. I had no such experience. What flashed across my mind were the different flavors of ice cream I had never tasted. "I don't want to die," I cried. "I haven't tasted Mississippi Mud or Pistachio Passion. I want to live so I can taste those flavors!"

While I was still speaking, a voice so sweet, so compassionate, so life-giving—a voice I knew then, as I do now, to be that of my Lord and Saviour, Jesus Christ—broke through the barrier of sin and said, "Come with Me, and I will give you peace and joy forever more!"

I quickly answered, "Yes!" and promised to follow, no matter what the cost.

He replied, "You will know that I spoke to you on this occasion because the following will come to pass. First, from this day forward, as long as you live upon this earth, wherever you go, no matter what the season or occasion, you will always find a flower and be reminded of this moment."

(I could fill volumes with these incidents.)

"Second," He continued, "you will know beyond a shadow of doubt that I have spoken to you because someone will come to your home and say, 'I have come to take you home!' And you must go." Afterward, I was to tell the world what He had done for me. At the time, this had no meaning because I had nothing to show what He had done. I was still immersed in sin, sometimes boasting that I was the wife of the devil to whom I had gladly given what was left of my soul. I would later come to recognize this instruction to be my call to ministry, especially since He secures many opportunities for me to give my testimony as I preach and teach His Word around the world.

I was not to repeat the third promise to anyone. It was a personal message for my life alone. However, on one occasion, years later, I felt as though it wouldn't matter if I shared it with some close friends. But when I tried to tell it, I was visibly confounded and couldn't remember the details of any part of my story. Now I obey!

The next morning my friend tried to shake me into consciousness. When her efforts to revive me failed, she thought I must be in a coma and was about to call an ambulance. At the same time, my secretary was on the phone, frantic from a disturbing dream she had had, in which she saw me being pushed from a porch, several stories above the ground. She said I was wearing a silk nightgown that blew in the breeze as my limp body crashed to the ground, where it lay broken in a pool of blood. The dream had been so real and frightening she immediately called to warn me of impending danger. I took her dream seriously, especially since, unknown to her, I was wearing the very nightgown she described.

Convinced that something supernatural had happened to me, and encouraged by Elizabeth, a friend from Egypt who gave me books on metaphysical phenomena, I bought a long, green gown from Elizabeth's boutique. I put it on and stood on a street corner in the north end of Hartford shouting, "Jesus saves!"

Someone tipped off my friends in the press that I was having a nervous breakdown in public. They told my political advisors who came and dragged me, kicking and screaming, to a safe house. There they administered a few friendly slaps to my face to stop the hysteria, as well as generous doses of alcohol to mellow me out.

For weeks after this episode I refused to smoke, touch alcohol, or use foul language. I began to speak in the language of the King James Bible because that's what I thought good Christians did. "How art thou?" I greeted my friends, and everything was "thee" and "thine." I didn't know how to pray, so I hung my head out an upstairs window, focused on the stars, and shouted with all my might, "Hey, J. C.!" (I was too scared to call His name, Jesus Christ, being aware, in a primitive way, that I was a sinner and He a Holy God.) "This is Hyveth Williams! Remember me?" I supplied my Social Security number and address, in case that would help place me. "I'm the one You spoke to the other day." Then I shared my gratitude and grievances. As primal as that praying was, it was invested with a spiritual power I sometimes long for these days.

For weeks I was "holier than thou." I walked about in my long green gown trying to convince everyone that Jesus saves. I tried to manipulate people into saying, "I have come to take you home," the magic words from my dream. But nobody ever did. My few remaining friends thought I had gone stark, raving mad.

It was right in the middle of all this that the ambitious intern from my office gave my "fireplace" files to her reporter friend. And he, eager to score points by coming up with a big scoop, took the files to his editor. Upon reviewing the documents, the editor decided he had no choice but to run a story about the corruption in city government. I will never forget the taste of fear that filled my mouth and spread like gall into my stomach when I received the telephone call that "all hell was about to break loose when the morning papers hit the street."

I discovered that evening that God was with me. I went to a secluded place on the campus of Trinity College, near my home, and sat on a huge rock overlooking the skyline of West Hartford. There I laid my fractured heart before God and cried out for His intervention, interlacing my pleas with promises of good behavior for ever and ever. I left that hallowed hill hours later to beg the editor to give me a break—or at least a few days to get out of town. I was too emotionally devastated to face the music. My pleas seemed to make him more determined than ever to publish the story. The substance of the files he had examined had whetted his appetite to uncover the source of the corruption at city hall. Many careers would be made and destroyed in the city as a result of the ensuing series of articles filed by his top investigative reporter, who uncovered much more than they had gotten from me. Only after I shared how his reporter had acquired my files did the editor agree to modify the headline.

Now it was no longer a secret that I had had a role in the newspaper reports. As a result, I became *persona non grata* in the city I had come to love. By this time, I was no longer affiliated with the mayor's office. I was hired by Channel 3 TV and sent on assignment with one of their star reporters. We were to interview Harvard University students who had organized a sit-in support of a union that had called a strike among all the nonfaculty employees. We spent the entire day roaming the halls of that Ivy League institution before returning to the office to edit our videotape for the evening news.

While I was waiting for another reporter to complete his edits, Emily, the woman who was responsible for the various story assignments, came in to speak to me. She accused me of trying to steal her boyfriend, the reporter I had worked with that day. When she identified him as her secret lover, I blurted out, "But he's a married man!" I immediately realized the probable outcome of that remark when Emily angrily reminded me that her father was an important reporter at CBS news and she had the power to make or break me.

Sure enough, the next day the station manager informed me that he had to let me go because they couldn't afford insurance coverage for me. I was sure Emily had had something to do with it, but I later learned that the station manager was yielding to political pressure because I had been blacklisted.

It was impossible for me to find work in a city where, a few weeks before, I couldn't keep up with the demand for my time and talents or avoid the press that seemed to follow me everywhere I went. No one returned my telephone calls; no one accepted my invitations to lunch. I was being isolated and punished. The stress of being publicly ignored and privately scrutinized became almost unbearable. I drank more alcohol and ate less food. I looked like a skeleton on heels, so my political advisors agreed that I should drop out of the public eye and quietly check into the Institute of Living, a mental hospital near my home. There I could receive the best psychiatric care available in the state. I was terrified at this prospect because of what had happened to a local TV personality of my acquaintance who had been hospitalized at the institute. When this once-stunning beauty came out, she looked like a senseless, bloated, zombie as a result of Thorazine injections she had been given to stabilize her unbalanced mind. The thought of being institutionalized helped snap me back to my senses. I began to reproach myself for ever believing in God when I was an active atheist. I began to smoke again and celebrated my return to sanity with alcoholic toasts when I asked my secretary to help me get my life and crumbling public relations company back on track.

By then it had become difficult to drive all the way to Norwich to consult my personal astrologer, so I began consulting with a tarot card reader Elizabeth had introduced me to. That is where I turned for comfort and affirmation the day Channel 3 let me go. Even though he charged $40 an hour, he acted as though he was a friend who had my best interest at heart, and at the time that's exactly what I needed. So it was easy to believe him when he told me the storm would soon pass, along with the one who was making my life difficult.

Soon I was consulting him every day, checking all my plans with him before taking action. One day he advised me of a cloud of abundant riches that would be coming over my life to rain unlimited opportunities on me. I felt like celebrating! I began the celebration by taking my secretary to an expensive restaurant. Then we danced with passionate abandon until dawn at my favorite discos. I didn't know this would be my last dance as I wriggled like a worm in the cesspool of sin, blinded to my lostness by the strobe lights, and numbed by the noises of the blaring sound system that blocked out the tragic reality of my empty, haunted existence.

Instead of working the next day, we nursed our hangovers, reliving the night's escapades, snickering like silly schoolgirls. We meant to chill a few bottles of champagne in the refrigerator, but were too giddy to notice that we'd put them in the freezer instead. As the evening wore on we drank ourselves senseless, completely forgetting about the champagne in the freezer until the frozen bottles burst open, shooting corks and glass into the freezer door with the sound and fury of a machine gun. We began running around the house, half-scared and half-crazy, spilling drinks, screaming wildly, pushing each other over in mock terror as we scrambled for a place to hide.

The doorbell rang in the middle of this pandemonium, instantly interrupting our playful madness. I staggered to open it. There stood my friend Michael and his wife, Janice, whom I hadn't seen in about 10 years.

"We've come to take you home," Michael said.

Instantly, I was sober. The dream had been real! Jesus Christ had spoken to me, and now I must go as directed. Asking my secretary to clean up and lock the door, I left with Jan and Michael. The interesting thing was, they were not even Christians, but I went home with them anyway, too frightened to question God.

I sat on the edge of their bed watching the evening news while Jan fixed supper. When the lottery number 0-4-0 was displayed on the screen, Michael said, "That is your number. It means out of nothing comes forth something, and it will go back to nothing."

If you knew me then you would know how important it was to be "something" or "somebody." You would understand the fear that gripped my heart as Michael continued to speak.

"Jesus Christ wants your decision today," he said.

I looked at him quizzically. "What do you know about me and Jesus Christ?"

"Hyveth, you know I don't believe that stuff, so why are you talking to me about Jesus Christ?"

What was going on? I was definitely hearing Michael say things that he claimed he was not saying, accusing me of pushing my fanatic ideas on him. When he began to tell me about the life of Jesus as a boy in Egypt, I became very confused. He kept interspersing his remarks with repeated reminders that "Jesus wanted my decision" that day.

What decision?

Feeling trapped, I frantically fled from Michael and Jan's house, running into the night, not knowing where I was going. Anywhere to get away from God.

Michael found me at the bar of a local club, trying to drown my fear in a glass of alcohol. Carefully peeling my fingers from the sweaty glass, he guided me toward the door. Once outside, he scolded me, warning that running away was not the answer, because wherever I went Jesus would already be there, waiting for my answer.

"There's no place to run or hide, Hyveth. This time you must pay the piper!" Michael said. He led me back to his home.

It was a troubled woman who laid her head on the little cot in Jan and Michael's guest room that night. Since sleep was impossible, I laid there reviewing the history of my life, especially the past few months. I began to be afraid with an indescribable fear. Not the fear one has when facing an approaching enemy. A different, all-consuming, inner fear that brought the holiness of God clearly to my mind.

As I lay in that little room, the family's two Doberman pinschers came to the window and began to howl. As a child growing up in Jamaica I was told that when dogs howled it was a sign that someone in that household was about to die. I was sure it was going to be me. All night the dogs howled. Even the weather seemed to reflect the torment of my soul. As the wind whipped the trees into a frenzy their snow-laden limbs lashed against the roof of the house with dry, scratching fingers.

That was the night of my Jacob experience. I wrestled with God for my soul. He wanted to rescue me from the darkness, to pull me back from the gaping abyss of sin, but I was reluctant to let go. I was familiar with the devil, and even though my lifestyle had robbed me of every shred of human dignity, at least it was familiar territory. I was not ready, or willing, to venture into the unknown by allowing God to have His way with my life. I was afraid of Him! I didn't want to become like the Christian zombies I knew.

But early in the morning I knelt at the side of the cot. "You're bigger than me, God. You win!" With a sigh I gave up. I believe it was at that moment my carnal nature died. The dogs ceased their howling, the wind and the storm stopped, and an incredible calm came over me and the elements. Feeling both exhausted and exhilarated from the long night of struggle, I raised my fist to heaven, declaring at the top of my nicotine-filled lungs, "In the silence of this moment, I swear with every breath I take that if You don't keep Your promise to me I will spend the rest of my life telling people You are not to be trusted!"

He has never failed me. God is the only being in this universe whom I say is to be absolutely trusted.

When I left Jan and Michael's house that day I was a different person, in no way related to the one who had come there the evening before. I could see colors in the sky, as I had never seen the sky before, clear and blue, like a dome of hope above me. I sat in my living room to celebrate the newness of life with a cigarette. I had just bought a new carton. (Chain smokers can't afford to run out of cigarettes.) I opened a pack, flipped one out, and put it in my mouth. Just as I flicked the lighter, I heard a voice.

"Don't you know your body is the temple of God?"

I knew I was alone, and I thought the decision I had made the night before meant that I wouldn't be disturbed again by this voice. But here it was again, loud and clear, challenging my sanity. The hair on my arms stood at attention and my heart tripled its beat. I put the unlit cigarette on the mantle over the fireplace. Running upstairs, I checked each room, calling out, "Who's there? Come out and face me!"

I returned to the living room shaken, more sure than ever that I needed a cigarette. Again, as I attempted to light it the same voice repeated the same question. This time I ran to the basement and checked everything very carefully before going back upstairs to check the closets, under the beds, the bathroom, the attic. I was, as I already knew, all alone in the house.

I leaned against the fireplace and said aloud, "Boy, I really need a cigarette now!"

"Hyveth, would you go into a church and spit at the altar?" the voice asked. "Every time you smoke you desecrate My temple, your body, in which I now live!"

I put that cigarette down and never picked one up again.

There were other incredible miracles, but the greatest miracle occurred one day while returning from a trip to Rockville, Connecticut, with Elizabeth. We drove past a field of beautiful, tall grass swaying in the wind like wheat waiting to be harvested. I had always wanted grass like that for decoration in my home, so we stopped the car and I impulsively ran over to harvest some, unaware that the bamboo-like stalks would be as sharp as razor blades. Grasping a bundle firmly in my right hand, I pulled with all my might. I felt a sting in my little finger but paid no attention until the blood began spurting out.

I had severed my finger at the joint. I screamed for Elizabeth. Seeing the blood that now covered my hand and dripped onto my foot, she looked around for something to use as a tourniquet. Finding nothing, we pulled off my slip and wrapped my hand snugly, agreeing that the best action would be to rush to a hospital.

As I sat in the passenger's seat cradling my hand, it dawned on me that I now served a God of tremendous power. Squeezing my fingers together, I made a sweeping motion with my hand and commanded, "In the name of Jesus Christ, be healed!"

Carefully, I unwrapped my hand and looked. My finger had been completely healed—there wasn't even a scar where it had been severed at the joint. The only evidence of my accident was my bloody slip. To this day, all I have to show for this accident is a slightly deformed finger—I did not think to straighten it before praying for healing.

For once, neither Elizabeth nor I had anything to say. We drove home in silence. When she seemed to be in a great hurry to drop me off at home, I thought the whole incident must have been more unnerving than she was acknowledging. But within the hour she was knocking on my door with her 80-year-old mother in tow. Literally dragging the poor woman into the house, Elizabeth begged me to touch her mother so that her teeth, which she had lost through the natural process of aging, would grow again! Thank God, I was not foolish enough then to misuse the precious gift of healing He has given me. And in time, I would learn that not all of God's healing empowerment comes through the physical realm. He also does a mighty work of healing through spiritual rejuvenation as we turn our eyes upon Jesus, the Author and Finisher of our faith!

I was to grow in many different areas. Here is how God cleaned up my obsessive use of profanity. The week following my encounter with God in Michael and Jan's home, I woke up to the discovery that I was unable to speak. No matter how hard I tried there was no voice in me. My tongue was a swollen, red mass that burned as though I had eaten a pound of cayenne peppers. To get relief from the pain, I filled my mouth with ice. For seven days my only method of communication was writing everything on paper. By the second day I was so frustrated that I stayed in bed for the rest of the week, crying and praying for help.

One morning my housekeeper found me on the floor near my bed where I had spent the night attempting to pray. I was soaked in water from melted ice, and my eyes were swollen shut from crying for nearly 24 hours. She didn't know what had happened to me. It took some doing to convince her I was having an unusual experience with God, and not a stroke. I had to write sentence after sentence to keep up with her questions. She did what many were to do when I later shared my story—she shook her head and declared, "God never works that way! Something is physically wrong with you!"

But time has proven that God lives and speaks to His people, even me, the "chief of sinners," in the only way they will hear. Because of this experience I don't reject any person out of hand when he or she tells me that God has spoken to him or her. After all, the Bible clearly states that when God speaks, worlds are formed and lives are transformed. For me, the best proof that one has heard the voice of God is whether he or she remains the same, or becomes a new creation, from the inside out.

I didn't eat anything all week. I just lay there as God ministered to me. By the end of the week the swelling of my tongue decreased significantly. I was very thirsty and hungry, so I crawled downstairs to the refrigerator. The only food there was an unopened pack of bacon in the freezer. As I reached for it I became so violently sick to my stomach that I never touched any kind of pork again. (Perhaps we don't have to coerce people into adopting our lifestyle. When God comes into our lives He often changes us in ways that will be permanent.)

The only thing I could keep down was warm tea, which I carefully spooned through the side of my mouth. I did not want to irritate my tongue again. When the pain finally left I found myself speaking differently, almost with a new tongue. I had to enunciate my words in such a way that they would not irritate my tongue again, and have not used foul language since. As a result of this experience, I've thought that in addition to being a language, the disciples' "other tongues," mentioned in Acts 2:4, could also refer to the new language that comes with conversion. As we are transformed into new creatures we no longer use the language of the carnal nature that is so intertwined with profanity, lies, and dirty jokes.

Now I wanted to see God. I was so in love with Him I wanted to see Him, especially since He had told me I had been specifically chosen to do a task for Him. I remember sobbing out loud, giving Him names of people whom I thought were more worthy to be so selected than myself. I felt I, the product of a poor family with some tragic, shameful experiences in my past, could never be good enough to be chosen by a holy God. But He assured me that He wanted me, not those other "good" people. Still, I begged Him to reveal Himself to me. The more I studied the Bible, the more urgent this desire became.

One morning as I lay in bed pleading for this gift that I knew would help me maintain my walk with Him, He invited me into the backyard where, He promised, He would show Himself to me. I was beyond excitement! I had this image in my mind that God would appear like a huge angel of light, brilliantly shining, wearing blindingly bright, white clothing. (Perhaps He might even pose for a picture as validation to my story when I told it later.) I couldn't wait to get into the backyard to see God.

I waited for hours. Nothing happened. Not what I was expecting, anyway. So I began to look around. I noticed the sun. Its rays seemed to penetrate through the leaves with a life-giving force I had never noticed before—warm, energizing, dancing through the branches to caress my face, drawing me into nature's heart. A bird lit on the fence nearby. At first it seemed to be daring me to make it move, bobbing back and forth as if unable to control its balance. Then it began to sing a glorious morning aria. I just had to touch that delicate, little creature. When I reached out my hand, it stepped onto my fingers without hesitation, never missing a note of its song. Sometime during this enchanting performance a squirrel wandered by. He paused, watching me quizzically, twisting his head in quick, jerky movements. Assured there was no danger, he joined the party, scampering across my shoulders and over my head, tail waving like a fan.

It was incredible! But still I waited for the revelation of my image of God, unable to really focus and absorb the miracle unfolding before me. Not until I was baptized nearly three years later, and shared this experience with my Sabbath school teacher, did I come to understand that God had visited me that day. He had revealed Himself to me in the only way I was capable of handling. How often I wish I could repeat that event! I would pay more attention, not just with my eyes, but with my mind focused on the grandeur of our great God!

I had withdrawn from public life and become a recluse. For three months I stayed at home reading my Bible, waiting for the Lord to speak to me, to teach and guide me. Once in a while I would go out at night to get groceries. The phone no longer rang. Friends thought I had returned to England. Eventually, I decided to hire someone to work in my yard because my neighbors began to complain about my unkempt lawn.

Mr. O'Brian was an elderly Irishman who knew everything about everyone in city hall since, at one time or another, he had worked as their handyman. I had known him when I worked at city hall. I knew he would be only too happy to work for me because he hoped to glean some juicy stories about me. (Well, if we're to be honest, I was also interested in more than his gardening skills. He was an endless source of information, especially about the back room political scenarios to which I was still addicted.)

He did everything to pry information out of me. One day he reported there was to be a neighborhood meeting to discuss the upcoming gubernatorial elections. I could not resist the temptation to at least attend and listen, even though the Lord instructed me not to go. I thought, *What could a few hours of sitting and listening do to me?*

I arrived just as the lieutenant governor was about to step out of his car into a small crowd of agitated people. Mr. O'Brian and I were watching from the vantage point of a flight of steps, just above street level. Without warning, unseen hands hoisted me into the air and threw me to the pavement in the street below. As I lay there, screaming in pain, people gathered around, excitedly describing to each other the astonishing phenomenon of seeing me sailing through the air.

I was rushed to the emergency room where the physician on duty described the event as a "hyperkinetic happening." When pressed to tell me, in lay language, what that might be, he said, "If I were a Christian, I'd say you had been attacked by the devil, my dear!"

It was not too far-fetched to believe that Satan would attack me. After all, I had a track record as one of his best soldiers. I had obeyed him implicitly; I had served him unreservedly. There were times when I had boasted proudly that I had sold him my soul, so it was no surprise that he was putting up a fight for his property.

At home that evening I stood at a window screaming at Satan. I demanded a divorce from him. "It's over! The one thing I ever really wanted, you couldn't give to me. How often I begged you for the peace of mind that comes from self-respect, and you failed to provide it!"

I felt in my heart that I had severed the relationship with the devil and his evil world, but would later learn the paradox of becoming a new creature living in an old, sin-addicted body. I didn't know the daily devotion and determination it would take to put aside my carnal nature and nurture the divine.

The next Sunday I was back in church. It had been more than three months and no one there remembered me. I had not attended since the night I professed my faith in Christ, but this encounter with the devil had really shaken me. I couldn't wait to be back in church. I was shocked to see people stubbing out cigarettes in the parking lot before entering the sanctuary to sing praises to God. I was even more disturbed to share a pew with a couple who reeked with alcohol. In a whisper, they explained that their bloodshot eyes and lack of sleep were due to an all-night party.

Somewhere in my heart I knew that the Word of God was true, that when converted Christians become new creatures in Christ this is demonstrated by a transformed life. When the minister gave an appeal I was the first one on my feet and literally ran down to the front to proclaim my newfound faith, followed by several other people. To my great surprise, the minister wanted to baptize all of us then and there. The others were led to the baptistry and were baptized in a very emotional ceremony. I refused to participate.

As I was waiting for the service to begin the next week, the minister took me aside and asked if I would come forward again when he made the appeal, cautioning me in the name of the Lord to submit to his desire to baptize me. I realized that he had recognized who I was, and the talk among the congregation was that he had caught a "big fish." When I didn't go forward the end of the service, I could tell he was really angry with me by the disapproving glances he cast my way as he baptized others. He announced that those who refused to be baptized that day would be lost because they were committing the unpardonable sin.

That struck a chord! The one thing I was most afraid of was death. And even though I had no concept of the second death, I did not want to be "lost" forever, whatever that really meant. He invited me to his office after the service. I went with fear and trembling in my heart. He began shouting that I had embarrassed him before his entire congregation when I refused to be baptized. I was too afraid to argue, but somehow got up enough gumption to tell him that I felt I needed Bible studies before I would be baptized. Then I began to cry as I explained how I had spent my life running from one excitement to the other; that I had become so jaded with life, and how I didn't want to start being a Christian until someone told me what it all meant and exactly what would be required of me. This time I did not want to turn back from this journey, like I had done with so many other activities in my life.

The minister interrupted me, tossing a small pamphlet across his desk.

"Read this," he commanded. "If you understand it, I guess something is really happening between you and God."

On the cover of the booklet, in bold black letters against a glossy gold background, was the word "Hebrews." When I asked what it was about he informed me that it was a contemporary translation of the book of Hebrews, adding, "Hardly anyone can understand this book, so if you read it and you can, then you must be converted."

I ventured to ask if he understood it. He didn't answer, only showed me to the door. That was the last time I attended that church. And I did read that book and understood it!

The next Sunday I continued my search for a church to which I could permanently belong by attending the 10:00 mass at the Catholic church, a few blocks from my home. I was surprised at how empty that huge sanctuary was.

The following week I attended the 8:00 mass. There were a few more people, including the lieutenant governor, who lived nearby.

The third Sunday I decided to participate. When the time came to go forward to receive the communion sacrament, I noticed that the priest hesitated to serve me. After the service, Mr. O'Brian told me everyone had noticed the priest's hesitation. According to my handyman, some parishioners were putting pressure on the priest to ask me not to attend anymore. They were uncomfortable with a Black person sipping from their common Communion cup. That's all I needed to hear to make me stay. Even though I was not being spiritually nurtured, I dug my heels in and attended that church for nearly six months.

God was still speaking to me from time to time. He told me to sell my home, pay off my debts, and give away everything I owned, including any profit from the sale of the house. My business was nearly bankrupt, and I could barely pay my mortgage, but I was reluctant to obey. Instead, I borrowed a large sum of money from a friend, convincing him it was a worthy investment in my business. I figured that if I could resuscitate my public relations company I could secure a lot of business and be financially fit again. But all this time, the Lord kept insisting that I sell everything and leave the country.

Instead, I poured more money into my business. I rented a huge hall and decided to have another fashion show for local designers, since the first had been so financially lucrative. I tried to sell tickets and get people interested; I bought TV and newspaper ads, but on the night of the event barely a dozen people showed up. Now I was doubly bankrupt. I couldn't pay the advertising bills, I was late with my mortgage, and I couldn't meet payroll for my employees.

I decided to pray. God's first response was that I should trust and obey Him. I was desperate. Finally, I put my home up for sale, and within a few weeks it was sold for nearly three times the amount I had originally paid for it. I paid off all my debts, sent all my clothing to my family in Jamaica, and held an open house where I gave away almost all the furniture. I called the United Moving Company to pack and ship the rest to London, since that was the next destination marked out for me by God.

# Chapter Two

# Out of Darkness

**M**y decision to return to England was made out of fear, rather than faith. After three months of self-imposed isolation the situation came to a head one day when I visited downtown Hartford. I was sitting in the atrium of the civic center, recalling the days when I walked like a giant through that facility. Hardly anyone recognized me now. Amazing! After so many years of being the spokesperson for the mayor, being on radio and television, and countless personal and public appearances, it had taken only three months to be forgotten. The harsh reality was that I was no longer a sought-after local personality. It was an uncomfortable, unsettling feeling.

I couldn't stop the waves of memories that sometimes evoked tears and sighs of regret. There were the times I had attended concerts and ball games at the civic center without tickets, or as a personal guest of the promoters, always receiving royal treatment. We once hosted a dinner at the plush restaurant upstairs for gymnast Nadia Comeneci and her entourage. I remembered her as being exhausted and bratty, but we all fawned over her and tried to accede to her every whim, even while cursing her under our breath. Elvis Presley also performed there. I believe it turned out to be his last public appearance. Donald (not his real name), the promoter, invited me to a private party for the legendary star when I told him that Elvis was my mother's favorite singer.

It was arranged that I would attend the party and get my photo taken with the King of Rock 'N' Roll so that I could give the framed copy to my mother as a birthday present. Even though it was to be a top secret party, I told my secretary, swearing her to secrecy. She couldn't wait to tell her mother, whom she, of course, also swore to secrecy. Her mother immediately called her sister, who worked in the typing pool of one of the insurance companies. She, in turn, was very excited, thinking that it was her niece, not me, who had been given the special invitation and announced the good news to everyone.

Before long, more than 100 phone calls had been made announcing the arrival of Elvis and broadcasting the name of his hotel. Security at the hotel that evening was a nightmare. The press and hundreds of screaming fans made it impossible for Elvis to stay there, and the party was moved before I could be notified. The sad part of this whole event was that I was not even able to stay for the concert because I got into a fight with my date and stormed out of the auditorium minutes after a very overweight Elvis arrived. He was driven onto the floor in a black Cadillac under the escort of several slick-looking, leather-clad motorcyclists.

Yes, a lot had happened in this place. With an air of sadness, I walked outside and looked up at the hotel adjoining the civic center. I remembered that January morning in 1978 when winter storms dumped more than a foot of snow on New England. That ice storm, the worst in the history of the region, blanketed the city, leaving thousands of residents without heat or electricity. The public works department had worked frantically to clear the streets and have everything ready for the big University of Connecticut basketball game scheduled to start in a few hours.

I had worked late that evening. The roads were so bad I was driven home in a police cruiser with chains on its tires. Even this well-equipped car had difficulty maneuvering. My whole world was cold and gloomy. Even though many people in the city envied what appeared to be my glamorous job, I longed to be relieved of it, especially the long hours and thankless paper-pushing tasks that came with it. I couldn't seem to shake a terrific sense of foreboding as I fell into a restless sleep that night.

The shrill ring of the telephone jarred me awake. The city's civil defense director quickly instructed me to call the mayor while he contacted the governor, to tell him that the roof of the new Civic Center had collapsed. He hung up so quickly I didn't get a chance to ask if anyone had been injured. I quickly made the phone call, dressed, and in minutes was speeding in a police cruiser toward the Civic Center with the mayor. We were silent as we rode the elevator to the penthouse of the adjoining Hilton Hotel. Governor Ella Grasso and her staff were already there. As we stepped into the cold night air, a distant clock chimed the 12 strokes of midnight, an eerie sound in the stillness of that wintery night. The civil defense director focused the floodlights on a gaping hole where a tangled network of concrete and steel beams hung like a broken spider web over the newly-installed red-cushioned seats.

I dropped my half-smoked cigarette into a cup of lukewarm coffee someone had handed me for the mayor. The sound hissed through the uncomfortable tension. Everyone looked at me as though I had dropped a bomb. I said what everyone was thinking. "This could have been the greatest tragedy in the history of New England, had fate not intervened."

The fans and two competing basketball teams had left the Civic Center literally minutes before the roof caved in. Looking down at the twisted steel sticking up through slabs of broken concrete of this massive structure, we all concluded that no one would have survived.

The press went wild the next morning, everyone pointing fingers at various local officials and architects. We also made the national news, but the mayor was very disappointed with the reports, complaining that a similar incident in another mall the day before had preempted us! Months later, after intensive public scrutiny and private investigations, it was concluded that the innovative space-age structure, whose roof was designed to easily shift weight from one trestle to another, had malfunctioned and dumped its load of ice, snow, and freezing rain on the more than 40,000 recently installed, but empty, seats.

I took the incident to be a warning against the corruption within the local leadership in city government. Philip Helms, my assistant, claimed they had approved the use of low-grade materials in the construction. He and I had carefully traced the diversion of approximately $6 million from the capital improvements fund of the city budget. We had presented our findings to some of the city councillors, but they were reluctant to pursue the matter, perhaps because they were afraid of indicting friends or even themselves. In our frustration and eagerness for public exposure, we gave the information to the manager of a local television station, begging him to do an editorial about the missing funds. When he refused, I allowed Phillip to talk me into what became a dangerous game of leaking information to the press.

The investigation was still ongoing, although there were signs of major cover-ups. The roof was almost completely replaced, along with some major restructuring of the entire premises.

So here I was, out of a job and out of the political loop, standing and staring at the giant symbol of my own failure to motivate people toward change and renewal, not even recognized by the very people for whom I felt I had given up everything to protect.

By the time I turned to walk away I was full of remorse and angry recrimination. There had been many opportunities I had allowed to slip through my fingers because I permitted my heart, not my head, to influence my actions.

I was so deep in thought about all these events that I had walked several blocks before realizing I was standing by the G. Fox & Company department store. Right there on the street another life-changing experience unfolded. One moment I was remembering events from my past, and the next moment . . .

I heard my name called in heaven. It wasn't that I heard my name called in the skies above or in my head as I stood below, it was called *in heaven*. It seemed as though there was a court in session, and I had been investigated and found guilty. Before sentencing, my name was called by the judge. Without understanding why, I knew my response to this call would have eternal consequences. In that instant I admitted my guilt as a sinner before the whole universe . . .

I was devastated. I sought refuge in the church across the street, but it was closed. I tried to speak to people milling around me on the busy street, but no one seemed to care. My behavior must have been pretty erratic because some people brushed me off gruffly, saying I must have recently escaped from an insane asylum. Others thought I was just another drunken nuisance. My world was coming to an end! God was after me, and I could no longer resist Him.

I don't remember how I made it home. I only remember the cold sweat on my forehead after I leaned against the fence of the churchyard to vomit. At home, the Lord emphasized again the importance of leaving for England, where He would lead me to a church that would explain these spiritual phenomena I was experiencing.

When I had calmed down enough to articulate this latest revelation, I called Elizabeth, who listened intently as I recounted every detail.

That night I had a tremendous dream that seemed to outline my life until Jesus comes. I dreamed I was in a huge, palatial residence, much like a governor's mansion, when I became very bored with my existence. There had to be more to life than sitting around giving orders to a myriad of servants who were at my beck and call. I looked around at the lavish, expensive furniture and made up my mind to give it all up and go out into the unfamiliar world outside to find my purpose in life.

As I walked outside, the pathway was wide and beautifully landscaped. Flowers of every imaginable variety bloomed in beautiful profusion. I was so excited by the potential opportunities that I began to skip along the path, not realizing it had narrowed significantly, turning into what seemed to be an orchard. The path became dark, but not foreboding, because the trees on both sides had grown so large their branches met in the middle to form a thick canopy. The trees were laden with huge grapefruit in varying degrees of ripeness. Before I could reach up to pick one, the branch bent down as though it was giving its fruit to me. I took it and skipped a few yards farther when the same thing happened again. The two grapefruit were so large they filled my arms, but as I skipped along a little farther I saw the biggest, most beautiful grapefruit of all, hanging low, inviting me to pick it. I put down the two I was carrying and reached up. I had to have that one to share with my friends. But then the fruit pulled back, its leaves waving vigorously to indicate No! I stretched and strained, groaning to reach it. Exerting every muscle in my back and arms, I finally touched it.

Then it spoke. "You may have me someday, but not now! You are not ready for me right now."

I was so disappointed that I sat down and began to cry. It made no difference that I already had two luscious fruits; I wanted that one!

Once again it spoke. "I'll always be here. Go, get ready for me and I will also give myself to you!"

Suddenly it dawned on me how selfish I was for crying like a spoiled child when I could not get my way. I began to remember some of the texts that spoke of the tremendous sacrifice Jesus made so that I might have eternal life, especially Isaiah 53:4, 5 (NASB):

"Surely our griefs He Himself bore, and our sorrows He carried; yet we ourselves esteemed Him stricken, smitten of God and afflicted. But He was pierced through for our transgressions, He was crushed for our iniquities; the chastening for our well-being fell upon Him, and by His scourging we are healed."

As the meaning of these passages pressed upon my heart I fell on my face and cried out to God to change me, no matter what it would take. At that moment, the fruit delivered itself to me, rolling to a place right in front of my face.

I was jarred awake from this dream, my body shaking with dry sobs. I felt a tremendous tension in my chest from the intensity of the experience. I knew right away that God was speaking to me through my dream, but instead of waiting for Him to interpret it I gave it my own spin and almost drove myself insane in the process. For the next few months, I tried to manipulate my life to bring the dream to fulfillment, but finally became too frustrated and gave up.

I have since come to understand that the mansion represented my life in Hartford, which God directed me to leave and strike out like Abraham, not knowing where I was going, believing in Him and depending on His guidance, abandoning my hopes in His will.

The pathway represented the transformation of my life from man-made roads, well-manicured, but never satisfying, to God-created, canopied paths.

The leaves represented the tremendous regeneration and spiritual growth which would be my continued experience, while the fruit represented the last three careers I would have until Jesus comes, or I pass away. My first career was as personnel director in Washington, D.C. When I share how it came about you will understand how, by the grace of God, it was handed to me. My second career is that which I am doing today—a minister. Again, when I recount how I came to it you will see that it gave itself to me, for I did not choose it. God called me and sent me to serve. The third career is my dream, an impossible dream: To serve God as chaplain of the United States Senate and pastor of this nation that has been such a blessing to me. This dream started out as a selfish replacement for my lost political ambitions but today represents a divinely-inspired desire. More will be said about this as my story unfolds.

Bright and early the morning after this challenging yet troubling dream, Elizabeth was on the phone, exhorting me to visit Harold, our tarot card spiritualist. I hadn't seen or spoken to Harold for a long time, though he had been my daily guide until I returned to church a few months before. She was eager to have him interpret the revelation I'd received on the city street about being judged in heaven. Besides, she said, Harold also needed to consult me on the very important project of purchasing the television station that was being offered for sale. She fed my ego by telling me how he respected my opinion and knowledge in the communications industry. Since

I desperately needed a job and the professional stimulation, I reluctantly consented to a meeting the next Friday. I made it clear that as a born-again believer I did not intend to consult Harold's cards. I had read in the Bible that consulting witches and warlocks was an abomination to the Lord.

It was my plan to attend that meeting only as a consultant on the issue of purchasing the TV station. I drafted a prospectus and outlined my fee. However, when Friday morning came and Elizabeth and I drove to Harold's office in downtown Hartford, it became clear that I had been brought there under false pretenses.

A stranger dressed in black sat stiffly in the swivel chair behind Harold's desk, his back to the door, as though studying something fascinating outside the window. He did not turn around to greet us when Elizabeth and I were introduced to him. I quieted my fears by convincing myself that sometimes psychics, or those who confer with them, behave in very peculiar ways. Since I assumed he was one, I gave no further thought to his sinister behavior.

As we began the meeting, the stranger continued to stare out the window, still not acknowledging our presence. At first, the conversation was light, about the weather and my feelings on no longer being in the limelight at city hall. When I opened my briefcase and proceeded to outline my proposal, I was perplexed by Harold's apparent lack of interest in the presentation. Then he began to repeat incidents I had shared only with Elizabeth, such as the healing of my little finger and the persistent voice I was hearing. I realized Elizabeth had betrayed my confidences. The intense creaking of the swivel chair being turned from side to side indicated "Mr. Stranger" now seemed to be taking an interest in the proceedings, although he pretended not to. Eventually, he turned around. To my surprise, he was wearing a priest's collar. Harold introduced him as the high priest of the Black Catholics, an organization to which both Elizabeth and Harold belonged. Since they were all Caucasians, I guessed that "Black Catholic" must not be a racial designation. (I later learned it is a branch of a satanic cult.)

The meeting immediately changed from a discussion about acquiring a television station to an interrogation of me. Mr. Stranger stood up, a squat, balding man, with eyes that blinked rapidly behind thick, horned-rimmed glasses. Breath that had to be worse than the devil's flowed past brown, tobacco-stained teeth. He slowly walked around to the front of the desk, rapidly opening and closing his right fist as though he were considering punching me. He leaned over to look directly in my eyes, breathing his bad breath of death in my face. "Tell me the truth. Who are you?" he screamed.

That was a stupid question since we had just spent the past half hour talking about my job at the mayor's office and my subsequent unemployment and conversion. However, I thought I would humor him and repeated my name.

He interrupted me in mid-sentence, clamping a tobacco-stained hand over my mouth, shaking his head in disappointment. "You're not cooperating," he snarled. "I want to know the truth—who are you? I guarantee that you are going to tell me before I'm through with you, sweetheart!" He pinched my cheek so hard it burned, then cupping my face in both his hands he threatened, "Cooperate with me now—or face being forced to later!" He dropped his hands and hissed, "I don't give a ___ how you do it, just tell me who you are!"

Harold and Elizabeth joined him in a rhythmic march around the chair where I sat, chanting, "Say your name; say your name!"

By this time I was thoroughly frightened, gripping the chair with both hands, thinking desperately how I could get out of the situation. Holding up my hand, I stood, and in my most put-on, lighthearted tone said, "Enough, already, guys! This is a joke, right?"

Wrong! Harold pushed me back into the chair and commanded Elizabeth to lock the door and hand him the key. In the course of a few minutes the scene had changed from a cordial consulting opportunity to a kidnapping. I was terrified. I knew if I screamed no one would hear. Even if someone did, it was unlikely they'd respond because it wasn't uncommon to hear unusual sounds emanating from that office.

For the next several hours the three of them begged, pleaded, cajoled, threatened, and screamed at me to admit that I was the reincarnation of an angel who was closely connected with Lucifer, and who, in their minds, was the source of the voices and extraordinary events that had happened to me since my conversion. At one point they brought a marijuana plant out of a closet and commanded me to tell them where these were cultivated in Jamaica; they needed a contact to generate fresh supplies of the illegal narcotic. They tried to manipulate my mind by pretending that I was not seeing and hearing what I knew I saw and heard. They tried to force me to demonstrate the power Elizabeth had described to them that had healed my finger and gifted me to see extraordinary colors in the atmosphere.

As the hours passed I became thirsty and hungry. They refused me water and food. When they did not get the information they wanted, they began to get very frantic. They tied me to the chair and forced me to sip a thick, sweet liquid that looked like espresso coffee, but must have been a mixture of drugs. I became very woozy. As I was blindfolded and taken to a car, I heard the clock in the old state house chiming. Nine o'clock.

We drove for what seemed to be about 45 minutes, but it could have been only 10. I tried to listen to the sounds outside. My abductors noticed and turned up the radio. All I could do was pray. I was sure this must be the meaning of the two roads the other psychic had seen. It was payback time for all the years of involvement with these crude, devil-worshiping people, and the price would be my life. We reached our destination and I was led into what seemed to be a hall. I was seated at a table and could smell a variety of cooked food. My head ached.

After about 10 minutes, the blindfold was removed. As soon as my eyes adjusted to the semi-darkened room, I could see I was sitting in the midst of a group of White men wearing black priestly gowns and collars. Women darted about looking after babies and replenishing the food and drinks at the table.

On my right, in the center of this group, sat a very corpulent man whose very eyes swam in a pool of evil. He smacked his lips, drooling a mixture of food and drink from the corners of his mouth as he ate and spoke with his mouth full, sometimes allowing particles of food to fly indiscriminately, landing on plates or persons. His chair was decorated with a variety of objects, including a half moon, what appeared to be masks of perverted human features, and shrunken human skulls. Evidently, he was the newly elected chief priest. He waved toward the table, inviting me to eat as much as I liked. As hungry as I was, I didn't want to risk being drugged or poisoned, so I pretended not to notice the invitation and prayed silently that my growling stomach would not give me away.

I was too newly converted to fully realize I was in serious danger. I chided myself for not calling on the powerful name of Jesus Christ when this whole thing began. But even then I felt I could not pray. I had gotten myself into this mess; I should get myself out and suffer the consequences.

When Harold and Mr. Stranger stood up and whispered in the high priest's ears, I became uneasy. The high priest shot a disapproving glance in my direction, chilling my blood, convincing me I was in trouble so deep I'd better bring it to God's attention. I began bargaining with God on a variety of promises if He would only get me out of this predicament.

About midnight the high priest clapped his hands to indicate to the 40 people in the room that the ceremony was about to begin. Several men jumped to their feet and opened the partitions to reveal the presence of perhaps 100 more participants of various racial/ethnic backgrounds. They were sequestered, but feasting, in the large adjoining room, faces flushed from too much alcohol, their laughter signifying the beginning of evil intentions. A large table was brought to the center of the room and spread with a gold cloth, woven with a black insignia of their satanic cult. The announcement that followed was grim: The table was for the new initiates who were to be inducted into the organization by public sexual intimacies with the high priest first and, after the high priest's degenerate desires were satisfied, an orgy with the top leaders.

Numb with fear, I suddenly spotted Dennis (not his real name), who had been my coproducer for the Sunday morning talk show on WINF radio. I mouthed a silent, *Help me!* He ignored my plea. I had always wondered about Dennis—his shiny bald head, the weird-smelling locket he wore around his neck, his penchant for stories about black magic. Now it all began to fall into place; he was deeply involved in this satanic cult. I tried again to catch his attention, but his eyes were glazed, as if he had overdosed on drugs and alcohol. *Even if he does see me,* I thought, *he's going to pretend he doesn't know me since one must not associate with initiates before they were touched by the high priest.*

There were six of us initiates, and I was first in line. I had the presence of mind to ask to use the rest room before being publicly violated in their mind-blowing ritual. Two women escorted me toward the back of the room. Dennis followed, still pretending not to know me. Just as we reached a small hallway leading to the rest rooms, he deftly distracted the women. I understood at once; he was going to help me! I groaned loudly and collapsed to the floor, pretending to faint. He sprang to my rescue. This six-foot-six-inch, 250-pound giant with the shiny head picked me up and carried me as though my 90-pound body were as light as a feather.

"What in blazes are you doing here?" he whispered through clenched teeth when he realized I hadn't really fainted.

The women pressed anxiously toward us, probably to help revive me. He spoke to them briskly. "Open the rest room door so I can get some cold water on her face!" he commanded. When someone protested that it was the men's room, Dennis pushed his way through the crowd of leering drunks and simply kicked the door open. Once inside, he almost threw me against the wall as he slammed the door shut and leaned against it.

"Open that window and get the ____ out of here!" he whispered hoarsely, "and don't come back! In fact, if I were you, I'd get as far away from this place as possible. Your life won't be worth ____ when they realize you've escaped." He turned on his heel and left. I was never to see Dennis again.

I scrambled through the window, dropped to the ground, and ran through a wooded area, not knowing where I was going. I thought I could hear dogs barking and feared they had called out the hounds on me. After what seemed like hours of picking my way through the dark, unfamiliar woods, I cried out to God, promising that if He should ever get me to safety I would never participate in witchcraft or spiritualism again.

He did, and I never did—except for one other time.

~

It was my final year at Columbia Union College. I was one of three women in the theology program. Carol (not her real name), the brightest and most promising of the three of us, could parse Greek verbs in her sleep. She also began to dabble in the occult. Before long, she was talking in strange voices, using the foulest language and representing herself as the channel for the spirits who invaded her body at will. One in particular, an eighteenth-century spirit who spoke with a thick, upper-class English accent, began to dominate her personality. She became belligerent and rude in class. She was very sensual and seductive, propositioning the male students, while at the same time being outrageously unkind to the female students. She boasted how she had built a shrine to the devil in her dorm room and talked freely of her moonlight rendezvous with him. Her one desire, she was always eager to say, was to have the devil's baby.

Prior to this, Carol seldom spoke to me. But as her obnoxious behavior increased she began to speak nicely to me, perhaps because I was the departmental secretary who graded some of her papers. She and the theology major she was dating (who is now a minister), would participate in some pretty explicit intimacies in the foyer of the religion department, as if to defy everyone's sense of propriety. Eventually, Carol's attitude and behavior with her boyfriend, added to the rumors of her drug abuse and occult activities, led the administration to recommend her suspension from the college.

One day Dr. Bill Liversidge, who was on campus conducting a spiritual gifts seminar, asked me and another theology major if we would join him, Carol, and her boyfriend in a season of prayer for her release from this satanic involvement. I agreed to participate because by then I felt sorry for Carol and was interceding on her behalf in the department. Still, I was most uncomfortable with any idea of confronting demons or participating in a deliverance ministry. This idea was gaining popularity on campus, allowing lazy, undisciplined students to escape responsibility by seeking to have "the demon of procrastination" cast out of them, and I would have none of it.

I stayed in the background, not being sure what was expected of me or what the outcome would be. Because of my past involvement and memories of my promise to God not to participate in these activities again, I believe I was more nervous than the others. I had awful flashes of the evening getting out of hand and my name becoming associated with the appalling "deliverance ministry" that was racing like a wildfire through our denomination. I feared that my entire future as a minister in the Adventist Church would be compromised. Because of this concern, I didn't mention my past, and only Dr. Liversidge knew a little about it from our previous conversations.

As the evening wore on and the various evil spirits took over Carol's being, things became very scary. I must admit that until that moment I wasn't sure but that Carol had been faking some of her experiences and using others to manipulate those who paid attention to her misbehavior. Some in the group felt Carol was orchestrating the events while we were constant in prayer. She began to gurgle and scream, then her accent, body language, and tone of voice changed. She identified herself as an eighteenth-century young English woman, speaking with a perfect English accent as she described her intentions to use Carol to accomplish her selfish goals. The evil spirit continued speaking through Carol as she convulsed and rolled on the floor, as if in a drug-induced withdrawal. Sometimes she curled up quietly in a fetal position with a finger in her mouth. At other times she thrashed about on the floor, pronouncing the foulest of invectives as she demanded that we leave her alone to enjoy her late-night rendezvous with the devil.

As we prayed harder, she screamed louder. I stood up, about to excuse myself and leave, when Carol pointed an accusing finger at me and shrieked, "Go! Get out of here, you pretentious _____! You're not going to be a pastor some day!" Her voice dripped with sarcasm. "Get the ___ out of here! They don't know, but I know about your past ring and card activities with the psychics."

I was speechless. How did she know this? I had not shared this particular detail with Dr. Liversidge. He later confirmed he had revealed nothing to her; he was not in any friendly communications with her at all, believing that our sole purpose was to pray for her release from the clutches of the enemy.

What should I do? My first instinct was to run out of the room and slam the door—the door of the room, and the door of my mind which was now being flooded with some long-disregarded memories. In the end, my faith in God won over my fear of exposure and I decided to stay and tell my own story, rather than to allow a fallen angel to intimidate me with my darkened past.

I shuffled to the center of the group and meekly said, "Yes, I danced with the devil. That I cannot deny. I did even more: I sold my soul to the devil and, if you would believe it, I married him! But when I asked him for the one thing I wanted most—self-respect and a sense of dignity—he couldn't give them to me. So I left him. Today I'm married to someone else. I took unto myself a husband, and He is none other than Jesus Christ, my Lord!" By now I was shouting through tears, with a voice that trembled, not with fear, but with an all-consuming confidence that God was with me.

The mood had suddenly changed. Dr. Liversidge and the other two participants pulled closer to me, laid their hands on me, and we prayed as we had never prayed before, all of us crying shamelessly. I can't say we were victorious, although several hours later it seemed so. Carol was once more a model student for a few weeks. The administration reconsidered their suspension and placed her on probation instead. Although we were sworn to secrecy, some of us could not keep this incredible event to ourselves. We rejoiced in the power of prayer.

As for Carol, she sold her car and purchased a hearse. She was eventually suspended from Columbia Union College to, according to her own later testimony, return to her occult rituals, romance with black magic, and fellowship with the prince of darkness in the cemeteries of Silver Spring.

I refocused on my studies for the ministry, determined to never be drawn into another such situation, no matter how high the compassion quotient. As the word got around about what had happened that evening, however, I was repeatedly sought out to participate in a variety of deliverance ministries. But I never did again. I felt that spiritualism was the new excitement generator for the fringe elements who dabble in this dangerous phenomena, not realizing that it is a massive, organized movement where real and present dangers threaten the lives of those who become involved in it. Having been knee-deep in spiritualism since I was a child, I have no desire to be presumptuous with the grace of God by becoming involved again, even if it is in the name of setting someone free from the clutches of an evil spirit. I came out of that darkness into the marvelous light of Christ and now rely totally on the power of the Holy Spirit, through prayer, to loosen the grip of evil on the lives of those who seek Jesus earnestly.

~

God heard my cry for deliverance that dark night in the Connecticut woods. I ran toward the lights of cars speeding by on the unlit street ahead of me, praying as I ran, promising God that I would never associate myself with Satan-worshiping people again. Car after car went by, but I was too terrified to try to flag one of them down, fearful that the Black Catholics had patrols out trying to find me. I was sure they would hunt me down and destroy me. But the Lord was with me. Eventually, an elderly couple picked me up and delivered me to my door.

I didn't sleep that night. I sat in a chair in the middle of the living room with my Bible on my lap, waiting for an invasion of evil spirits or a knock on the door from agents of the Black Catholics. I read my Bible and prayed for the opportunity to live to see the morning so that I could begin again to live for Jesus. I knew the words of only one song, and sang it over and over again. "Living for Jesus a life that is true, striving to please Him in all that I do." When I got tired of singing, I imagined I was a movie producer, casting and directing the twenty-third psalm, then the Lord's Prayer. By God's grace I made it through that long, dark night.

When the new day finally dawned, I knew I would now obey God and leave Hartford, Connecticut, for my divinely-designated destination in London, England. It took only a few days to get my affairs in order. As I was driving in my car on one of my final errands, I heard a minister preaching on one of the local radio stations. He mentioned how God wants to heal His people, and if we have faith, no matter how small, we will be healed.

I was suffering from a very bad case of bursitis in both shoulders as a result of shoveling too much snow at my home in Hartford. It had been especially irritated the past few days by my rushing around and lifting things as I cleared out my house. In the past, I had undergone all sorts of laser heat and cortisone treatments with little or no results. My shoulders were swollen and uncomfortable. I couldn't lift my hands above my waist without experiencing the most excruciating pain. I couldn't wear anything that required lifting my hands above my head or reaching for zippers and buttons in the back.

I was in tremendous pain, so I put my hand on the dashboard and prayed, "Lord, I have abused my body so much I don't deserve to be healed, but I know You are merciful and forgiving, so please give me some relief from the pain in my shoulders."

I really can't pinpoint the specific moment when the pain stopped, but it did. Even though one of my shoulders remains larger than the other as a result of the cortisone treatment, I have not suffered from bursitis since I offered that prayer.

I arrived back home that evening, exhausted from the long drive, but free from the pain in my shoulders. I opened my front door to find Elizabeth, or someone who looked like Elizabeth, sitting in my living room. I tried to compose myself, even though my heart felt as though it would pump itself right out of my throat and cold sweat trickled down the back of my neck. How had she gotten in without a key? Before I could ask for an explanation, she stood up to greet me with open arms, smiling broadly. I turned away quickly to close the door behind me, almost overcome by the scent of evil as she began to speak in a soft voice so unlike Elizabeth's. My suspicions increased when she appealed for my help in "restoring her mother's teeth." In my confusion and alarm, I didn't know how to respond. Then she came to the point.

"Hyveth, why did you run away the other night?"

I didn't answer, but focused my eyes on a spot on the floor and concentrated on calling on Jesus in my mind.

"Do you know how much trouble you've caused Harold and me? Why don't you come back and apologize, and we'll let bygones be bygones."

The Elizabeth I knew certainly would not say something like that. Who, or what, was this?

"Tonight is the last of the convention," she went on with a knowing wink as she reached out to grab my arm.

I shrugged her off and moved away as confidence in Christ flowed into me again. I felt sure this was not a human; this was a demon. "Get out of my house, Elizabeth!" I commanded, pointing to the door, trying my best to not show any fear or intimidation. "Jesus Christ is Lord of my life, and I don't need your satanic stuff anymore!"

At the name of Jesus she screamed with the harsh sounds my grandmother's pigs used to make when they were alarmed. My worst fears were confirmed: This was not Elizabeth, but an evil spirit that had taken her form.

"Jesus Christ, help me; save me!" I cried over and over.

The thing which I thought was Elizabeth began to whine, but it didn't sound like a human. If you've ever heard a cat "meowing" in the early hours of the morning, sometimes it sounds as if it is saying words. That's what "Elizabeth" sounded like to me. She reached up and plucked off her silver hair, which was cut and combed like Elizabeth's, exposing a wrinkled, bald head. She screamed, and her teeth fell out.

I stood transfixed, staring as this demon shriveled away, bending over like an old hag. She plucked her eyes out, one by one, producing a sucking sound as the eyeballs were pulled from their sockets. All that time she kept telling me that was what would be done to me if I tried to defy her.

A foul odor filled the room. I shivered from the iciness that had permeated the atmosphere. As I found my voice again and began shouting the name of Jesus, confessing my sins, seeking forgiveness, declaring my commitment and love for God, that thing skulked past me toward the door, disappearing before it reached it. Shaking uncontrollably, I turned to make sure it had not slithered up the stairs to hide in the attic. As I leaned to look up the stairs, I rested my hand on top of the radiator, on something cold and chilling: A tubular vial, filled with mercury that formed itself into the letters d-e-a-d. I picked it up, screaming, and hurled it outside with all my might. As it splattered in the middle of the street, I could hear the wailing of the evil spirit receding over the park across the street. I turned around and fell to my knees.

I never saw Elizabeth again, but when I returned to the United States a year later I called her. She was surprised to hear from me, but seemed very distant on the telephone. She told me that she had never seen me again since the night I ran from the Black Catholic meeting. She said she had been severely beaten and raped as punishment for doing such a poor recruiting job with me. I knew the bond of friendship had been broken, never to be restored again.

~

The next morning I was on an airplane bound for London. It was so good to be reunited with my son, Steven! My plan was to quickly find a job and purchase a home for us, in spite of the fact that God had instructed me not to keep any of the money from the sale of my Connecticut house. I gave my sister some money and put some in the bank. My sister's apartment was a small, two-bedroom flat on the twenty-first floor that she shared with her son, my son, and now, suddenly, me. It was unspeakably difficult to tote groceries up to the apartment, especially since the only elevator was usually out of order.

Within a week I landed a job in the West End business district. (I was to stay there less than a month.) One morning as I slowly made my way down to the ground floor (the elevator was out of service again) to go to work, I was impressed by the Lord to return to the apartment and change my clothes and remove my rings and makeup. Now one would have had to see me to understand why this was important to the Lord. I used to wear two or three colors of eye shadow, bright red lipstick, and matching red fingernails that were about an inch and a half long and were my pride and joy. Many times people in Hartford would stop me on the street to ask if they were real. I had rings on every finger, even a specially made thumb ring for my right hand. I wore big, bold earrings, plus many chains around my neck and bracelets around my wrists and ankles.

Now God was telling me to return to the apartment and change all that? I was definitely not prepared for this part of the transformation process. I looked at my watch, then up at the sky, and exclaimed, "Why now, Lord? I'll be late for work!"

But something seemed to propel me back up the stairs. I struggled breathlessly up those 21 flights of stairs, complaining all the way about the demands God was putting on me. I thought they were grossly unfair, especially since earlier that week I had met with a "messenger of God" from the Bible Way Temple in London. She informed me that God never asked His people to do some of the things I claimed He had asked of me. "And He never would," she insisted. So now I was arguing with God, demanding to know why He treated me worse than He did His other children by making these demands on me.

By the time I got to the apartment I was properly worked up; nevertheless, I took off the jewelry, washed my face, and once more headed out the door. Then I heard Him say that my beautiful fingernails had to go, too. I was not only an obnoxious new believer, but a real spiritual juvenile in those days. I sat down and clipped my nails off all right, but with such wails and groans one would think I was being savagely brutalized. I did not make it to work that day. That evening my sister found me weeping, my shorn fingernails lying at my feet. That was the beginning of a radical transformation that worried my family so deeply they would consider putting me away in a mental institution.

After I had stripped myself of these external adornments, the Spirit urged me to dispose of my enormous collection of jewelry. I was still far, far from learning that when God speaks I must obey. I gave a few pieces away (those that I really didn't like or had not used in a long time), but the special pieces I kept hidden in a jewelry box that I took out from time to time, just to let them run through my fingers as I reminisced about wearing them.

I did eventually give the majority of my collection to a friend, but I kept the expensive jade ring, the one that was regularly featured in my psychic visits. I wouldn't wear it to church on Sabbath, of course, but I did wear it around the house. One Sabbath afternoon when I was at home studying, the Spirit convicted me of my error. Instead of taking the ring to a pawn shop, I threw it in the trash compactor. I am wiser today and don't react to His will as fanatically as I did then. I have learned that when the inside is right with God the outside is not too far behind as the Holy Spirit works out the process of sanctification, that continuous regeneration spoken of in Titus 3:5.

My first Sunday in London I visited a Lutheran church near my sister's flat. About 15 people gathered in a large, dark, Gothic building. The minister did not once open a Bible or a hymnal. Instead, he gave a discourse about his recent vacation. The following week was part two of the vacation saga. I was frustrated, but I sat through the entire sermon, pinching my son when he wriggled too much out of boredom. The third week the building was closed. A sign on the door indicated the minister was gathering more sermon material. "Gone on vacation—back in a fortnight," it said.

I turned around and left, seething with frustration against God. On the way home, we passed a pub. Laughter spilled through the half-opened door, suggesting that at least a lot of fun was happening there. Angrily, I dragged Steven by the hand because he wouldn't keep up with me, fussing and fuming until we reached the apartment building. When I discovered that the elevator was on the blink again, I lost it.

Running out onto the concrete walkway leading to the front door of the building I looked up into the sky and screamed, "Now look here, God, I never wanted to be a Christian! I was satisfied being an atheist, then You came into my life and turned it upside down, inside out! You won't let me get baptized; You won't even let me find a church to worship in. Are You trying to drive me crazy? So guess what? I'm going upstairs and I'm getting into bed. I will not move, I will not breathe, until You tell me what to do. Do You hear me, God? I'm going to hold my breath till You answer, and if I die it'll be Your fault!"

I stormed into the building, pushing my bewildered son out of the way as I marched up those 21 flights of stairs like a woman possessed. With my last energy I flung open the apartment door and fell on the living room floor in front of my sister who was watching television. I was sobbing so hard she didn't know what to do. She asked Steven what had happened, but the bewildered boy couldn't explain, so she just grabbed me and shook me before helping me upstairs to the bedroom where I collapsed into a heap, still sobbing. I spent a restless night of praying and crying, reading my Bible and seeking the Lord.

# Chapter Three

# Meeting Marie

I woke up early the next morning, dressed quickly, and left before my sister emerged from her bedroom. I didn't want to tell her that I was about to resign from the job I had held for less than a month so that I could come home to wait for the Lord's directives. She already thought I was both obnoxious and fanatical.

Michael, my supervisor, was already there when I arrived at work. I was very nervous, but gathered up enough courage to tell him I was quitting. After a perfunctory attempt to persuade me not to resign, he asked me the question I had hoped would not be brought up.

"So, Hyveth," he said, tilting back in his chair, "tell me the truth. Why are you really resigning?"

I gulped hard, clenching my fists in my lap. "I need to be in a quiet place so I can find out what God wants me to do," I blurted out. There, I'd said it.

For a long moment, Michael gave me a scrutinizing stare. I expected ridicule; instead he gave a testimony of his own emptiness. He said he wished he had my courage to stop and get out of the rat race to find himself, but he was owned by an expensive E-type Jaguar and a newly acquired condominium in the exclusive Hampstead Heath neighborhood. He couldn't take the risk I was taking.

I was too new at this Christianity thing to realize that he was a prime prospect for witnessing, but God worked it out that we kept in touch, and a few years later I was able to share my faith with him.

I left his office feeling alternately fearful and excited. I knew when I walked out the front door I would be stepping into an unknown world. I hesitated in the foyer. Maybe I shouldn't leave . . .

A pleasant young woman stopped in front of me. "Hello, my name is Marie McIntrye," she said, sticking out her hand.

I was in no mood for her pleasantries, and I didn't accept her outstretched hand. I just knew if I shook it she would take it as an invitation to talk.

Not in the least put off by my rudeness, she continued. "Is this your first day at work?"

"No, it's my last!" I snapped, moving toward the front door.

"It's my last day, too!" she smiled. "Where are you going now?"

"Home, if it's any of your business."

"May I walk with you a little?"

"No!" I almost screamed. "I'm a Christian, and I don't walk with heathens!" I waved my hand in a gesture of dismissal. "And I'm not interested in anything you have to say. I definitely don't want to hear all the worldly garbage you people talk about." I pushed past her, ignoring the hurt look on her face and the tears in her eyes.

"But I'm a Christian too!" She reached into her purse and pulled out a well-worn Bible. "Every day I go across the street to that little park and read my Bible during lunch."

"Well, bully for you!" I said, pushing my way, shoulder first, through the door. I really wanted her out of my face.

She didn't budge. Thank God, she didn't budge.

"I live over in Bermondsy. Where do you live?" By now I was walking fast, so she spoke breathlessly, trying to keep up with me.

I didn't answer, just kept walking toward the bus stop. "This is where I catch my bus to go home," I said.

"Me too!" she exclaimed with delight, as though that was the greatest revelation for the day.

"Well, I live in Bermondsy, but today I'm going to walk home, all right?" At this point it didn't matter how far it was, how long it would take, or that I had no idea of the direction. I just wanted to get away and sort through the thoughts muddling my mind. I turned and walked away quickly.

"I'll walk with you," Marie said. "It will give us a chance to talk and get to know each other."

I rolled my eyes toward heaven in utter frustration. How was I to know she was God's answer to last night's prayers? I knew God was talking to me, personally, but it had never occurred to me that He might also use other human beings to communicate with me. I was so wrapped up in my own selfish world of "I-must-be-special-to-God-like-no-one-else-because-He-talks-to-me-personally" that I was completely blind to the fact that I was hurting one of His children. He was about to teach me a most significant lesson which, I must confess, would have to be repeated many times before I finally got it.

Since it appeared I was to be saddled with Marie's company, I decided I would at least control the conversation. After all, I was the older, more experienced one and, I was sure, Christian or not, God had never talked to *her* personally!

So I began with my conversion story. I told of my life in the mayor's office, my deferred political dreams, and how I was just getting my act together to return to the scene of my greatest professional accomplishment, better and stronger than when I left. I shared the joy of knowing Jesus and the depression of losing everything I had worked so hard to acquire. To my surprise, she listened intently and didn't interrupt as I spoke for more than an hour.

By the time I had finished we were in a park near where we both lived. I had warmed to Marie and didn't think she was such a nuisance anymore. In fact, she was very bright, articulate, intellectually stimulating, and able to discuss a variety of subjects I threw at her. I tried to apologize for being so unbearable when we first met.

"Let's begin again," I suggested, extending my hand to her. "My name is Hyveth Williams, and I'm very pleased to meet you, Marie McIntrye."

She clasped my hand and smiled the beautiful smile of forgiveness. "I live not too far from here," she said in her sweet English accent. "Would you like to come home with me for a moment? I have something I'd like to share with you."

As we walked, she told of her family who had moved from Jamaica to find a better life in England. I realized that our lives had many similarities.

Once at her home, she gestured for me to sit on the sofa. "I have something interesting to show you that I read recently," she began, taking her Bible from her purse. "But before I do, let me just read this passage. Have you ever heard this before? 'If because of the sabbath, you turn your foot, from doing your own pleasure on My holy day, and call the sabbath a delight, the holy day of the Lord honorable, and shall honor it, desisting from your own ways, from seeking your own pleasure, and speaking your own word—'" (Isa. 58:13, NASB). She stopped reading and looked at me, her face full of concern. I had begun to cry as she read, silent tears trickling down my cheeks. Had she said something to upset me? Was I feeling sick?

I shook my head emphatically.

"Well, perhaps this isn't the right time to show you what I had planned," she said gently, easing me off her sofa and leading me to the door.

I turned to her, my eyes overflowing with tears. "I went to work this morning to quit my job because I wanted to just go home and hold my breath till God tells me what He wants me to do . . ." My words trailed off into loud sniffles. "As soon as you began to read that passage I knew it was God speaking to me. I know now what I have to do."

She showed me out the door and promised to call me. Frankly, as I look back on that encounter, I am convinced that it was only by the grace of God that she contacted me again, because my strange behavior should have permanently put her off.

I walked out of her flat into the mid-afternoon haze of a London day, feeling as light as a feather. I knew that the Sabbath was Saturday. I had many cousins in Jamaica who claimed to be Seventh-day Adventists, but they were awful people. I wondered if Marie was an Adventist; she hadn't said. She really hadn't had an opportunity to after I broke down crying. But how could such a nice person be "one of them"?

~

Ours was a poor family who literally lived off the land. We lived in a place called Esher, surrounded by Seventh-day Adventists. Perhaps we were the only non-Adventists among at least 100 families. We grew our own fruits and vegetables on a piece of parched property my grandmother had inherited. Money was so scarce that only one Sunday of each month were we able to buy meat to make curry goat. Every Christmas Grandmother cooked tender beef so deliciously that even though I've not eaten it since becoming a vegetarian more than a decade ago, I can almost taste it as I write. Every other Sunday, as a special treat, we ate either chicken or pork that we raised ourselves. During the week we ate eggs and fished for crayfish from the river that ran through our property. We had either exhausted the crayfish supply in our part of the river or they figured out our fishing habits, because after a while we could find nothing in our water.

Then one day my pet goat strayed onto our Adventist cousins' property. As I was searching for her, I came upon a part of the river where crayfish of every size—some so big my eyes popped wide open—were literally jumping out of the water. I forgot all about the goat and ran to my aunts to breathlessly share my discovery.

"Mabel, Thelma! I know where all the crayfish are! They're over there in the Peters' river!"

Mabel and Thelma, who were just a few years older than I, ran to see for themselves. They were back in a flash to tell my grandmother about the treasure. Grandmother didn't seem at all surprised to learn that the crayfish were plentiful on her family's property. She calmly explained that because of their religion the cousins couldn't eat them.

That sounded crazy to me. Why would anyone in their right mind not love those delicious crayfish? I sure was glad Grandmother's God didn't stop her from eating them. And I was glad that our cousins' God stopped them from eating crayfish because now we could have them all for ourselves! Mabel, Thelma, and I decided it would be all right with the cousins if we fished in their part of the river and relieve them of those crayfish they didn't want. And then they wouldn't be tempted to eat them.

When Grandmother didn't say no, we dashed through the bushes, swinging our pails and homemade nets, yelling and laughing and rolling in the long grass, happy to be on the way to a harvest of crayfish. As we fished and played in the water, making enough noise to drive the birds out of the trees, Thelma thought she saw someone lurking behind some banana trees, but we teased her, saying it was a ghost, and carried on with our play. We filled our pails, and even ate some of the young crayfish raw, and plucked the black eggs out of others. We chattered about the different ways we would prepare and preserve them, since we didn't have a fridge and only bought ice on Sundays.

After a few hours, we walked home with great satisfaction. But when we walked into our yard, there sat the cousins on our veranda with Grandmother.

"Children, come here!" When my grandmother spoke in that tone, we all knew there was trouble.

We set down our crayfish-full pails.

Mr. Peters, our cousin's husband, walked over to one pail and said, "See what I mean? They are little thieves, and the Bible says stealing is breaking the commandment!"

_What's a commandment?_ I thought. _Was it like one of the glass lamps that got broken in the last earthquake?_ "I didn't see anything like that in the river, and we certainly didn't break it," I explained nervously.

He ignored me and picked up a handful of crayfish, shaking them in Mabel's face. "These crayfish are unclean. And you are not going to eat them, now or ever!"

We all knew they weren't clean, but we always cleaned them properly before eating them.

His wife, who looked a little like a crayfish herself, nodded her approval.

"You little thieves!" he yelled, grabbing Thelma and shaking her.

Grandmother sprang to her defense. "Take your hands off her before I kick you off my veranda!" she shouted.

He eyed all of us coldly. "You are not going to have these—they belong to us. You girls stole them, and you have to put them back." Grabbing Thelma by the arm, he dragged her, kicking and screaming, toward their property. Mabel and I followed behind them, belting out all the noise our little lungs could summon. Grandmother added her fair share to the general melee, shouting for Mr. Peters to put her daughter down and calling him names too ugly to record. But nothing we did swerved him from his righteous purpose.

Once we reached the river, his wife took two pails of squirming crayfish and dumped them in the water while her husband forced Mabel to pour out the last pailful herself, to teach us a lesson. Sadly, we watched the fish float downstream with the current.

My family was devastated by this event. We couldn't understand how anyone—especially people who went to church each week—could be so cruel to children. We talked about that encounter for years.

I sat down under an almond tree in the yard and cried for a long, long time. I thought about the Friday nights we had gone to the cousins' house to listen to them read the Bible and pray. It always bothered me that they never smiled or said a kind word to us children, unless it was to tell us how to behave. My little heart hardened against their God. He must be as mean as they were.

My grandmother was so angry that as we got ready for bed that evening she made us promise that we would never become Seventh-day Adventists, because they were the meanest people she knew.

The property adjoining ours on the other side also belonged to relatives who were Adventists. The matriarch of that family went to church every Saturday morning. In the evenings she would visit her husband's grave, calling him up from the dead to listen to her troubles and to send him to wreak havoc on her enemies, like my grandmother.

By the time I was 15, I had made up my own mind that I wouldn't be a part of that church to which it seemed almost every Jamaican was flocking. Especially when the Americans came with huge tents and moving pictures of horrible beasts that they flashed on the screen in the darkened tent. Many nights I would go to bed trembling with fear that one of those beasts would come to eat me.

But the event that affected my mind most negatively occurred when I was about 8 years old. I had climbed an ackee tree that overlooked another Adventist family's property. I was spying on their home, as we children often did, trying to see what they were doing. They were reasonably well-to-do, at least better off than we were. The husband had gone to America as a farm worker and had returned only the week before.

Suddenly his wife rushed out of the house. Her husband was in hot pursuit, waving a machete whose blade glistened in the sunlight. I knew something bad was about to happen. As they screamed at each other, the husband lifted that machete and brought it down with a thud across his wife's neck and back.

I closed my eyes against the awful sight, but it replayed again and again in my mind.

Our cousin, the crayfish-faced wife, ran across the narrow street and into their yard. When she saw what had happened she dashed back to her house and brought sheets to wrap around the wife. There were no phones or cars, so she quickly called a few men from the fields. They constructed a litter from branches and carried the poor woman away, singing in rhythm as they walked to a place where they could hire a car and take her to the hospital.

She never came home again. Neither did her husband. Their house stood empty for years, its furniture still inside, and overgrown grass outside. I never went near it by myself, and our family never spoke of the event. Every time I tried to talk about what I had seen my grandmother would gently put her finger across my mouth and whisper, "Hush up, chile!" I took that to mean that the husband might come and kill me, too. So that fear, plus the beasts on the silver screen in the evangelistic tent, produced nightmares more frightening than anything Hollywood has produced to date.

With the words Marie had read from the Bible still ringing in my ears, I rummaged through these recollections. I decided I would obey God, but I would never worship with "those people." There had to be other Sabbathkeepers.

~

I began searching for work with a new enthusiasm. I accepted a position at an American firm as administrative assistant to a man named Michael Rosenthal. This company had been started by a Connecticut man who had parlayed a $10,000 loan into a billion-dollar stockbroking empire by trading gold, silver, and other commodities on the international market.

My new boss, an aggressive, 25-year-old executive, told me he was a very "spiritual" Jew and agreed I would not have to work on Saturdays. Nor would he. As we talked about the Sabbath, for reasons I still can't explain, I began to concoct a story, telling him I was the descendant of Jews. I was happy to report that in Hebrew my name meant either "house of life" or "house of love." And it does.

Michael was immediately attracted to me and did nothing to hide it. I knew I was playing with fire by accepting the position, but I rationalized that I needed to know if God had cured me of my past weakness for good-looking men, even if all they wanted was a quick, free fling. In my broken-ness, I had often convinced myself I could make someone like that love me for life and settle down and have a family. We would live like the couples in the romantic novels I used to feast on as a teenager. But after a few of these failed relationships, added to a history of being sexually violated by relatives as a child, I had become hopelessly addicted to sex and pornography, habits I secretly indulged.

As soon as I gave my life to Christ, He made it clear to me that I had to immediately give up three things: profanity, smoking, and sex outside of marriage. The first two were reasonably easy, but I felt the last was harsh and incredibly difficult, if not impossible. I used to joke with my friends that I could figure out a way to live without food, water, and air, but not without sex. Not that I was a loose woman. I consoled myself that I wasn't promis-cuous because I wouldn't date more than one man at a time or sleep with him on the first date. Such is the reasoning of an addict.

Now God was demanding a higher ideal from me, and I didn't think I could do it. At first, I thought I would go absolutely crazy. The worst times were at night when my dreams were often filled with wild sexual fantasies. I would wake up in a cold sweat, begging God to ask anything else of me. But I stuck with His program, and through the grace of God and the powerful presence of His Spirit, I overcame even that addiction. Today, I do seminars on human sexuality in the plan of salvation, teaching people, mostly young people, why it is so important to follow God's rule. I have a very low threshold of tolerance for people who make it seem as though God isn't able to take away these desires and replace them with the gift of celibacy. I am living proof of the fact that God can, and will, cure a sexual addiction, just as He does any other addiction. And He cures us to the uttermost!

Isaiah 54:4 (NASB) is a promise to which I cling and renew every morning: "Fear not, for you will not be put to shame; neither feel humiliated, for you will not be disgraced; but you will forget the shame of your youth, and the reproach of your widowhood you will remember no more."

Not only does God cure us, He restores our dignity and all that which the locusts of sin have eaten (Joel 2:25). He heals our broken emotions and builds up our self-esteem. With our new heart He gives us a new attitude so we can live like virgins again as the Holy Spirit does His work of regeneration in us.

In time, the dreams came less frequently, but I needed to know, in a tangible way, if God had indeed given me the now much-desired gift of celibacy. And where better to prove it, I thought in my misguided ignorance, than in a setting where this weakness would be highlighted with a man to whom I was also hopelessly attracted? So I accepted the job Michael offered, both as a professional and personal challenge.

Michael "wined and dined" me daily, and I did not object. It felt good being a sought-after lady again. No other administrative assistant in London was taken out to lunch and dinner as often as I was, and to some of the finest, most expensive restaurants in the city. Michael was a gracious date who sent me flowers regularly, accompanied by some of the most seductive, romantic words I have ever heard. Sometimes I kidded myself that he was sincere, but I didn't yield. It irritated him that I wouldn't even allow him to kiss me, but I had made a promise to Jesus that if He cured me of this addiction, the next man I kissed would be my husband.

At my first lunch with Michael I said no to a glass of wine when he wanted to toast our "budding relationship." I never touched the stuff again. I couldn't believe it! Was this really me? Before, I would never consider having lunch or supper without a glass of wine or some other kind of alcoholic fortification.

When Michael realized I was successfully overcoming my initial attraction to him, he took another tack. He tried to convince me that through my witness he had turned his life over to God. When we ate lunch together in the office, he began to read from a prayer book as I read my Bible. We ate in a lot now that I was no longer playing the I-may-someday-be-available game. Gullible new Christian that I was, I was thrilled to learn of the influence he claimed I was having on his life. (I've since gotten smarter, realizing some people will fake anything for sex, including conversion.) His conversion didn't last too long. For about a month all his conversations were laced with things about God. He even invited me to Friday night services at his family's synagogue, to the surprise of his twin brother who was not too happy about the "mixed relationship." Even though Michael and I never talked about marriage, his brother's greatest concern was about the children of a racially mixed marriage.

Soon Michael began to date other women in an effort to make me jealous. When it didn't work, he became strictly businesslike, though still "keeping the door open, in case I changed my mind," as he would often say with a broad grin and wink.

I was so happy with the way my life was changing, surprised by the opportunities of becoming a whole, healthy person in Christ. I celebrated every possible moment, immersing myself deeper and deeper in the Word and in obedience to the will of God.

The first two Saturdays after I met Marie I stayed at home and did nothing but read and sleep. I talked with Michael about attending the synagogue with him, but it never happened. I soon figured out he didn't have the courage to bring a Black woman with him, even though he had no problem with desperately trying to get that same woman into his posh apartment and, hopefully, into his "fantastic" bed.

The third weekend, I got a telephone call from Marie. For the first time, she told me she was a Seventh-day Adventist and invited me to her church the next day. As much as I wanted to say no, I didn't. She had no way of knowing about my childhood memories of Seventh-day Adventists. Besides, after my strange behavior the day we met, I felt I needed to prove to her that I was a normal, sane person.

But my old fears seemed to be confirmed shortly after we arrived at the church. The pews were packed, so we were shown to the front pew. The greeter had pinned a shabby-looking paper to my lapel that proclaimed "VISITOR" in bold, black letters. As I sat skeptically on the edge of my seat, I wondered if this was their version of the scarlet letter.

We had just sat down when I looked up at the platform. One of the men seated there welcomed me with the broadest smile. I courteously returned his smile, but when he followed up with a wink I quickly averted my eyes. He did everything short of standing on his head to attract my attention, and every time our eyes met, he winked. I knew something awful was about to happen, so I picked up the hymnal and forced my eyes down the page. After a few minutes, I began to wonder if I could have possibly seen what I had seen. Carefully, I glanced up, and there was that sordidly sensual wink again, but this time it was accompanied by a mouth puckered into a silent kiss. Can you believe it? Right there on the platform during the worship service that man was attempting to seduce me!

After church, as Marie introduced me to her young friends, the boys circled us like scavengers around a fresh carcass. Within my hearing they were joking about who would be the one to win me for a date. Because I looked very young, they thought I was about their age, never suspecting I had a 13-year-old son at home. I was so outraged by their behavior that I walked out of the church with Marie close behind. A lady called out to Marie, inquiring whether or not she was still planning to come for lunch.

Marie pointed to me and replied, "I have my American friend with me; is it all right if I bring her, too?"

The woman, not knowing I am Jamaican, put her hands on her hips in a defiant stance, and speaking in Jamaican patois asked, "Gal, you tink me a feed de five towsand tiday? (Girl, do you think I'm feeding the five thousand today?)"

That was the last straw. I marched away from that church declaring, "God, I will never, ever become a Seventh-day Adventist! Do You hear me? Never, ever!"

I have since learned two important lessons. The first is to never tell God what you will, or will not, do. The second is that the devil and his evil angels are always ready to pluck a new believer out of the hands of God and away from His church.

I didn't have much at home to offer Marie for lunch, but she stayed anyway, profusely apologizing for my difficult introduction to the church. She tried to explain that Satan was attempting to thwart God's plan for my life, but I would have none of her explanations. I had made up my mind to find other Sabbathkeeping congregations, and that was that. By then, I was so turned off from organized religion I didn't even try to find another church. I decided to stay in my bed on Sabbath and study the Bible. This I did for almost a month, making my sister's life miserable.

My sister, Renita, is one of the most peaceful, reasonable people one could ever meet. Being the middle child, she was the most neglected in our family, in spite of the fact she was a brilliant student who, at 14, won a place in college in London. Nobody in the family made a fuss about it. They were too busy expressing their disappointment over the fact that I was pursuing a career as an actress. Renita stuck by me through this and other experiences, but being self-absorbed as I was, I took her for granted. Even after I moved out of our mother's house and the family was forbidden to talk to me, she would sneak over and keep me up-to-date on what was happening. She wasn't much of a talker, but she showed me her love by always supporting me, and later in looking after my son when I needed help. As a new Christian I was very harsh to her. I don't deserve the love and forgiveness she has given me.

I knew that God wanted me to keep the Sabbath; therefore, I decided that everyone around me would have to do the same. I didn't talk to them or solicit their input, I just decided. One Friday evening my sister was watching *Dallas,* her favorite program. It was about the time when everyone was wondering who had shot JR. Since the living room doubled as my bedroom, I had to stay in the room my son shared with his cousin until she was through watching TV. I tried to read the Bible, but couldn't concentrate. I tossed and turned on the lower bunk bed, all the time getting angrier and angrier that Renita should be breaking the Sabbath by watching that ungodly stuff. Finally, I jumped out of bed, ran downstairs, and turned off the TV just when an important scene began to unravel. That wasn't all that unraveled.

"What on earth do you think you're doing?" Renita screamed, jumping up from the sofa.

Bravely, I shielded the TV behind me and spoke piously. "This is the Sabbath, and we should be resting, not watching this—this—"

I tried to find words to describe the program, but before I could she pushed me away from her television, and in a voice louder than I had ever heard her use before, she said, "You listen to me, you obnoxious, selfish twit!"

Her nose almost touched mine. I had never seen her so agitated and it scared me a little.

"You think what you're doing is worshiping God? You run around here forcing everyone to follow you. You think you're the only person who knows anything about God. You make my son miserable, and your own son is a nervous wreck! You make me sick!" She spat those last words out slowly like slaps in my face.

For the first time in the months I had been living in her home, I realized how un-Christlike and selfish I had been, imposing myself and my lifestyle on her without considering her feelings. All my self-indulgent incidents flashed through my mind, making me even sicker than she seemed to be. She, too, had an experience with God, but not once had I asked about her story. No wonder she left me alone and said very little to me when we were at home. I still experience moments of deep regret because I know those early impressions and my poor model of Sabbathkeeping affected her and added to the negative impressions about Adventists she had heard as she grew up. I feel responsible for her reluctance to join the Adventist Church, even though she attends often and has become quite friendly with several members.

I was too dumbfounded to apologize that day, but the Lord gave me strength to do so in a more meaningful way than just saying "I'm sorry." I determined there would be noticeable changes in my attitude and actions. I did eventually apologize, but I could tell by her response that even though she sincerely accepted it, she would have to wait and see if changes would really follow.

A few weeks later, I knew we were beginning a better, more honest relationship. She invited a friend from her church over, and for the first time I sat and listened to my sister's story. She had given her life to the Lord, and while searching for a place to belong, a coworker had invited her to a Pentecostal church where the people accepted her and treated her with love and respect (much more than I had done since returning to England). She no longer belongs to that church, since their doctrines are not sufficiently biblically based to hold her. Also, the noise and expressions of speaking in tongues frightened her son. But, praise God, she is on a renewed quest to find a home church, and now that our relationship is better than it has ever been before, I am convinced that one day she will follow her mother and sister into this marvelous message.

I wish I could excuse my excessive, insufferable behavior by saying my conversion experience was dramatic and had overwhelmed me. But the truth is, I had been a very self-centered person all my life, and God was using these events to bring me face-to-face with who I really was. Only then could He effect a permanent change and heal the brokenness that had dragged me to this lowest common denominator in my personality.

About three weeks after my encounter with the Adventist Church, I received another telephone call from Marie. This time she wanted to meet me on Friday evening so we could walk in the park and pray together. I saw no harm in that, so I agreed. Once again the Holy Spirit was using her to reach me and teach me God's ways.

We walked in the park for some time, admiring the beautiful flowers and the heady scent of spring right there in the middle of the concrete jungle of Bermondsy. As the sun set, we sat on a bench and Marie prayed, thanking God for the Sabbath. I became nervous; I didn't want to talk about going to church with her. But I was caught off guard when she said, "Hyveth, I need to understand something because I'm only a young girl. I have never heard a testimony like yours. You've inspired me—and even scared me— with the tremendous experiences you've had with God. I've never known anyone before to whom God has spoken audibly. A few weeks ago when I read from Isaiah 58:13, you cried and confessed that God was speaking directly to you and instructing you to keep the Sabbath, right?"

"Right."

"Well, tell me how it is possible for you to have heard the voice of God directing you to do something, and then you allow a few little incidents by people to turn you from doing it?"

Those words flew like bullets into my heart. I almost fell off the bench. I couldn't answer.

She stood up, challenging me. "Well, since you won't—or can't—answer me, you can come to church with me tomorrow and start all over again!"

I found my voice in a hurry and protested vigorously.

She would have none of it. Quietly, but firmly, she stated, "Well, my dear, you can stay at home disobeying God and end up losing Him and everything else. But as for me, I will keep His Sabbath holy!" Then she walked away.

"Lose God?" I yelled after her disappearing back. "Never!" But I was shaken to my innermost being as I ran from the park to my sister's flat.

All night the Holy Spirit added weight to her words. I dreamed I was drowning, and Marie, standing on the bank of the river, turned and walked away every time I reached out to her. All I could see was the faint shadow of her figure receding into the darkness.

She was right. Why was I allowing people to turn me away from what God said? I called her early the next morning to tell her I would go to church with her. I wasn't ready to say I would join, but I wanted to follow God and see where He would lead me. I needed to show her that my testimony was true. God had dramatically intervened in my life, and I wouldn't turn away from Him for any reason.

By the time we met at the bus stop, we had missed the bus.

"I'm sorry, Hyveth," Marie apologized as we waited for another bus. "After that big speech last night, I cause us to miss the bus to church. By the time the next one comes along in 15 minutes we will be too late even for the worship service."

"It's OK," I said, actually relieved that we wouldn't be going back to that church.

Then she brightened. "But wait! There's a little company that meets in Deptford, and here comes the bus to take us there!"

We arrived at Deptford in time to see a little group of people carrying a small portable organ, flowers, and books into a pool hall that they weekly transformed into a sanctuary. Pastor David Hughes, from California, gave an incredible sermon, reading from a book entitled *The Desire of Ages.* I had never heard words more powerful! I had to get a copy of that book. Sister Russell, the Bible worker, gave me a copy, and I couldn't wait to get home to start reading.

I stayed up all night, finishing the book late the next morning. It was the most insightful book I had ever read about the life and ministry of my Lord, whom I now loved beyond words. I felt I had just been personally introduced to my Saviour all over again as the Scriptures came alive and my understanding of salvation deepened.

My life changed significantly as I discovered other books by Ellen White to read. I learned that no form of lying is acceptable to God, no matter how good the intention. (That was a major problem for me—I exaggerated everything.) Well. I would have to tell Michael the truth, that I was not a descendant of Ethiopian Jews. This would be very difficult. I prayed hard—and kept putting it off. One day he returned from Germany with a beautiful gift for me. Almost without thinking, I blurted, "Michael, I'm not really an Ethiopian Jew." I cringed, waiting for his response.

He smiled. "Is that all you can say to a man who's just come back from a great trip? I would prefer hearing that you at least missed me a little," he teased, trying to pull me into a hug.

I stiffened, avoiding his embrace, wanting to know if he had heard what I had said. I expected to be fired on the spot. Instead, he got up and left the room. I couldn't figure it out. Was he so angry he had to go for a walk to cool down? I looked in the adjoining offices and checked the hallway, but he was nowhere in sight.

Before long, here he came into the office carrying the largest, richest cheesecake I had ever seen. "Let's celebrate!" he laughed. When he couldn't find a knife, he began breaking off pieces, spilling cherries on the desk and floor.

"Celebrate?" I asked cautiously.

"Yes, you dummy!" He tweaked my cheek affectionately. "Finally, Hyveth Williams, you trust me enough to tell me the truth! I always knew you were making up that Ethiopian story, but I felt you probably needed to." He shrugged and sat down. "I'm glad you've finally admitted it. Now you are ready for this." He pulled a paper out of his pocket. On it was the combination to the safe where all the company's confidential bank records were kept.

Michael never made advances to me again. We became great friends and coworkers. Even after I returned to the United States, he called me at least once a week to ask my opinion on different things because he said he knew that I truly walked with God. I was the first to know when he proposed to his future wife.

That day was the beginning of my struggle to stop lying and exaggerating the truth. Along the way, I learned that even worse than lying is not owning up and telling the truth.

After 10 months in London I still hadn't found suitable housing for my son and myself. All that time, I had been sleeping on the floor in my sister's living room. Against God's clear instructions I had kept some of the funds from the sale of my house in Hartford, Connecticut, thinking I would try to buy a flat through the London Housing Council. But that failed. I was depressed because while I could see the hand of God preventing my progress, I couldn't understand why. I am very seldom melancholy, but when I am, I'm suicidal. It had been months since I had felt so bleak, and here came all those old feelings, flooding my mind, overwhelming my world. It began to really bother me that I had sold my house where I sometimes had a live-in

maid, and given away my furniture and my clothes in order to obey and follow God, only to end up sleeping on the floor of my sister's house.

Soon my prayer and study time began to decrease and my resentment
toward how God had led me increased. I was becoming impossible to live
with. My sister began complaining again about my selfishness and spiritually odious behavior. My son began to bite his fingernails to the quick because of how miserable I was making his life. Exasperated, I decided that my
problem must be in thinking that an atheist could ever be converted to
Christ. I decided to return to my old ways and give up this whole idea about
God. I was too numb from an indescribable inner pain to consider the consequences of that decision.

As I was walking from the train station later that week, I saw where a terrible accident had happened. For safety reasons, the rule on British trains is
that no hands or heads are to be put outside the train windows. (These were
the days when the windows could be opened by passengers.) On that particular day a young man had opened a window and put his head through at
the very moment a train rushed by in the opposite direction. Although I was
not in the same car, the bloody carnage was evident as I walked past the
emergency teams.

It should have scared me, but instead it seemed to be the answer to my
own problems. I began thinking about how I could execute a similar "accident." I thought that if I made it look like an accident my son would inherit
quite a bit of money, and that would somehow compensate for the loss of
his mother. I knew my sister loved him and would care for him until he
could be on his own. Having satisfied my mind that he would be taken care
of, I began planning how it would happen, perhaps the next day on my way
to work.

I trudged toward home in the darkening London evening, my eyes lowered to the pavement, awash in low self-esteem and haunting dark thoughts.
I glanced up for a moment and noticed an elderly man leaning against a wall
across the street near a bus stop. I paid no further attention to him, but in a
moment he was at my side, greeting me in the gentlest manner.

"You are too young and beautiful to be so sad."

I glared at him, thinking his next move would be a come-on.

He ignored my dirty look and continued calmly. "There is so much in
life to be thankful for . . . Why are you so sad? Hasn't God been good to you?"

I took a long look at him. His well-worn clothes were clean enough, but he looked like he had no family and needed to be cared for more than I did. I resented his attempts to minimize my experience when he didn't know anything about me. I opened my mouth to give him a proper "Hyveth tongue-lashing" when he smiled and melted my heart. For at least five minutes this precious man spoke the sweetest, most encouraging words to me. He urged me to not give up on God, to just hold on because the Lord had great plans for my life if I would only trust and obey Him.

As we walked, he talked about God just like Ellen White writes about Him, confidently, as though he knew Him personally. I told him I was thinking of killing myself the same way as the young train victim had. I shared everything about my disappointment with God, and he consoled me with Scriptures, emphasizing, "just trust and obey God, my young friend." My heart was lifted up as though a huge burden had been removed. When I turned to share my joy with him, I discovered I was walking and talking to myself. I whirled around quickly, just in time to see him disappear along a path toward the apartment buildings. How awful of me not to have expressed my appreciation! I dashed after him, but when I came to the place where he had stood only seconds before, he was nowhere in sight. I stopped passersby who must have seen him because they were walking on the same path at the same time, but no one had seen an elderly man fitting the description I gave. Though I searched everywhere within a block of that place, I didn't find him. A delightful thought began to work its way into my consciousness . . . He had to have been an angel, sent by God to console me in one of my darkest hours!

Hurrying to work the next morning, I took the escalator to the third level to catch an underground train. Above the noise of the trains I heard the sweetest voice singing a lovely song. As I listened, the singing changed to whistling. Forgetting all about my mad dash to work, I followed the sound of the voice to a part of the station that had been blocked off to the public. I walked along the deserted platform until I could go no farther. In the echoing stillness I heard God's voice saying, "It's time to return to the United States. Go to Washington, D.C., and wait for My instructions." Then the voice began singing that beautiful song again.

I couldn't concentrate on anything at work. As soon as I could, I did exactly what I shouldn't have—I called my friend Diane Lyman who was then living in North Carolina, and told her I was planning to return to the United States. I asked her to find a house there for both of us to share and to keep her eyes open for a job for me. I didn't mention the instructions I had to go to Washington, D.C., for two reasons: I had never been there before and didn't know anyone, and second, if Diane knew about this she'd probably think I was going crazy. She was so thrilled about our potential plans that I felt affirmed in not revealing what really happened that morning.

About a month later, I was invited to the home of Sister Newton after church. Sister Newton was a colporteur whose dream had founded, and sustained, the little Deptford church. Men were noticeably absent from that lunch because, as the older women explained, they had been either left behind in Jamaica or no longer practiced their faith. The conversation focused on the absence of men and on my singleness, and one of the women began to share what she thought would be my future in the church. She insisted she was not a prophet, or the daughter of a prophet, but could boldly declare that I would spend my life in the gospel ministry. I wasn't even baptized yet, so I smiled sweetly and turned my attention back to my rebellious taste buds and the vegetarian repast.

A few weeks later, the Sabbath school teacher asked how many in the class were ready to be baptized. Only then did I realize that not everyone there was Adventist. And since I had no real reason to delay the decision, I said I was ready. Several others also agreed. I later learned I had been carefully steered to that class of new believers. This happened so matter-of-factly that it momentarily scared me, in light of the fact that all my other attempts to be baptized had been divinely foiled. But to my surprise, the ensuing days were without the usual divine intervention, and I became confident that my baptism had the Lord's blessing, even though my family vehemently disapproved.

I was baptized Sunday evening, December 31, 1979. On Friday afternoon I decided to celebrate the impending occasion with a feast of the best crabs London could offer. I had never been given a formal Bible study, other than what I heard in Sabbath school, because the Deptford members assumed that since I knew so much about the Bible I must have had studies before coming to their church.

My sister, Renita, was helping my son and me prepare this delicious meal when the doorbell rang. It was Sister Russell, whose job it was to talk to each candidate before baptism. I happily invited her to share our feast and began to describe the delicious crabs. The dear saint let out a scream and sank to the sofa with a heavy sigh like she'd just been told that a favorite friend had suddenly passed away. In time she collected herself enough to tell me that if I ate the crabs I couldn't be baptized.

"No crab-eating people will be admitted into heaven!" she declared.

Such was my introduction to the Adventist health message. Although I didn't eat any of the crabs, I may as well have, because I watched the rest of my family with lust in my eyes and longing in my heart as they finished off every one of those delicious, handpicked delicacies.

That was not all I learned that evening. Many other things in my life would have to change if I was to be baptized, Sister Russell said. I can scarcely bear to tell about what happened next, but because of this incident I determined to spend my life living and teaching others the joy of freedom in Christ, without compromising biblical principles, as we worship God in spirit and truth.

My son owned a pet hamster, Charlie, whom he lovingly referred to as my "grandson." As Sister Russell was giving me my final instructions, my son brought Charlie in for his goodnight kiss. I took that little pet and spoke to it, then gave it my usual affectionate kiss that made my little son laugh like bells were ringing in his heart. But as I handed Charlie back to Steven, Sister Russell gave me a look of strong disapproval.

"You must get rid of that rat!" she insisted.

I tried to tell her it was a hamster, not a rat, but she wouldn't hear me and ordered me to take that rodent away immediately and throw it away because it was an abomination to the Lord to touch it. With tears in my eyes I obeyed her instructions. She wouldn't leave until I did, and I loved my Lord so much I thought whatever He asked of me I should do. I tried to explain things to Steven, but he couldn't understand. How he screamed as I took that little pet and ran out the door, down the 21 flights of stairs, and put it in the bushes outside. He wouldn't speak to me the next morning, but when the time came for me to be baptized, he was the only one from my family who came.

Sister Russell finally left, instructing me to take my bath before going to bed, a habit she counseled me to follow from that day forward since it was a sin to bathe on Sabbath mornings. "Sister White said it's too much work on the Sabbath."

I was emotionally confused about hurting my son and being given all these last-minute rules that I must follow in order to be baptized. I couldn't help wondering who Sister White was and why she had so much authority over what I would do from now on. Amazingly, it never occurred to me then that Sister Russell was referring to Ellen White, because the person she described didn't fit the picture of the woman whose books thrilled me so much.

My son forgave me but was unable to forget what I had done to Charlie. I still keep a photograph of that little hamster to remind me that God is more concerned about His little children and creatures than about rules made up by human beings.

The evening of my baptism was rich with emotional symbols. Michael sent a dozen red roses with a note: *I hope your new life will be filled with more roses and less thorns.* Because of our family's history with Adventists and my family's determination never to affiliate with them, neither my mother nor sister would attend my baptism. Since there was no baptistry where our little company met, I was to be baptized in the very same church where I vowed I would never become an Adventist. My son gave me a small silver cross he had made as a class project for the occasion. His gift was more meaningful to me than anything I could remember. I tucked it into my purse to remind me of the tremendous change that was taking place in my life.

Pastor Hughes asked the six candidates to give a brief testimony of our journey to this point. When my turn came I said, "I am taking unto myself a husband from whom I will never part, even in death!" Even so, let it be, Lord Jesus!

I spent the next day at my mother's house with our family. I woke up early and decided to prepare breakfast for the family. As I reached into the fridge to take out the sausages (vegetarianism had not yet taken hold on me), I accidentally bumped the handle of the frying pan, spilling hot oil over my hands. My loud yelp brought everyone running. I was begging God for relief from the searing pain. My mother had once taken her house keys from me because of my foul language and blasphemous talk about God. She feared that one day He would strike me dead, and she didn't want it to happen in her home. So when she saw me praying, instead of cursing, she was stunned. In that second, she was convinced that something special had happened in my life. She told me how she had planned to put me in a mental institution because I was acting so crazy, and when I decided to be baptized as an Adventist, she was afraid her worst fears were confirmed. Now she was praising God, saying, "I can't believe that God has chosen my own daughter and touched her in such a special way." She began reading her Bible faithfully and later became actively involved in a nearby Baptist church.

I hadn't told my family that the Lord had instructed me to return to America. I also had kept my conversations with Diane a secret. But I had to tell them now, though, because Diane had found a house and would be expecting me in a few days. When I finally shared the news, Steven went into a depression that would take him more than 10 years to recover from. He was happy in England and did not want to leave his friends. He was angry because he used to have so much when we had our own home, and now he had settled down to so little, but he didn't want to move again—things might get worse. It would be almost 15 years before I learned the reasons for this reaction. I was crushed by his response and decided to leave him with my sister while I went to get things ready for his comfortable return to America. I would live to regret leaving him behind, but at that moment I was determined to leave England.

# Chapter Four

# Go Where I Send You!

**E**ven though the divine instruction was to go to Washington, D.C., I made plans to go to North Carolina. Had I been more familiar with Jonah's story I would have known that when God says go to Nineveh, Tarshish is not an acceptable alternative.

When I told the members of Deptford church that I was returning to the United States, they gave me the most touching farewell at a vespers service, and presented me with several Ellen White books. But the most meaningful gift was the song "Trust and Obey," which they sang with tears and much love. Pastor David Hughes, in expressing his sadness about my leaving, said that my story should be told to the entire denomination. He gave me a letter of introduction to someone he knew well at the General Conference headquarters and I left, determined to obey God and go to Washington, D.C.

I called Wilson Gaitor, the former city manager of Hartford, asking him for contacts in Washington, D.C. Through his daughter, who worked for the federal government, he was able to secure temporary lodging for me at a Baptist boarding house for Senate pages, two blocks from Capitol Hill. A few days later, however, when the emotions of saying goodbye had worn off, I bought a ticket to Hartford, Connecticut, and made reservations to fly from there to North Carolina. The day before I left I spoke to Diane and confirmed that we had indeed secured a house in North Carolina, and we made plans to see each other in a few days.

I arrived in Hartford without fanfare. Gone were the days when a limousine and members of the local press corps would meet the mayor and me at the airport. It had been nearly a year since I had left Hartford, but the emotions that now overwhelmed me were as fresh as the day I left. I confirmed my reservations to fly out on Wednesday, but Diane called Tuesday evening and dropped a bombshell. The owner of the house had decided not to rent after all, and due to some personal problems, Diane had decided this was not a good time for me to come stay with her. Through her tears she regretfully advised me to go to Washington, D.C. I was stunned! She knew nothing of the divine directives I had received, yet she was suggesting I go to the very same city. I held the phone aloft and stared at the receiver in utter dismay. Are there no lengths to which God will not go to get us to obey Him? With fear and trembling, I changed my airline reservation from North Carolina to Washington, D.C.

I got to Washington around midnight. I had cancelled the room at the Baptist girls' dorm when Diane confirmed our North Carolina plans, so had no place to go and no one to meet me. I remembered that the U.S. Conference of Mayors' office was on I Street and thought I would find a hotel there. I hailed a taxi and asked to be taken to a reasonably inexpensive motel on I Street. As we drove along, the seedy look of the neighborhood concerned me a little, but I comforted myself that it was dark and everything looks bad at night, especially in the winter. However, as I stepped inside the hotel the odor of stale urine and alcohol mingled together confirmed my fears. I should have turned around and left, but I was so tired. All I could think about was a good shower and curling up between clean sheets. Certainly the potential danger of a woman being alone in this unfamiliar city never entered my mind. I paid for a room and asked to have someone help me with my bags. The desk clerk informed me that for $21 all I got was a room, not service. So I dragged my suitcases up two flights of stairs. When I put the key in the lock I realized the door was open.

I couldn't see much from the dimly lit hallway, so I pushed the door open, dropped the heavy suitcases on the floor, and switched on the light. A man leaped out of the shower stall like a surprised cockroach. He had been shooting up drugs; he held a needle in his hand and the rubber tubing was still wrapped tightly around his arm. His long, greasy, blond hair stuck to his sweaty neck as he fled past me down the hall. I screamed and ran out of the room in total shock and fled down the stairs to the cubby hole that served as the front desk. When I demanded a refund, the clerk, an old woman whose face reflected the mean streets of the neighborhood, mentioned something about the lower regions freezing over before she would give me a refund.

There was no way I could stay in that place. I decided to call the Baptist girls' dorm. There was no pay phone, and the desk clerk refused to allow me to use hers, so I went back upstairs and threw myself on the mercy of God. Like Jonah, I was entangled inside the belly of the great fish of disobedience. I fell on my knees and cried out to God for forgiveness, then promised to do all that I had vowed. Picking up my suitcases, I walked down the stairs and was about to push my way through the double doors when the desk clerk came after me. In a pleasant voice she offered to call a cab, and then gave me my refund.

Her sudden change of heart was an affirmation that God had heard my prayer and was helping me out of this predicament. Just as Samson's hair became a sign of restoration when it began to grow again (Judges 16:22), the clerk's out-of-character kindness was a definite indication that my prayer was not only heard by God, but I was being guided again by His divine agencies. I used her phone to call the Baptist girls' dorm and was told that although my room had been assigned to someone else, I would be given temporary shelter.

Even in the dark of night I could see that the dorm was one of those opulent old mansions filled with antiques. A large living room and the dean's quarters occupied the first floor. The second and third floors were dorms for 20 women, and the basement housed the kitchen and common dining room where occupants ate together every Wednesday evening. The men's dorm was located in the adjoining building. In this place I was to learn how to become a practical Christian and a vegetarian. I'd also learn how to share my faith in a meaningful way as I counseled many of the young ladies who were on their own and in trouble in the big city.

I arrived so late I was left to bunk in the living room so as not to disturb the other occupants. The next morning I was assigned a room with Fay, a young woman from South Carolina, who had never shared anything with a Black person before. She complained for two days, and it seemed that I would have to move out. Then Gloria, a young lady who had just started her first job with the federal government, offered to share her room with me. It was my intention to stay there for about a week, but it was God's will that I stay six months.

The house rules seemed simple, but they were strictly administered by the dean. Since some of the Senate pages were only 16 to 18 years old, an 11:00 curfew was strictly enforced. The use of alcohol and tobacco were absolutely prohibited, and we all had an assigned day to clean the common kitchen and a Wednesday to prepare supper. Anyone caught in the slightest infraction of these rules would be immediately evicted from the house. As it turned out, that rule would work in my favor regarding Fay.

Belligerent about my being there, Fay began to openly use foul language and alcohol. When she discovered I was Adventist, she cooked cabbage with bacon fat, since the only thing she knew about us was that we didn't eat pork. When I unknowingly ate it, she laughed at me and said how foolish my religion was. She eventually became so rebellious she was asked to leave. Then Gloria and I were given her second-floor room that had a view of the street and a congressman's house with its exquisite garden.

The day after I arrived I took a cab to the General Conference in Takoma Park to visit the man Pastor Hughes had referred me to. I sat in his office while he read the letter of introduction Pastor Hughes had sent with me. I didn't know what the letter said, but he seemed awkward after reading it. Pastor Hughes had indicated to me that he would suggest that my testimony be reported in the *Adventist Review,* but I was not sure what other information had been passed on to the reader. His discomfort became more obvious when he began to detail to me the various churches to which I would be welcome. Having never been a person to whom skin color or race is an issue, and having been incorporated into the Deptford church where people from different races and cultures were happily serving the Lord, it was a jarring discovery that the mother church in America was separated by races. He told me about Black conferences (the need for which I now understand but believe should not exist among God's chosen people, who are to live and share all resources as one family on earth as it will be in heaven). He cautioned me not to attend certain White churches, as I would not be welcome. But he thought that I would be right at home at Dupont Park church, even though it was way across town. He didn't even mention the struggling Capitol Hill congregation that was less than a block from where I was staying. Perhaps he was not aware of it. (Pastor Wintley Phipps would put it on the map a few years later.)

I couldn't leave that building fast enough. What had I gotten myself into? The thought of leaving the Adventist Church sprang to mind again, but I forced it out. I focused on finding a job. I felt that no meaningful help would come from the Adventist community, which seemed to me to be fragmented by racial concerns.

I decided to attend a Baptist church that first weekend in Washington, but when Sabbath morning arrived I could not rest. I began to pace the floor, not knowing what to do with myself. Finally, I decided to check out a church for myself and not rely on the words of my General Conference contact. By the time I found the Pennsylvania Avenue Seventh-day Adventist Church in the yellow pages, it was about 8:00. I dialed the number, not really expecting anyone to answer, but I wanted to be able to say that I had at least tried to call. A gruff voice rumbled in my ear. In my mind I immediately identified its owner as White.

"Do you allow Black people to attend your church?" I asked, skipping all perfunctory telephone courtesies.

"What did you say?" He seemed stunned by my question.

I repeated myself, this time slower and with more emphasis.

"Well, come on over and see for yourself that everyone is welcome!" he urged. He gave me directions and the time of service, then asked, "How will I identify you when you arrive?"

"I'll be wearing a yellow cab," I said, laughing.

It had to be the most beautiful church I had ever seen. I had once attended a program at the Gallery in London, but it was an old building. This was a relatively new one surrounded by well-manicured lawns and had a driveway that led right up to the front door. Brother Schack, my phone friend, *was* White and was so tall he seemed to have to bend his neck to get through every door. Sure enough, he was waiting for me and welcomed me warmly. He became my spiritual mentor until his death from cancer several years later.

Although the majority of the congregation of approximately four hundred was also White, the senior pastor, Harry Sabnani, was Indian, and his associate, C. D. Henry, African-American. From these men I learned the pillars of pastoral formation and parish ministry, especially from C. D. Henry, whose way with the young people is better caught than taught. I was also pleased to meet several Black families, including Ralph and Barbara McClain who later "adopted" my son and me. Bob and Diane Freeman and their two children, Tiki and Bobbie, supported me through school. Maryann Sanders, and her two children, and Virginia Logan became my neighbors and friends.

I spent that entire first Sabbath with Brother Schack, who introduced me to the other members, telling and retelling the story of my telephone call. When he became ill several years later, everyone who visited him in the hospital had to hear that story again, no matter how often they already had. I left that church that first Sabbath feeling as though the denomination had been vindicated of all possible shortcomings simply by the warmth of the church people.

The next morning I bought a Washington *Post* and quickly began to scrutinize the employment section. The very first ad I saw was for an administrative assistant. I called, even though it was Sunday. The woman who answered mentioned that she was just on her way out when the phone rang. This was the first and only ad she had placed, she said, and if I could be in her office at 9:00 the next morning she would interview me.

I dressed carefully for the interview. The Center for Community Change was part of a consortium of quasi-government offices that distributed federal funds to rural Americans for housing and farm workers. I was hired on the spot to work with the personnel director. By the end of the second week, my boss, the woman who had hired me, accepted a better-paying position across the street and the director said I could have her job. This was a miracle, the first fulfillment of my dream with the grapefruit! Life was unfolding even better than I had hoped.

I could now afford my own place, so I decided to leave the Baptist girls' dorm, despite the promptings of the Spirit to not do so. I argued back with a dozen reasons why I should leave. Many of my housemates ate pork, visited night clubs, used foul language and alcohol, and listened to unacceptable music. Another bone of contention was the required attendance at Sunday morning or evening services in the church behind the dorm. True, one Christian young lady introduced me to the sermon tapes of her teacher, Chuck Swindoll, who became a favorite author of mine. And I met Susan Speers, who would become a lifetime friend.

Nevertheless, when I answered an ad in the newspaper for a place I was delighted to learn that the landlady was Adventist. I convinced myself this must be God's will for me. Gloria, the only person in the dorm who owned a car, drove me to Clinton, Maryland, to look at the room. I failed to notice how far it was because we were too busy talking about her secret love affair with a man she was planning to marry soon.

The house was beautiful. Nestled in a new subdivision, it had a big yard and many trees. It was a dream! I immediately took it. Sonia Green, the landlady, picked me up the next day after work, and I moved to Clinton without a car and without knowing the bus timetable or routes. I wasn't worried about such mundane things; Sonia promised to give me a ride to the bus stop the next morning. Unfortunately, she wasn't familiar with the routes or buses, either, and left me at the wrong place. I was stranded out in the middle of nowhere on my first day on my new job. An hour before I was to be at my office, I was still stuck in Clinton. I couldn't find a cab and had no idea where I was or how to get to where I needed to be. I was so exasperated I leaned against a light post and asked God what it was about Christianity that had turned me into such a rootless fool.

I was still in that posture when a car pulled up and a flamboyantly-dressed woman stepped out to see if I was all right. When she learned I was lost she immediately offered to drive me to the nearest station so I could catch a train to Washington, D.C. She introduced herself as Ella Murphy, who was in the personnel business, providing temporary help to various companies. And she was an Adventist, too! As we drove along, I told her this was my first day as personnel director and shared my need to find a replacement for the position I had just vacated. We exchanged phone numbers and I thought that would be the last I'd see or hear of her. That afternoon she called to get the information about the job, and as we talked she concluded that *she* should interview for the position. I hired her at the end of our interview and the next Monday morning she began to work for me, becoming another lifelong friend.

Ella started me on the road to hiring Adventists during my professional tenure in Washington, D.C. And it was Ella who got me my first speaking appointment in the Adventist Church. After she heard my conversion story, she arranged for me to tell it at an Adventist Youth Society (AYS) program at the Dupont Park church. There we met Esther Maddox, a teacher who was between assignments. Ella quickly helped me hire her. Ella, Esther, and I became the fearsome threesome for the Lord. God would use Esther a few years later to help me keep my son in an Adventist school. She provided much-needed spiritual and financial support during my difficult transition from a high-profile executive to a poor college student.

After three weeks of struggling to get to the office from the house in Clinton, I realized that I had to move. But where? I could afford only $300 per month, but where in the city would I find such a deal? Only one place. So I put my proverbial tail between my legs and returned to the Baptist dorm. It was tough confessing to the dean that my declaration that "God had led me" to the house in Clinton had really been my own selfish desires. Fortunately, she had not yet reassigned my bed, so I was able to return to my room with Gloria. I was now ready to follow the Lord's instructions carefully.

Shortly after I returned, I met a new resident from the boys' dorm. He called himself NK because his Hindu name was so difficult to pronounce. NK was completing his master's degree, preparing to becoming a Methodist minister. He was a devoted disciple of Elton Trueblood, whom he talked about in every conversation. Sometimes I would ask him if he had any thoughts of his own because he began every statement with "Elton Trueblood says." He complained that all I talked about was Ellen White. To remedy this problem we agreed to exchange books. We would sit for hours on the steps of the Library of Congress or the Supreme Court building to read and discuss this material. As time passed, Elton Trueblood, though a great author, could not hold up to the teachings of Ellen White, so NK turned to the Adventist faith.

This was the first time I had successfully shared my Adventist beliefs. Just as Paul regarded Timothy as his son in the Lord, so I related to NK, but the church members thought we were dating. They didn't know I was adamantly single because I was still recovering from a very bad relationship that had ended when I was converted. Nevertheless, I became very awkward around NK and defensive when people mentioned his name. Soon I didn't even want to study with him. So I introduced him to Pastor Sabnani, who took over the studies. Today NK is married to a physician, and he and his wife have a beautiful daughter. When he couldn't find opportunities for ministry after he joined our church, he became a successful businessman.

Before long, I felt right at home in the Pennsylvania Avenue church. In fact, I soon became very aggressive in Sabbath school, sometimes interrupting to correct the teacher or to proudly display my "extensive knowledge" of materials I had independently researched. I also became very involved in helping Ralph McClain with the youth group that now included my son, Steven, newly arrived from London. I was so self-absorbed I didn't notice that the people thought I was a prickly pear in their midst. I knew that Pastor Sabnani was keeping a wary eye on me because he would regularly invite me to his office to correct some of my strange views, but that never deterred me. Years later, while speaking at a youth federation in New York, I met Pastor Sabnani again. He confessed that if someone had told him I would become the person I am today he would not have believed it. I'm so glad that God never lets go of us, but works with us to wash and regenerate us to draw out our utmost for His highest.

Almost a year later I was promoted to the position of personnel director of Rural America, the largest office in our company, serving all 50 states, with offices also in Mississippi and Texas. I was given a large travel budget and assigned to provide training and expertise to all three offices, plus all the smaller grant recipient agencies in the field.

Meanwhile, I became even more unbearable at church. I boasted loudly of big opportunities and exciting travel experiences. People would sometimes groan and cover their faces when I stood up at prayer meeting because they knew I was going to tell how wonderful I thought I was to God who "speaks to me personally." Well, the truth was that God had not communicated audibly with me in months. His silence was devastating. I thought I had committed the unpardonable sin and was lost forever. I decided to fast for a week until I heard from Him again.

The last day of my fast was a Sabbath. In the quiet of early morning, God called my name. I was elated! I stood at the window, listening, as He talked to me. I was saddened when He said He no longer needed to speak to me audibly. He explained that in the beginning my heart was so hardened by sin that audible communication was the only way He could reach me. But now that I was learning His Word and was being instructed in His church, He was letting me go, like a parent encouraging a child to walk for the first time. He assured me that He would always be with me, holding His outstretched arms to catch me if I should fall, and urged me to listen for His voice in Scripture, in the works of Christian authors, and the guidance of principled men and women.

After God explained why He would no longer address me audibly, I dressed and went to church. I had forgotten about an all-night prayer meeting being held, but decided to join in after breaking my long fast at lunch. As usual, I seized the leadership, even though I had never conducted one before. About 11:00 p.m., as we were singing and praying, Gerry, an elderly woman, stood up to speak.

"I have something I need to confess before we go on," she said.

All eyes were on her because she had been so quiet all evening.

"There's someone here whom I dislike. In fact, I hate her because she is so obnoxious."

I had heard that word before, but this time I was sure it wasn't me—I was always polite to Gerry. I nestled into the deep sofa and closed my eyes as I listened.

"She's a know-it-all, and when I'm around her I feel like she's trying to put me down. I can't tell you how many Sabbaths I have to pray for strength to come to church because I don't want to see her."

By this time we were all like Judas at the last supper, asking, "Is it I?" She shook her head vigorously to each inquiry until I asked. Then she stood stiffly, not responding at all.

"It can't be me!" I protested. "I've never said a bad word to Gerry! Have I, Gerry?" I needed her to say No because here I was bleeding in front of these people. I really needed them to see me as an important leader in the community. Things took a turn for the worse when others chimed in to confirm Gerry's speech.

Ralph McClain, always observant, always the peacemaker, took me into the kitchen. He carefully pointed out that I had been at least overbearing, if not obnoxious. But he helped me see that God wanted to use me in a mighty way. I clung to that small consolation like a drowning woman. He said the way I handled this situation would determine whether or not I would be forgiven and accepted by the community, or excoriated and rejected.

Oh, how I hated that divine discipline. The little girl inside me whose spirit had been broken so many times, who was hurting and crying for recognition and help to be nurtured into wholeness, rebelled against what was going on. I didn't know how to articulate the pain, so I clenched my teeth and decided to just listen. I yielded my will because the bottom line was that I loved the Lord more than life itself. I loved that church, and God knows I needed a place to belong. We must have talked for about an hour, but when we emerged from the kitchen I had made peace with God and was ready to apologize to Gerry and the others. The pain of rejection would take a long time to heal, but I needed to begin anew. And I did, sincerely.

If anyone asks, I am always quick to point to that event as the moment when I truly surrendered myself to God and trusted that He would take care of the hurt I was experiencing. It is too self-serving to describe the incredible transformation that followed. I will only say that Gerry and I became fast friends.

Soon after this event I read again in one of Ellen White's books that to not tell the truth in every situation, in precept or example, by silent assent or verbal consent, was an abomination to the Lord. This was an area that the Holy Spirit had brought to my attention more than once, because I used my sanguine inclination to exaggerate as an excuse to cover up this sin. Now God was urging me to change my behavior. I tried everything to overcome this habit. I would set my jaw against it. I would sometimes bite my tongue until it bled, following Paul's example of "buffet[ing]" his "body and make[ing] it [his] slave" (1 Cor. 9:27, NASB). I began correcting myself in midsentence, even when it was embarrassing. I even told people that I didn't tell the truth. But nothing worked. Instead of diminishing, the problem grew to gigantic proportions.

I was so frustrated that one day while alone in the foyer of the church I threw up my hands in despair and cried, "Lord, I'm a liar! Please, help me because I can't help myself." I couldn't tell you when that habit stopped controlling me, but the day did come when it no longer ruled over me. Although I haven't quite learned the secret of totally controlling my tongue, I now find myself naturally preferring to die than lie!

Being an extremist, I couldn't allow God to change me on His own or in His time. So I became instrumental in forming a group called "The Repairers of the Breach," based on Isaiah 58:12. I became a strict vegetarian, expounding that cheese was forbidden by Ellen White because it was such a filthy thing. And it wasn't enough that I wore a hat to church all the time, I insisted that all the women who joined our study group had to wear hats to church.

Helen Hawley, my former roommate, still remembers how uncomfortable she was with this rule. She had been a Roman Catholic before becoming an Adventist. She did not own a hat, but had some little black handkerchiefs Catholic women sometimes use to cover their heads as a sign of reverence when taking Communion. "The Repairers of the Breach" never said she had to wear them, but we made it clear that she did have to cover her head. We can laugh at ourselves now, but back then it wasn't funny as we imposed our will on others, no matter how much they protested.

I stopped caring for my hair and wore long, dark dresses with high necks and long sleeves to show how modest I had become. We met for long Bible studies and prayer after church every week. I would have been a candidate ripe for plucking by the likes of a David Koresh. I would sit in church, evaluating members to determine whose appearance made them (in my opinion) unlikely candidates for heaven. All this time I was becoming angrier and angrier and covering it up with a false piety too rigid in its legalism to describe. The pendulum had swung further than the far right; I was now a certifiable fanatic.

I reached the end of my rope when I could find no peace in prayer or worship. I decided there was too much sin around me and I would quit the Adventist Church to either find one that followed Ellen White's writings completely, or else start my own study group.

After making that decision, I had three consecutive dreams, two of which were the same. The first two dreams both began on a train ride. I sat across from a handsome man and his secretary, both very well-dressed and businesslike. In the first dream, I was intrigued by them and followed them, not thinking that they saw me. I discovered that they lived in a palace to which they were always driven by a chauffeur in a Rolls Royce.

In the second dream, they stopped the car and invited me to come with them. As we talked I discovered that they were leaders of a worshiping community which they described as being heaven on earth. And it was. I walked into a white marble heaven, so clean the brightness of lights and colors were hard on my eyes. Since I was homeless, I accepted their invitation to stay. They took me to a room upstairs that was so large that my entire apartment would fit into it and still have space to spare. But when I came down to supper, I saw that the couple had undergone drastic changes. They were listening to blood-curdling music, and the handsome prince was now a toothless old man reading pornographic material, while his secretary trudged about like an old hag. I hid behind a wall and overheard them discussing how they were going to sell me into an underground slavery ring and use the money to lure others to their den of iniquity. I had to escape, but as I tried to run I was caught and locked into a basement dungeon from which there was no escape. Since no one knew where I was, I was lost forever. After both dreams, I woke up in a cold sweat, shaken by how real it all seemed.

The third dream was different. I had been in a house that looked like the Pennsylvania Avenue church. It was filthy inside, and no matter what I did to clean it, it just became dirtier. I finally decided to hire a strong servant to clean the entire place, scouring out all the dirt hidden in every nook and cranny. I heard that there was a place "over yonder" where people went to find good servants, so I set off to find it. I swam across rivers filled with alligators that snapped at my heels. I climbed mountains made out of soft sulphurous brimstone that crumbled beneath my touch. I crossed pits and scaled precipices where huge snakes slithered along the bottom, lunging to bite me with their poisoned fangs.

I finally came to the top of a mountain. There I found a huge hall, filled with thousands of servants, all dressed alike. I was tired and confused. How would I ever find the one who could clean out the house I had left behind? I became desperate, grabbing people and asking them for their help. Then I came to the center of a room where a Man stood, whose face I couldn't see. Although dressed like the others, He was different. There was something distinctive about His demeanor and an authority He brought to the position of servanthood. When He turned to look at me, His eyes were filled with unspeakable compassion. I was immediately transported to the judgment hall scene described in Matthew 26. I had once seen an illustration of Jesus looking at Peter, after his denial, with tremendous tenderness. Suddenly I was in Peter's place as Jesus tenderly looked at me and said, "If I, the Lord of the universe, your sinless Saviour, can live in that house, who do you think you are to leave it? Take any of these human servants and follow him to eternal ruin, or follow Me and enjoy eternal life! I will never leave you or forsake you."

I reached out to touch Him, but He had already disappeared into the crowd, His words hanging like ripe berries from a branch, waiting to be harvested. I woke up, realizing that providence had once again intervened in my life.

I interpreted these dreams to mean that God had brought me into the Adventist Church, and in spite of the many things which were not going as I expected or wanted, I was not perfect either, and should stay and learn from my Lord and His people. These dreams were to have a profound impact on the rest of my life, especially during the debates about women's ordination.

I stopped participating in the Repairers of the Breach movement and recommitted my life to Christ. That was the last time I ever even toyed with the idea of leaving the Adventist Church. If one day I should leave, it will be because God tells me in clear, specific terms, just as He has guided my life in the past, and not because of a scandal or the lack of principle-centered leadership or the failure to ordain women.

~

I met a man at church. Eugene, a French-American, was not a Christian, but attended one Sabbath to please his mother's friend. He drove a Fiat X19 with the license plate WOW. His company, Wash on Wheels, power washed the outside of buildings. He was immediately drawn to me, and my Messianic syndrome went into overdrive as I determined to save his unconsecrated soul.

We spent an inordinate amount of time together, and no matter how much I pleaded, Eugene would not quit drinking or smoking. Though he loved my company and the way I talked about God, I can't remember him ever studying the Bible on his own. Even when I tried to study with him he would make excuses, yet he would not miss a Sabbath or the afternoon Christian Growth class taught by Ralph McClain. Since he always sat beside me and I always drove his car when he was out of town, people began to think of us as a couple. But I had no personal "love" interest in this man.

One Sabbath afternoon during the discussion in Christian Growth class he stood up and declared his love and his desire to marry me. I was totally unprepared for those sentiments and very angry that he had placed me in such a difficult situation in public. Ralph talked to me after the study. He helped me understand that in the process of playing the great Bible worker I had given Eugene the wrong message. And he, in turn, had fallen in love with me. I would never marry a nonbeliever, not only because God says not to in 2 Corinthians 6:14, but because I was once a nonbeliever. I know from personal experience that an unbeliever is not capable of loving me in the unselfish, unconditional way I need to be loved. Second, even though Eugene fit the description of men to whom I was normally attracted, I had not smoked in years and wasn't about to be intimate with someone who did. Third, I needed to learn the lesson by which I now live in my ministry: God does not need me to use my feminine wiles to win converts to His kingdom. Neither should I give Bible studies to men alone, for when they are vulnerable and I'm weak, who knows what sin that combination will give birth to?

Ralph made it clear that I had a Christian responsibility to either follow through with Eugene or break off contact immediately. I chose the latter because I was not about to defy God on this one. I told him that Sabbath afternoon that I would not see or speak to him again. I referred him to Ralph for further Bible studies.

Eugene had been a respected undercover cop in the city. While on one of these assignments, someone discovered his identity and put poison in his drink. Although he didn't die, it caused a mental breakdown that manifested itself from time to time in hallucinations. These episodes could be triggered by a certain odor, a color, or a taste, and no one, including Eugene, knew when one would occur.

A week later I received a telephone call from Eugene, telling me he was in the hospital and needed to see me right away. I didn't make the connection when he said he was at St. Elizabeth's Hospital, the mental institution where the likes of John Hinckley are incarcerated. Of course, if I had read the morning paper or listened to the news I would have been prepared before the old Messianic button was pushed and I was off in a flash. I would have called my pastor and asked him to visit Eugene. Instead, I put the phone down, ran to my car, and raced to St. Elizabeth's.

It seems that Eugene had been wandering around in a stupor for several days after I said goodbye to him. He had neither slept nor eaten and something had triggered a hallucination. He felt that God was sending him to warn President Carter that someone was attempting to assassinate him. Somehow he found his way to the White House and tried to gain access. In the course of his police work he had once had White House clearance, but this privilege had been revoked years before. Like any other intruder, he was now *persona non grata*. Not satisfied with being sent away, however, he responded to the persistent voices in his head that urged him to go warn the president and drove his X19 through the wrought iron gates onto the White House front lawn, where he was arrested. As a result of this incident, concrete barriers are now a permanent part of the front facade of the White House. The whole sorry story was plastered on the front page of the Washington *Post* and headlined national television newscasts that day.

Eugene became violent when he was arrested, kicking, punching, and flailing at the authorities who took him off to St. Elizabeth's Hospital, where he was given several Thorazine injections to calm him down.

Now enters Messiah Williams. The nurse on duty told me that when given an opportunity to make a telephone call, Eugene called me instead of contacting his lawyer. He also explained that the Thorazine was not having the expected effect because Eugene was still wide awake, waiting to see me. He showed me to a room, and a few minutes later Eugene strolled in, gaunt, eyelids swollen, all of which further emphasized his haunted look. When the nurse left the room, Eugene put his head down on the small table and fell asleep. Even though he was unconscious, I felt I should read a few Psalms and talk to him about God, then I would leave.

When I stood up to leave, however, I discovered there was no handle on the door and I could not pull or push it open. So I sat down and read a little more, then tried the door again. It didn't budge. I began to panic, banging at it with my fists. That was futile—the room was soundproof. My heart began to pound. I was locked in a soundproof room in a mental institution and no one on the outside knew where I was!

I finally remembered that in the movies people sometimes used their shoulder to break down doors. So I walked to the opposite side of the room, tilted my shoulder, and took a running leap toward the door. I bounced off like a rubber ball and crumpled to the floor in agony. It felt like I had dislocated my shoulder. Now I was in unabashed panic. I screamed until I was hoarse, but no one heard me. And Eugene never even stirred.

Several hours later, after a shift change, the new nurse on duty conducted a bed count and found he was one patient short. Fortunately for me, he had the presence of mind to check every room before notifying the authorities. He apologized and told me to take the iron stairs to get out. The guard there would direct me to my car. When I got to the foot of the stairs, there stood a poor woman cowering against the wall and screaming, "Murder, murder! Don't hit me!" She slapped at her face as though brushing away a swarm of flies. I was already distraught and this frightened me even more. So I flattened my back against the opposite wall, both arms outstretched, and tried to slide past her, screaming my own plea for help.

There we stood, the woman and I, screaming antiphonally. Even when a nurse came out of a nearby room and barked orders to be quiet, we couldn't stop screaming. She became very annoyed. "I'm not going to tell you two one more time to *shut up!*"

Finally, she ordered us into a room that was full of other inmates. I protested, explaining that I was not a patient, but she wouldn't listen to me. "I'm going to count to three," she said angrily, "and if you are not in that room"—she pointed energetically toward the door—"I'm going to be forced to bring out the water hose."

I didn't know what that meant, but the other woman evidently did because she began to move.

"But I don't belong here!" I cried, tears running down my face. "I'm a business executive."

"And I'm the Virgin Mary!" the nurse snapped.

"My office is on Wisconsin Avenue—here, call this number." I rummaged frantically through my purse.

She grabbed us both by the wrists and shouted, "Just shut up and get into the room!"

I was sure this was it. No one would ever find me. I would be locked away for life. "Oh, God," I sobbed, "get me out of this!" My purse clattered to the floor, spewing out driver's license, business cards, and used tissue.

Now I know why we women carry big purses filled with things we haven't used in a long time. It is for such times as this. As the nurse helped me retrieve my scattered paraphernalia she realized I had been telling the truth. She called the guard, who escorted me to my car. I sat in the car for a long time before I trusted my trembling feet to operate the pedals well enough to drive away.

~

While personnel director of Rural America, I hired an Adventist secretary and, as the months went by, several other Adventists to work at various assignments in the office. There were also a few nonpracticing Adventists among our employees, including the vice president for financial affairs. These people were part of a group of more than 100 employees who had a soda machine installed, then converted it into a beer dispenser where the secretaries began the day with a Miller Lite. When they refused to comply with my written requests to convert the machine back to a soda machine, I called the company and had it hauled out of there. This action stirred up a hornets' nest of anger, and I became public enemy number one.

When I began staff evaluations, something that hadn't been done before my arrival, the support staff threatened to strike until I persuaded the administration that this would improve productivity. Change was difficult. Some had been receiving a salary for little or no work. When their game was shut down, they started rumors that I hired members of my church in order to receive a kickback. I ignored them, but when the rumors persisted, my boss called for an investigation. Some Adventists on staff were forced to resign.

About this time, the director offered me a promotion to deputy director. Flattered, I immediately accepted. Then the rumors became even more vicious. One day I spoke to a young receptionist who was repeatedly tardy and hung out with some of the known troublemakers on staff. I told her the Bible warns that "bad company corrupts good habits." She reported my remark to the director, accusing me of forcing my religion on her. As a quasi-government institution, religious proselytizing, or the appearance of it, was prohibited, especially by the personnel director and equal opportunity officer. The director was kind enough not to withdraw the offer of promotion but gave me a caution. As the harassment continued, I could tell I was now skating on thin ice.

When the director invited me to a party with some White House officials I asked if alcohol would be served. "Only wine," he said, explaining that while I didn't have to drink I was expected to hold a glass as though I was drinking. I refused to go. I felt that would compromise my testimony, especially since there were already four ministers of different denominations on staff who were an embarrassment to the Christian faith. The director's attitude toward me changed significantly after this incident. His subsequent unpleasant remarks indicated he rued the day he had offered me the promotion, but it was too late to retract the offer.

The time came for my promotion to be presented to the board, composed of members from each state who were flown to Washington, D.C., for a weekend series of presentations. I made my presentation on Thursday afternoon, and everyone seemed excited by it. I was told that I was a shoo-in for the post of deputy director. However, the director, who claimed he promoted me because of my excellent work, and especially my committed Christian lifestyle, scheduled the approval meeting for Saturday morning at 11:00. It's not that he was unaware of the Sabbath. As a backslidden Quaker, he had maintained that he knew what Sabbath meant to me. He had often urged me to leave well before sunset on Fridays, sometimes teasing that he didn't want God to punish him for encouraging me to break this commandment.

From the moment I was told of the appointment, I began to bargain with God. I promised to pay a double tithe, to do many more Bible studies, to obey without being told a second time. I was like a child facing a spanking, pleading and promising anything if God would only find a way to get me what I wanted. This was going to be the best, highest-paid position I would ever have in my life, and I wanted it so badly I could taste it. I wish that I could testify that I voluntarily stood for Jesus, but that wouldn't be true.

Sabbath morning I dressed in a new business suit, purchased for the occasion. I decided I would go to Sabbath school, then slip quietly away and attend the meeting, confirm my appointment, and return to church before the service was over. No one would have to know. Except God. But surely God would understand when the big bucks started coming in that I'd pay tithe on, plus the extra time I'd spend giving Bible studies. That would certainly make up for any spiritual problem this might cause . . .

Once again, the Lord used Ralph McClain to point me in the right direction. I had kept the entire incident to myself, but God has a way of bringing wisdom without revealing our weaknesses. In Sabbath school that morning, when Ralph spoke about the importance of not compromising faith for fortune, I felt as though the Lord was speaking to me personally. The conflict continued to rage in my heart and mind. What difference would it make if I took just one hour out of Sabbath to do something I believed was a gift from God? Oswald Chambers, in his commentary on Genesis, says, "Panic always forces Christians to do that which is wrong to accomplish what is right for God." (Remember Abraham and Sarah in Genesis 12? And Moses and the Egyptian in Exodus 2?) Perhaps this was a test Satan was using in an attempt to rob me of my commitment to God. I sat in the pew too troubled to move.

I didn't know that I wouldn't attend the meeting until I didn't go. When I didn't show up, my boss became incensed by "the rebuff," as he angrily described it, especially since I didn't call to let him know I would not be there. When I arrived at my office on Monday morning, everything, except a chair and the telephone, had been removed, including the file cabinet containing the confidential employee records. My secretary was forbidden to speak to me and was immediately assigned to someone else. The director left me a terse note, informing me that effective immediately my salary would be drastically reduced and that a staff meeting was scheduled. The rumor was he would choose this opportunity to expose me as a fraud and a religious fanatic who had broken the federal guidelines and accepted kickbacks.

I handled the first three problems reasonably well, even though I felt like an object of curiosity. As the news got around about my predicament, workers filed by my office to peer in at me sitting in an empty room. I decided I would go to work every day and tough it out. My boss wouldn't return my calls or see me when I visited his office. I was being shunned.

As I waited for D-day to arrive, I became less confident that God would be able to take me safely through and more afraid of the consequences if He didn't. Quitting and walking away from this crisis became a very attractive alternative, but I knew I had mishandled some things and felt I needed to stay and set the record right. No matter how hard I prayed, though, the situation kept getting worse. Whispered accusations became audible confrontations as some secretaries, emboldened by my declining popularity with the administration, spoke to me in the most demeaning manner. Some of my colleagues, still angry over the soda machine, grasped the opportunity to get even by making vicious remarks in my hearing.

The day of the staff meeting 60 people from the Washington office gathered in the conference room. I took a seat in the back corner. Prior to my fall from grace, I had always sat on the right hand of the director, who seldom made a decision without consulting me.

My former secretary handed me a lukewarm soda saying, "A last drink for the prisoner!"

Even though I was sure the allegations were all false, I was terrified because I had seen my boss rake innocent victims over the coals before and break the composure of accomplished senior executives by ruthlessly humiliating them in this public forum. I was so nervous that every pore in my body leaked. Every shred of hope that God would rescue me evaporated.

When the director took his place at the conference table, anyone standing or sitting close to me quickly moved a safe distance away so as not to be considered a sympathizer. I sat alone, eyes closed. The meeting was called to order and the director stood up to speak. He cleared his throat and glanced quickly in my direction.

"I've called this meeting to discuss the situation with Hyveth Williams," he said matter of factly into the deafening silence. He seemed to be struggling to articulate the charges against me. He stopped and started again. And again. After three attempts, the staff began to get restless. Whispers from the back became audible complaints.

"Get on with it, man!" someone called out.

The director seemed confused. He began to nervously pick at the skin of his thumb until it bled, a sure sign he was under duress. Suddenly, he dismissed the staff, promising to make good on his pledge to expose me. But the man has never said a word against me. In fact, when I finally resigned three months later, one of the best letters of recommendation I've ever received was authored by him. God also gave me an opportunity to apologize for not notifying him that I wouldn't attend the board meeting, and he expressed his gratitude that I did not exercise my equal opportunity rights in a lawsuit against him. He asked about the source of my strength through those terrible months, and I shared a most gratifying Bible study with my boss before I left that last day. Sadly, his troubles were only beginning, because within weeks the government accounting office accused him of mismanaging federal funds, the company was reduced to one office with three employees, and today is no longer in operation.

As long as I live, I will never forget how it felt as I waited for my world to collapse that day. Had I been naive in my decision to obey God's call to "remember the Sabbath day" over my boss' scheduled appointment? I was deeply disappointed when God did not ride in to rescue me and show those "heathens" that I was His chosen woman. Yet all the time God had gone before me to smooth out the situation and miraculously prevent the director from speaking falsely against me, publicly humiliating me, and shattering my already fragile ego.

After resigning, I was unemployed for nearly a year. All that time the Spirit kept impressing me to go to school to prepare for the ministry. I would not obey because to cover up the fact that I was struggling with such a call from God I had been teaching that women should not be ministers. I was sure I'd find a job quickly. While working at Rural America I was sought after by many "head hunters" in corporate America. One had recommended me to the late congressman, Mickey Leland, from Texas. He interviewed me and hired me to run his San Antonio office. But the Monday I reported to his office on Capitol Hill, I discovered that his administrative assistant had resigned on Friday and the office was in complete turmoil. The receptionist asked me to call later. When I did, the congressman said he needed a few weeks to hire a new administrative assistant and he would get back in touch with me. A few weeks later, the new administrative assistant decided that his friend would be better suited for the job in Texas than I was. I was disappointed, but I thought I had enough unemployment benefits to see me through to the next position.

Almost a year (and hundreds of applications and interviews) later, I was out of money. I didn't want to put my son in public school, so I tried to get a job, any job. Finally, I took a position as a janitor in a factory where handicapped people made simple toys. It was a demeaning task, especially having to wash away the feces that had been daubed on the walls by the employees. It was the only job from which I was ever fired in my life, not because I wasn't doing it well, but because I believe the Lord saw that I had learned the lesson of humility He had been trying to teach me since my conversion. It was time to move on to the next lesson.

I had to give up the house I had rented and move into a less expensive home. I searched for other jobs, even as a maid in a hotel. Nothing was available to me because the Lord had closed all doors while He called me to prepare for the ministry. I was so afraid when I thought of going back to college. I had dropped out more than a decade before. But eventually the unemployment benefits ran out and I was faced with no job, a dependent child, and absolutely no income.

The mail arrived one day as I stood on the back porch, crying and complaining to God about my situation. I opened one of the envelopes and there was a check for $221.34, pension reimbursement from the city of Hartford. It had been several years since I had worked for the city, so I accepted the funds as a providential gift. Unfortunately my financial life had fallen into such disarray that I no longer had a bank account and so couldn't cash this "heavenly" check. Having money I couldn't spend was even more frustrating than not having any at all. Why would God send help in this manner, knowing I had no way of cashing the check?

I lay curled up on the floor in my son's room like a helpless fetus when I got the idea to call my former secretary at Rural America. Jane shared the good news that she had been promoted to administrative assistant to the president. I ached to be back at my old desk, but pretended to her that things were going well for me also. I wasn't sure quite how to ask, but I needed her help in cashing my check. I mentioned that I was having some banking problems and needed a check cashed.

"I don't think I can help you, Hyveth . . ."

I could hear her rustling through her purse and counting.

"Actually, all I have left is $221—Wait a minute . . . here's 34 cents!"

I just broke down and cried. The exact amount of my check! This must be God's way of increasing my faith and giving me hope, while providing an opportunity for me to witness to my atheist friend. This event was so obviously supernatural to her that she invited me to her home in Baltimore. I spent the weekend studying the Bible with her and leading her to a personal understanding of Jesus Christ. A few months later I was notified that the Hartford finance department had made a mistake and I had to repay the money; nevertheless, it never diminished the miracle for me.

My material life did not improve after that incident. In fact, it became worse. I was so broke I can't tell you how desperate I became. There were days when I had nothing to feed my son and no gas in the car to get him home from school. I was at the end of my rope. I decided to go on welfare. Even though I lived in Upper Marlboro, Maryland, I was referred to the WIC program at the welfare office across from Prince George's Plaza, more than an hour and a half away. I filled out the necessary papers for food stamps and was interviewed by one of the case workers. As she asked me about my

# Album Photos

My grandmother, Satyra Page (Miss Sity), and a family friend. She was in her mid-60s in this picture.

1945: My beautiful mother, Margaret Page, when she was 26

1961: I was a 15-year-old school girl at Oberlin High School, Lawrence Tavern, Jamaica.

1959: I'm 13 years old here.

I sent this picture to the casting director of a London TV show. (I got the part!) I was 18.

1970: My first day of work in the mayor's office, Hartford, Connecticut

1968: John, baby Steven, and me in happier times

A birthday party for my boss, Hartford's Mayor Athanson. Nancy Mulroy and Ann Raymond were secretaries in the office.

1965: In London with my friend Maureen, who died tragically of a brain aneurysm.

1975: I was on a modeling assignment
(for a book of poetry).

1976: A special
reception at city
hall for the actress
Kay Medford. I'm
with Mayor
Athanson and local
TV/radio personality
Brad Davis.

1977: Opening night of the CIAN fashion show. I'm with my friend Diane Lyman, a designer, and two models.

1976: Trevor (brother), Margaret (mother), Renita (sister), and Steven (son) at my aunt's wedding

1977: My last day of work in the mayor's office, Hartford, Connecticut

1976: This is my home in Hartford, Connecticut, where I hid the infamous papers in my chimney flue.

1977: Marcel Marceau, the famous mime; Mayor Athanson; Pat Falletti; and Steven

1978: When the tarot card reader I consulted predicted "a cloud of abundant riches" would "rain unlimited opportunities" on me, my secretary and I went out and celebrated.

1978: I'm with Ella Grasso, governor of Connecticut, after a meeting to discuss my future in Connecticut politics.

1978: Drugs were a part of my pre-Christian lifestyle.

1982: With my dear friend Ralph McClain at the Pennsylvania Avenue church

Charlie, Steven's little pet hamster, who taught me that God is more concerned about His little children and creatures than about rules made up by human beings.

1986: The Andrews
University era

1986: My mother,
Margaret Page, and
me in Washington, D.C.

1988: My sister,
Renita, in Paris

1987: I conduct my first baptism, Sligo church.

1989: Freedom! I'm a graduate of the Seventh-day Adventist Theological Seminary!

1991: With my dear friend and secretary, Wendy Barahmian, at the Boston Temple

1993: I made a new friend in Australia!

1990: Teaching the Boston Temple "multitude," shortly after I arrived

1991: My office at the Boston Temple

Ella Taylor, who became my best friend at the Boston Temple, painted, spackled, and repaired my church office herself, so that her new pastor would have a pleasant place to work.

1990: In the newly renovated sanctuary

1995: With my son, Steven, at the Boston Temple's 125th anniversary celebration

1993: Associate pastor Matt Lombard and I are at the baptism of Dan and Barbara Kelsey. I also married them just before they were baptized! They now head up the Helping Hands program in our church, feeding scores of homeless people every week.

employment history, she became visibly infuriated.

"What are you doing here? Trying to rip off the government, huh? You should be out looking for a job!" she said in a nasty tone. "What have you been doing to find a job?"

I didn't respond. My self-esteem was too low to care.

She ran on. "People like you have all the luck in the world and never use it."

If she was attempting to motivate me, it wasn't working. Every word was like a hard blow to my already-defeated psyche.

"I shouldn't say this to you, but when I was 16 I joined the Seventh-day Adventist Church."

*What was this?*

"I was the only one in my family who joined. The people at the church tried to help me because they knew it was my dream to be a doctor. I remember one woman who was willing to pay my way through the Adventist school, but I refused. I wanted to stay home with my family." Her voice was filled with regret. "But all my family ever did for me was to help me backslide. Pretty soon I was eating and acting just like them again."

By then tears were flowing down my face.

"If I had stuck with the program and followed the way God was leading me I would be a physician today, and not some tired, frustrated welfare worker having to deal with ambitionless people like you!"

I began to talk to her. I told her how God had been trying to reach me. I shared how I was being impressed to go to school, but was running away instead. As she listened her countenance changed, then her attitude softened. She urged me to go register at Columbia Union College, promising to direct me to educational funding resources if I did my part.

As I got up to leave she asked, "Have you ever heard this song?" In a beautiful voice she began singing "Children, Go Where I Send You." When she finished singing she looked at me. "Do you believe God sends people?"

"Yes," I whispered.

"Then go where God sends *you*," she said softly. "You will never live long enough to regret it!"

# Chapter Five

# Coming to My Senses

left the welfare office that day literally skipping—until I came to the parking lot and discovered I had a flat tire. Every shred of hope and motivation dissolved. My high intentions to rush right over to Columbia Union College and register disappeared into a chasm of despair and depression. Satan had snatched away my joy. It took my last few dollars to repair the tire, and I drove home to wallow in the depths of self-pity.

By Sabbath I decided only worse things would happen if I had contact with other human beings, especially some of the other broken shards such as myself. I knew that even the smallest scrape would throw me into the manic depressive, suicidal mode from which I suffered so much before conversion.

But I went to church anyway, in body if not in mind. The guest speaker, Dr. Bill Liversidge, an Australian pastor and the newly appointed ministerial secretary of the Columbia Union, sat in our Sabbath school class. His sanguine personality began to seep in around the edges of my darkness as he encouraged us to explore our spiritual gifts. During the worship service he called me to the platform. He didn't know my name, only that we had been in the same class that morning. I stood there nervously, waiting for whatever he would do next. He announced to the church that I looked like a woman who was running away from God, adding that he was impressed that I should be preparing for the ministry. Based on our interaction in Sabbath school, he said, he sensed that some of my spiritual gifts would be best used in that area.

My mouth dropped open. I could only look up to God with a sigh. I could feel assurance returning; the burdens and fears of the past few days rolled away, and I began to recapture the vision I had the day before when I walked out of the welfare office. I can't recall much else that happened in that worship service, but as we ate lunch in the fellowship hall, Dr. Liversidge urged me to see Dr. Ken Stout, then chairman of the Religion Department at Columbia Union College, to discuss attending as a theology major. If I was too nervous to go alone, he promised he would accompany me.

Whether planned by Bill Liversidge or Providence, while I was talking with Dr. Stout on Monday morning, Bill bounced into the Religion Department office wearing the broadest smile and offering the warmest welcome. I can never describe how much this affirmed and encouraged me on that first leg of a very uncertain journey. I know Bill and the welfare worker were used by God to prompt me to obey His call.

Columbia Union College was a very intimidating campus. I had not been to school in well over a decade, and although the administration was more than generous, providing a start-up check and offers of employment, orientation was a terrifying experience. At thirtysomething, not only was I the oldest person in a freshman class that included a 14-year-old girl, I was the only one who was not recently graduated from an Adventist academy. I felt out of place, unable to understand the language of my twittering classmates or the complex forms we had to complete. Overcome by a fear of failure (which lasted weeks into the first semester), my self-confidence was very frail, but God was using this experience to bring me to my senses as a new creature in Christ for whom the past, and much of the manipulative manner by which I had earned success, was stripped away.

It didn't help to hear the counsel of some members of my church who were not too happy that I was going to study theology. Their beliefs about women in ministry, combined with my past reluctance to keep my opinions to myself, had them deeply concerned. And I, still afraid to admit that God was calling me to the ministry, joined them in a prayer meeting where they prayed that the spirit of teaching or nursing would capture my interest. I comforted them with the assurance I would prepare to be a missionary, not a minister. (Shortly after my first sermon, however, they would change their view and, empowered by the Holy Spirit, affirm my call to the ministry by their support as it became evident that God had indeed laid His hand upon me for this work.)

In the fall of 1982 I began college classes. To support myself I drove a school bus for the first time, transporting children from our church to Beltsville Elementary school. My Greek class began at 8:00 a.m., but by the time I dropped off the students and raced to the college, it was usually only a few minutes before the end of class. My classmates were not aware that I had made arrangements with Elder G. Arthur Keough, our teacher. To them, I was just another tardy student. Every time I arrived their grumbled protests and snide remarks elicited enough giggles and guffaws to make the peer pressure almost unendurable. Elder Keough, on the other hand, was more concerned that I would miss important concepts and fail the class.

One morning he decided to give me an impromptu test to determine whether or not he should recommend that I drop the class. As usual, I arrived with only a few minutes left before the bell would ring. Before I even put my book bag down, Elder Keough called on me to translate a passage from Greek to English. I was so nervous I didn't hear his exact instructions, but with all eyes trained on me I was too afraid to ask for clarification. I quickly opened the text book and began to read, translating a passage he had not yet covered. You could have heard a pin drop as I read. Elder Keough's face registered blank surprise. Ken Mulzac, the top student in the class, declares this incident was the defining moment in his experience with me in our short journey together at CUC. He said he held his breath in amazement at the incredible way the Greek rolled off my tongue that day. All I could do was utter a silent prayer of thanksgiving, because I knew this had not happened by my might or power, but by the Spirit of God—and the help of the children on my school bus.

It had become a game on the school van for the children to take turns asking me to recite the Greek alphabet. In exchange for the privilege of sitting in the front seat the older boys gave me English words from the vocabulary, and I would respond in Greek. Even though they didn't understand what I was saying, the exercise helped me tremendously. The front seat soon became a sought-after place in the van. I learned more and learned it faster than if I had been in class, trying to keep up with only the daily lessons.

From that day my classmates treated me with new respect, and when I became secretary of the Religion Department the next semester I was often asked to teach the Greek class in our teacher's absence.

I got to thinking about how I had wasted a whole year running from God and decided to double up my class load and graduate sooner. So for two semesters I took 20 credit hours each semester, and for two more semesters

I took 26 hours, completing the program in two years and graduating with honors. It was helpful that I was able to transfer 12 credits from the University of Hartford.

I soon became the spiritual mother on campus. I moved from Upper Marlboro into a four-bedroom house, owned by the school, on Garland Avenue. I first sublet rooms to Ken Mulzac and his cousin, Winston. When they moved out, I took in three more students: John Fritz, Tom Decker, and Jeff Richards. These three men were the tallest, most handsome men on campus, which only added to my popularity with the young ladies, who were always eager to accept invitations to my home.

I started a Friday evening vespers service for freshmen that became one of the most popular events on campus during my last year. It is so gratifying when I travel to encounter former CUC students who express their appreciation for those vespers and the important impact they had on their spiritual development.

My house also became the local watering hole for weary travelers. I should have kept a guest book to record the visiting students from Italy, Germany, France, and all over the United States who stayed in my home for days, weeks, and, in one case, months. The word got around that if one was in Washington, D.C., and had no place to stay, or just needed to freshen up, go to Garland Avenue. I finally began leaving my front door unlocked so as not to inconvenience visitors.

I came home from a late class one evening to find my friend Liz Tolland and a dozen students from Hartland Institute camped out in sleeping bags all over my living room. We had a blast, singing and sharing the good news of our Lord's unconditional regard for us.

I had the blessing of meeting the parents of my boarder Jeff Richards when I preached at the Williamsburg church where his father served as an elder. Jim and Sunny Richards often held prayer meeting in their luxurious home that overlooked a private lake. Jim invited me to speak at the prison where he operated one of the finest prison ministries I've ever seen. I'll never forget the first time I went inside that prison with Jim Richards.

We were carefully examined for contraband and instructed not to allow the men who came to the study to touch us, especially me, being a woman. Apparently, the men were incarcerated for violent crimes. For many of them, their only contact with the outside world was television, and most had not been in physical proximity to a woman in years.

We were ushered into a large room where two armed guards waited for the prisoners to be brought in. Some of them came, hoping to use us; others came to ridicule. I doubt too many came to hear the gospel, but that's what they were about to receive. I preached my heart out, ending with my own testimony. Many of those hardened criminals cried as they gave their lives to the Lord.

The one who made the greatest impression on me was a big African-American whom I will call Timothy, which means "to honor God," because he certainly has! *Mr. T,* the popular television show, was in its first year. Timothy was Mr. T, down to the haircut and muscles. The only things missing from Timothy were the reams of gold chain and gigantic finger rings.

Judging by the deferential treatment he received from the other prisoners, Timothy was obviously a feared man among his peers. When I began to speak, he stood up, even though the rule was that inmates had to sit in their places until they were escorted out. The moment he stood up the two guards raised their rifles. The sounds of the guns being readied for firing ricocheted around the room. You've heard of a shotgun wedding? Well, as they pointed their rifles at Timothy—and therefore in my direction—I was experiencing a shotgun sermon. When other prisoners stood up to block Timothy with their bodies, all strength left my knees. Somehow I had the presence of mind to keep on preaching. Then Timothy smiled, displaying a row of gold-capped teeth, and nodded his approval. The guards—and everyone else—breathed a sigh of relief as the tension abated and the preaching continued.

After many Bible studies, Timothy gave his life to the Lord and became a model prisoner. With Jim's help, he was put into the work release program. The last I heard, he had been paroled, was baptized, and is now a brother in Christ.

I began my student internship under senior pastor Al Konrad at the Pennsylvania Avenue church. In order to generate Bible studies, I wrote letters of condolence to families whose names I had garnered from the obituary page in the Washington *Post,* an old habit from my days of working in the mayor's office. One day my eyes caught some personal notices, and I wrote letters and enclosed a small tract. I received only one response, but what an incredible one it was!

Lewis, a patient in St. Elizabeth's hospital, wrote to say he was interested in Bible studies. I passed the information on to Lorine Bray, the Bible worker, for follow-up. Soon she was going with a group from the church to give this man Bible studies. After almost a year of studies, Lewis accepted Jesus Christ as his personal Saviour and requested baptism. Because he was serving a life sentence without parole or privilege to leave the hospital grounds, Pastor Konrad had to go to court to receive permission for Lewis to come to church for his baptism.

I had planned a youth revival and rally for that day around the theme "Jesus Is Practical." Dr. Liversidge, Ron Vanderhorst, and the late Dr. Victor Griffiths inspired more than 800 worshipers in the morning, and Pastor Wintley Phipps thrilled an audience of nearly 1,000 in the evening. This was an unprecedented, cooperative venture with the Potomac and Allegheny East conferences. Our church had never had this many people in attendance before, but we were well-organized and were able to feed everyone at lunch.

That afternoon Lewis gave his testimony. He was the son of a prominent physician, he told us, and had begun abusing alcohol in his teens. When he was in his early 20s, he had gotten very drunk and viciously murdered a senator's secretary. Through plea bargaining his family was able to avert the death penalty, but Lewis received a life sentence and was isolated from society in St. Elizabeth's mental institution. His attendance at this rally was his first time off the premises for other than medical purposes.

He concluded his story by expressing how deeply he understood what Jesus Christ had done for him by taking his place on the cross. "Every day since my conversion," he said, "I have wished I could give my life for the young woman's life I took." He had written letters of apology to her parents, seeking their forgiveness and sharing his faith. He wasn't seeking to be released; he felt he had a responsibility to accept the consequences of his actions. In moving words he expressed the tremendous difference it had made since Jesus Christ had come into his heart and forgiven him, bringing him back like the prodigal son to his Father's house. Now he could face the rest of his life with a heart filled with the love and peace of God.

"I may not look like much, being a murderer and a prisoner in a mental institution," he said, ending his testimony, "but in the eyes of God I'm special; I'm His son!"

Then he walked away from the microphone and embraced his father and mother, publicly asking their forgiveness before he was buried alive in Christ in baptism.

There wasn't a dry eye in the house.

Although I was an intern at the Pennsylvania Avenue church, I was sometimes asked to preach in other churches in the Potomac Conference. One weekend Dr. Norman Johnson, one of my teachers, was scheduled to speak at a church in Winchester, Maryland. When he became ill at the last minute he asked me to take his place. Dr. Johnson didn't mention to the folk in Winchester that I was a woman, and because my name does not readily identify my gender or race, they were about to receive the shock of their lives.

I asked Ken Mulzac, my compatriot from Greek class, and his wife, Belynda, one of the best singers in our church today, to accompany me to the Winchester church. Ken let Belynda and me off at the door while he parked the car. When we identified ourselves as coming from Columbia Union College, the greeter, though visibly taken aback by two Black visitors, regained her composure enough to graciously inquire which one of us was the speaker's wife.

"I'm the speaker," I replied with a smile.

"Welcome, Mrs. Williams!" She pumped my hand heartily. "As soon as your husband comes in, please send him right over there." She pointed toward the pastor's study.

At that very moment, Ken walked in. Pushing past me, the greeter reached her hand out to Ken. "Pastor Williams, we're so happy to have you speak to us today," she gushed, vigorously shaking one of his hands, while pressing a church bulletin into the other.

"I'm not Pastor Williams," Ken replied. "She's over there!"

Completely nonplussed, the poor woman abandoned her post and ran into the sanctuary. "Elder Bob is not going to like this!" she exclaimed over her shoulder.

Soon she was back with Elder Bob in tow. "This is the speaker." She pointed an accusing finger at me, as though I had committed some grave sacrilege for which he was going to have to discipline me.

"No one told me you were a woman!" the good elder exclaimed, pursing his lips and folding his arms tightly across his chest, leaving my unshook hand hanging limply in midair. "What am I going to do now?" He looked around distractedly, scratching his head. "Where can I find a speaker on such short notice? I'm not even prepared to preach today!"

I waited for his initial shock to subside a bit then suggested that we stick to the planned program.

"I don't think that's going to work," he objected firmly. "My daughter is here for the first time in a long time, and she's not going to listen to some woman."

Those last words reeked with such prejudice that I had to find a place to compose myself. I made my way across the lobby to the ladies' room with Belynda right behind me. We prayed together, thanking God for a safe journey, and asked for wisdom in this delicate situation. Then we rejoined the others in the lobby.

It was finally decided that since I had come such a long way I could speak—but only briefly, thereby reducing the length of discomfort for the congregation. Before her special music, Belynda was given a long introduction, but no one introduced me before I stood up to speak—probably to make it clear that women, while acceptable as singers, are not as preachers.

You could have cut the awkward tension with a knife. The elder sat on the front pew, intensely reading his Bible, determined not to give the impression that he approved of my presence by listening. I looked out over the blank, uninviting faces and trembled inside. Nervous stress has always done alarming things to my gastrointestinal tract. But God was with me. I gave it my best under the power of the Holy Spirit, and when I was finished the elder's daughter, who had long since dropped out of the Adventist Church, responded to an appeal to commit her life to Christ. That made her father so happy he invited us home for the most delicious vegetarian meal I have ever eaten.

The table settings of pure sterling silver and the expensive decor indicated the rich blessings this family enjoyed. We spent the afternoon in deep conversation, and they literally would not let us leave until we had had evening vespers with the family.

A few weeks later I received a letter from one of the elderly ladies of that congregation. She was the first person who ever addressed me as "pastor" as she thanked me for the ministry of the Word. I have moved often and lost some important artifacts, but I have kept that letter to remind me from whence I came so that I will keep my eyes on the prize which is the eternal hope and glory in Christ Jesus our Lord.

While working at the Center for Community Change, I was inspired, perhaps even impelled, by the Spirit to share the tremendous transformation I had experienced in Christ. I decided to put up a tent on 14th Street where the prostitutes hung out. I did all the research and received permission from the city. Since I had never done any type of evangelism, I needed to speak to an expert.

I called the General Conference and was referred to Elder William Scales, ministerial secretary. He invited me to share my dream. Though a soft-spoken man of God, he carried a big stick when it came to imparting the Word. After we talked, he suggested that I needed to have much more than just the "guts" to call up the city and secure a spot for a tent. He was planning an evangelism meeting for that summer in Virginia and felt I could gain valuable experience with him. So he signed me up as a Bible worker. That crusade was my first, and I learned to knock on doors and invite people, share my testimony, give Bible studies, and greet people as they came to the meetings.

As I got to know Elder Scales, I shared my dream of one day becoming a missionary and, perhaps, even a pastor. From the very beginning, he introduced me publicly at the crusade as Evangelist Williams. It made a big difference in the way the other workers related to me. On the long drive from Virginia to Upper Marlboro, I often let the title "Evangelist Williams" roll off my tongue, repeating it out loud with warm satisfaction.

One of the Bible workers was a woman in her late 70s. She had been badly bitten by a dog in her younger days while knocking on doors for another crusade. The injury caused her to walk with a noticeable limp, and when some of the young theologians assisting with the crusade saw her, they began snickering and making snide remarks about her apparent feebleness. I'm very sorry to say that I joined in. However, as the days ran into weeks, she was the one with the most people attending the meetings. As the sun got hotter and hotter, many of us who had teased her behind her back dropped out or constantly complained, while she patiently continued to present candidate after candidate for baptism.

One day I had the opportunity to work with her and asked for the secret of her success.

"Perseverance will make you prosper," she answered cryptically.

I had not yet become familiar enough with Joshua, chapter 1, to realize that this was an excellent summary of what God meant when He encouraged His leader to "be strong and very courageous." Since I didn't understand what she meant, and she wasn't about to explain, I decided to watch her carefully and discover her technique.

I noticed that when the sun was hot, she quietly praised God for the opportunity to be alive and healthy to feel its warmth, sometimes counting off her many friends who could no longer enjoy this gift since they were dead and buried.

When she walked up a long flight of stairs in one of the many apartment buildings we had to visit, she took them carefully, stopping often to sing a prayer as she climbed.

When we knocked on a door, she breathed a prayer for the souls on the other side who needed to know Jesus Christ as their personal Saviour.

All of this slowed us down. In fact, we visited only five homes in the time that I normally covered 15. But we never left a home without a commitment for either Bible studies or a promise to attend the crusade. By the end of the crusade nearly all her candidates had been baptized.

Eventually, I would learn the lesson that personal perseverance in prayer will make anyone prosper, no matter what their circumstances, disabilities, or disadvantages.

I met every variety of person and beliefs that summer. I discovered the thrill of victory when a candidate surrendered to Christ—and the agony of defeat when one refused.

Sally (not her real name) was in her mid-50s when we met. She soaked up the good news like a dry sponge. Unfortunately, she was living with a handsome young man 20 years her junior, and for whom she had bought a house and a car. In spite of her generosity, he had grown tired of "living with an old woman" and was betraying her by seeing other women, some of whom he brought to their home, even while she was there. He had also begun beating her. On one of our visits we had to rescue her from his wrath.

Mitzi Smith, a junior theology major at CUC, was my Bible worker partner. We prayed with Sally, we counseled her, we shared the power of God to make a difference in her life, and His ability to give her strength to abandon this destructive relationship. She believed. Sally accepted Jesus Christ as her personal Saviour and never missed a meeting—until the last week of the crusade as we prepared her for baptism.

That week was horrible. During a brief visit with me, my sister had bought me a white station wagon, a huge bus of a thing, from one of the Bible workers. I didn't yet have the title to that gas-guzzling, transmission fluid-absorbing beast, but I needed transportation and drove it anyway. Mitzi was driving us to an appointment with Sally when someone ran the stop sign and smashed into the side of the wagon. Although we were not hurt, we were badly shaken, and the station wagon was thoroughly dented. After the trauma of exchanging insurance information with the other driver, we took off again, anticipating a good study with Sally. We were going to deliver a baptismal bag to her with instructions for the upcoming grand celebration.

When we arrived at Sally's home we were still a little shaken, but joyous about the prospect of securing her final commitment to be baptized. What a total surprise when she told us that she had changed her mind and would not be attending the meetings anymore. When we pressed her to explain, she said that her boyfriend had agreed to attend her Sunday church with her. She had already spoken to the pastor, who had assured her she could be baptized and still continue to live with her boyfriend.

We knew she had struggled with our instructions to either marry him or ask him to move, and were almost certain that when he told her, in our presence, that he would never marry her she would make the only other obvious choice and throw him out of her house. Instead, she exchanged the most precious gift any human being can ever receive, a relationship with God, for a destructive relationship with a man.

We were so sad. We spoke about her to some of the other Bible workers. One of them, Steve, went with me to see her. But she never changed her mind. That was a tough loss.

Then there was the interesting encounter with a Jehovah's Witness. She invited us in, planning to win us over to her beliefs. As she talked, my partner and I discovered that we were clearly out of our league with her. So I promised to return in a few days, telling her that if she could convince me from her Bible that Jesus was not God, I would join the Jehovah's Witnesses. I really meant it! I didn't know this was God's way of preparing me for another incredible encounter. I went home and read everything I could find on her denomination. I went back to her home several times but she wouldn't see me. Perhaps she realized she couldn't prove what I had asked. However, the information I gathered was to serve me well during my second semester at CUC.

A group of Jehovah's Witnesses heard that I was giving Bible studies and came to the college one evening to challenge me. The leader, a bright woman who had been a very effective Witness, said that I was teaching heresy and she would like to study with me to set me straight. We agreed to meet on Thursdays.

The first week she showed up with 17 people; I had invited only two. Soon things became intense, but to my surprise they asked to meet again, absolutely convinced they could win me over. To tell the truth, I was scared my challenge to my first Jehovah's Witness contact during the crusade would come back to haunt me. I don't think I have prayed and fasted more than during those weeks we studied together.

About four weeks into our studies they asked me not to use their Bible during the study anymore. I knew then that I had them. We baptized five at first, two sisters and their three daughters, and over the years several others were baptized after studying with other ministers at the Pennsylvania Avenue church.

That semester also brought many other changes into my life. I moved to Takoma Park, transferred my son, Steven, to Takoma Academy, and gave up bus driving. I began working as the Religion Department secretary and served as student intern at the Pennsylvania Avenue church to gain field education experience during my crash program. I was so busy being a "spiritual mother" to the students, an efficient departmental secretary, tutor, pastoral intern, and full-time student that I failed to realize that I was neglecting the most important responsibility of all—my son, Steven.

By the time he was 16, Steven had gotten in with the wrong crowd at Takoma Academy and had begun to use alcohol, tobacco, and foul language. His grades were suffering tremendously and his attitude toward me was outrageous. My son had never raised his voice or talked back to me. But now we had to negotiate and keep written agreements as to how we would relate to each other. He began leaving the house at night and taking my car without permission. I started hiding the keys and confiscated his learner's permit. He once took my car and allowed an unlicensed friend to drive it. As they sped through Silver Spring at 2:00 one morning, a drunken driver slammed into them. My car was totaled, but fortunately the only injury was his friend's broken hand. I didn't know what to do. So I ignored the problems, hoping they would go away.

I heard about Highland View Academy's reputation as a school where love and discipline were administered in balanced doses. I decided to send Steven there, in the hopes that getting away from Takoma Park would help him work through some of the issues that had turned him into such a rebellious young man. Sometimes I would look at him and find nothing in his face of the sweet child I had raised. Steven went out of his way to defy all authority.

We went to Highland View for an interview, and he was accepted. We argued all the way back home and then some more when we arrived in Takoma Park. He had less than one year left to complete high school, but seemed determined not to go. Nevertheless, we shopped for the things he would need at a boarding academy.

The next morning Steven left the house for school before I had time to speak to him. About 11:00 I received a call from the police, asking me to meet them at Washington Adventist Hospital, where my son had been rushed in an ambulance. I was sure he must have been in another accident. Too frightened to ask for details, I dashed out to my car and sped to the emergency room. I'm not sure what I expected, but certainly not what I found.

Medical personnel were pumping his stomach after an attempted suicide. I collapsed to the floor. After we had returned from Highland View Academy, Steven had gone to the medicine cabinet and taken everything he could find, including a new bottle containing 100 Tylenol tablets. When he woke up in the morning and realized the pills hadn't worked, he consumed alcohol that mixed with the chemicals in his stomach. He passed out in class. The police were called in and here we all were, waiting for the prognosis.

After several hours of stomach pumping and counseling, we left the hospital. He did not speak to me on the short drive home. That night as I slept, he packed his clothes and moved away to his friend's apartment in Takoma Park. A week went by before I finally located him—a week filled with hundreds of telephone calls and hours of driving around the streets of Takoma Park late into the night.

I never shared the details of my son's attempted suicide with anyone except my boss, Dr. Stout. I was so emotionally fractured myself that I didn't view the community as a safe place in which to expose my problems. So I kept them to myself, continuing to minister, work, and study. The fact that I did not have a nervous breakdown is all due to the grace of God which lifted me up and carried me through.

I came home one day, exhausted and desperate, realizing that I would have to notify the police about my missing son. He might be lying dead somewhere. He wasn't. He had returned home and was holed up in an unfinished room in our basement. His stay in that room was even more painful than his being away, because he would not go to school or talk to me or clean up after himself.

When Pastor Maurice Battle, Jr., then pastor of Pennsylvania Avenue church, came to visit him one day, I escorted him to the basement where my son was ensconced in that terrible room that looked like a pigsty. I still struggle with the feelings I had on that occasion. I just couldn't tell the pastor the whole sordid story that had led to that situation.

Steven no longer attended church. He became involved in break dancing and now proudly wore a huge bruise on his forehead, caused by spinning on it while doing break dancing tricks. I offered to send him to a dance school, if that was what he really wanted. He was very surprised because he expected me to take a rigid position, as I would have in the past. Within a week he stopped break dancing. When I asked him why, he first said it was because he'd lost interest, but finally confessed that since I approved it was no longer all that great. I had learned something important.

When he came home with his head shaved in a Mohawk, I said nothing. On Sabbath morning he surprised me by being dressed and ready to go to church. I asked him to drive and never said a word about his hair. Halfway across the beltway he asked me if I was really going to allow him to attend church with his Mohawk.

I looked at him and smiled, lovingly patting his knee. "Son, I carried you for nine months in my womb, and nothing you can ever do or say will make me ashamed of you."

I could tell he was beginning to get cold feet—he wasn't sure how he would be received. His fears were well-founded. His friends did not like his haircut, and neither did the church members. I was taken aside so many times I finally began saying to anyone who raised the subject, "I approve of his haircut, so sue me!"

No one is more cruel to pastors' children than members who can scarcely control their own. They foist their unrealistic expectations on preachers' kids like a vicarious discipline because they have no authority over their own. And I had let them. For the most part, I had been raising my son according to the reactions of the congregation. When he was small, I would sometimes pinch him hard to make him sit still because people complained to me after service if he flicked an eyelid. When he wanted to have a hamburger (I was the vegetarian, he wasn't), I wouldn't let him for fear someone would see me going into McDonald's. Ralph McClain finally told me to quit forcing my habits on him and, instead, teach him the reasons why being a vegetarian is important. What an eye opener to realize that some of the "rules" I imposed on him were because I didn't want the members to think I wasn't a good Christian or a good mother!

I was now determined to raise my son my way, loving him the same way Jesus loved me. As long as he came to church, even if his hairstyle was not one I would wear, I wouldn't say anything to turn him away. And I fiercely protected his rights to do so, like a lioness guarding her cub. Further, I decided to end the double standard of being nice to other people's children, no matter what they did or how they looked, while being so legalistic with my own child. He was going to be treated with love and respect, as he deserved.

As we left church that day Steven turned to me with a wry smile. "Mom, have you no shame? You allowed me to go to church looking like *this!*" He pointed to his hair. "Why didn't you stop me?" He told me his friends didn't like it, and he was anxious for it to grow out.

As I softened my harsh expectations, things began to get a little better between us, though still nowhere near where I wanted them to be. One evening as I prayed, the Lord promised me that this child would also be His. After that, I had some peace of mind. However, it would take a stint in the U.S. Marines and a nearly fatal motorcycle accident to tame the tiger that roared in his youthful breast. Although my son is not yet a committed Christian, he is quick to assure me that he thinks about God often. We are enjoying the best relationship we've ever had, but I can testify that it's not easy for single women to raise sons, or for newly converted Christian single mothers to raise boys who have not given their lives to the Lord. Satan, like a roaring lion, is always at hand to use them to draw us away from our commitment to God.

~

Once a year our church went to Camp Blue Ridge for a weekend retreat. This was to be my first experience, and I was looking forward to it. That Sabbath, Diane Freeman shared with me that the Lord had put it on her heart to befriend me. At the time I had no idea what this would mean—and neither did Diane. But over the years we have discovered that God had appointed her as my "raven" who would feed me as the birds fed Elijah. She did it so subtly, it took me weeks of careful sleuthing to find out that she was my benefactor.

One Sabbath I drove to church on an almost-empty tank. I had just enough gas to get me from Takoma Park to the Pennsylvania Avenue church, about 25 miles away, and no money to buy more. I was too embarrassed to share my plight with anyone. I didn't want to become a ward of the church. I laid my purse and Bible on a pew near the door while I hung up my coat. When I returned, my purse was gone. I stepped into the foyer to ask the greeter if she had seen anyone suspicious come into the church. When I returned, my purse was back—with a $20 bill tucked inside. I quietly asked around, but no one owned up to it. The money made it possible to buy gas and food that week.

This happened every Sabbath for three weeks, and there would always be a $10 or $20 bill when the purse was returned. I decided to find out who was doing this, so one week I hid behind the door. I saw Diane Freeman take my purse, open it, and place the money inside. Just when she turned around, I entered the sanctuary and hugged her. She was quite embarrassed, but told me how God had impressed her to help me. And help me she did for the two years I was in college. When I left for the seminary she prepared a beautiful, comfortable room in her home for me to come back to during breaks.

Many other people contributed to my well-being while I was in college—including Debra Carter, Virginia Logan, Ralph and Barbara McClain, Jerry Davis, and Wilson Gaitor. Their reward is indeed in heaven because I can never repay them except with heartfelt gratitude.

By the summer of 1984, my life began to settle down. Whenever the college was closed for holiday breaks, I worked at the General Conference. Jenny Stevenson, one of the unsung heroines of our church, worked in the personnel department there. She always made sure there was something for me to do and sent me from department to department on temporary assignments. I was not computer literate, so I was usually a "gopher," filling in for secretaries who were on vacation or maternity leave.

I remember Annette Stephenson, who was then secretary to Elder Bradford, North American Division president. Annette used to smile so sweetly as she encouraged me to give up trying to become a pastor. "Our church will never hire women pastors," she told me.

"Well, at my age, if I want to throw my life away it's all right, especially if I throw it away on the Lord!" I'd laugh.

Nowadays, whenever I run into Annette, she tells me how wrong she was and how impressed she is with my ministry.

I also worked a couple weeks for Bert Holoviak in the archives during the period he was researching his presentation in support of the ordination of women. A couple years later, his daughter, Kendra, then a student pastor, would spend a summer as an intern in my office at Sligo church.

But I spent most of my time working in the ministerial department.

Elder Robert Spangler was editor of *Ministry* magazine, and Mary Louise McDowell, my pastor's wife, served as his administrative assistant and taught me to use the computer. A few years ago, Elder Spangler and I were both speakers at the same event. As we talked together, some of the others present were surprised that we knew each other. I was happy to tell them that I had served as his "chief gopher" for almost two summers. He was quick to remind me that because of my accomplishments there was no need to say that. I objected, saying that I had to. Though I didn't tell him, the following experience was why . . .

A short time before I began working in the mayor's office, I spent six months in the home of Merilee G as her live-in baby-sitter and helper. Before the state of Connecticut purchased it, her father was the owner of the bus company. Financially, the family was more than comfortable.

Not long after I began working in the mayor's office, the bus drivers went on strike and the mayor decided to help bring it to an end. A meeting was called with Mr. G, state and city transportation officers, representatives from the city's corporation council's office union, and a variety of local leaders. Of course, the ever-present media was also there. I avoided going to the meeting because I was uncomfortable seeing Mr. G under these circumstances. I would have been embarrassed if others found out that I, now confidential secretary to the mayor, had worked for Mr. G's daughter as a maid, and had served him at table on many occasions.

The mayor buzzed me on the intercom and asked me to bring coffee to the meeting. I sent the receptionist in to get the orders, but she returned with a terse note from the mayor ordering me to do it. I entered the room with my heart in my mouth. Mr. G recognized me the moment I walked in.

"Hi, Hyveth! I didn't know you had anything to do with these people!" His sweeping gesture included the mayor and all the city officials.

"You know my confidential secretary?" asked the mayor, incredulously.

"Yes," said Mr. G, getting up from his seat to rest a hand on my shoulder in a friendly greeting.

*Here it comes!* I thought, closing my eyes.

"Hyveth and I are old friends, right?" He gave my shoulder an affectionate little shake.

"Ye-yes, sir," I stammered, not sure what to say or do because he still held me captive.

"I'm Bill," he whispered in my ear, "not sir. We're old friends, remember?"

*He wasn't going to tell them!*

He returned to his seat with a smile. I was about to walk out of the room when he said, "Excuse me, gentlemen, I just want to ask Hyveth something. I'll be right back."

We stepped out of the room together and he closed the door carefully behind us. "Tell me, Hyveth, what do you think about what's going on in there?"

He was asking *my* opinion? This was a man to whom I had barely spoken except to ask if he wanted me to freshen up his coffee or should I serve him another helping at the dinner table.

"Mr. G—"

He shot me a disapproving glance.

"I mean, well, Bill—" My confidence was returning to its normally bold level. "I think if you don't make an agreement you will be the bigger loser in the end. These drivers have the union on their side and they are ready to fight you. Why not surprise them and take the initiative and the sting out of their bite by offering a settlement?"

He looked at me for a second, then nodded his head. "You've got something there." He opened the door. "By the way," he said as he reentered the meeting, "how about lunch sometime?"

The next morning the papers proclaimed in bold headlines: MAYOR SETTLES BUS STRIKE! I never said a word about our conversation in the hall, and Mr. G took our little secret to his grave.

Later, Mr. G told me how his father used to sweep the bus depot for years, saving enough money from that and moonlighting at several odd jobs until he had enough to buy the company.

"Hyveth," he said, looking me in the eye, "never let your past impede your progress into the future!"

Ellen White says it this way: "We have nothing to fear for the future, except as we shall forget the way the Lord has led us, and His teaching in our past history" *(Testimonies for the Church*, vol. 9, p. 10). Most of the time we use this statement to refer to our church's history, but I believe it is also true of our personal history. Since I was healed, emotionally, by the Lord I have no reason to keep secrets about where I came from because I know where I'm going.

~

The confidence I now had was no longer in myself but in the fact that

God is always with me. His promise of prosperity is in both small and great events. With renewed hope I began to dream of evangelism.

The concept of Revelation seminars had become very popular, and I wanted to conduct one. I developed a proposal and presented it to our pastor, Lyndon McDowell. He approved it and I received funding from the Potomac Conference for the $2,000 budget and secured a room in an elementary school. Then I waited for a response to the thousands of brochures that were mass-mailed.

We had more than 70 people in attendance, and by the end of the summer we had prepared 28 candidates for baptism. Most were later baptized, and a number of them continue to attend, and actively participate in, churches in the area.

The success of this seminar blazed through the Potomac Conference like a forest fire. Many of my classmates said I was sure to be hired by a conference, even before college graduation. I was in two honor societies, I had a successful evangelism effort under my belt, and was very much in demand as a speaker. In fact, it was my privilege to be the first theology major to be invited to speak at one of the most prestigious pulpits in the area.

On that Sabbath morning, I just knew it was going to be a perfect day. I woke up with a song in my heart. I jumped out of bed like an Olympic gymnast and looked up to the ceiling, half expecting to see a panel of angels raise scorecards showing perfect 10s. I smiled to myself as I laid out a new beige silk skirt with permanent pleats, purchased especially for this occasion. I selected a matching silk shirt with a bow at the neck before running to the shower. My friend Sherry Shand says I can't carry a tune in a wheelbarrow, but that morning I was singing in the shower, even though I was out-of-tune and making up words.

I dressed carefully, topping the beige skirt and blouse with a black, short-waisted jacket to accentuate my figure. I admired myself in a full-length mirror, swaying and singing "Color-coordinated and I'm looking good!"

I ran from the house to my car and sang all the way to the church, arriving just in time to be ushered into the small back room where platform participants meet for final instructions. I noticed that the three men who would accompany me to the platform were all dressed in dark suits and congratulated my good taste in choosing something with a little life and color. As we walked to the sanctuary we passed an old mirror on the wall. I paused, as though I were examining the mirror, but I was really looking at myself again, stroking my clothes with self-confidence. I almost had to force myself not to blow a narcissistic kiss at the woman in the mirror. Arriving at the door leading to the platform, I tugged hard on the bottom of my jacket, stuck my chest out, and threw my shoulders back. In the words of a Brooklyn buddy, I thought, *Home girl is gonna blow today!*

We knelt before the congregation as the organist played the introit. While the others prayed, I plucked imaginary pieces of lint from my jacket because someone as cute as I felt should exhibit no imperfections. It was at this moment that God chose to teach me an unforgettable lesson in humility.

When the introit ended, the platform participants stood up to move to their seats. I did, too. Or at least I tried. Unfortunately, the high heels of my shoes were firmly caught in the hem of my skirt. The moment I stood up, my skirt (remember the elastic waistband?) slid down in the back, almost to my thighs. I slipped to the floor and began to shake my legs, each in turn, frantically trying to loosen my heels from the skirt. The pastor, not understanding why I was shaking like a leaf in a wind storm, cleared his throat and gestured for me to stand up. Oh, how I wanted to, but I couldn't. With a face full of disapproval, he gestured and cleared his throat a second time.

By now the congregation sensed something was amiss up front. Like people in an old V-8 commercial, they leaned to the left, then to the right, trying to see around the pulpit where I knelt like a disabled track star with one knee on the floor, wildly shaking the other leg.

By the time the pastor cleared his throat and gestured a third time, he finally realized I was in trouble and bent down and freed my skirt. I humbly backed up to my seat. My sermon was entitled "An Attitude of Fortitude," and I guarantee that's what it took to preach it.

So when the news of the Revelation seminar hit the airwaves I gave God the glory. I would not allow myself to think, as my classmates did, that this success would immediately result in an offer of employment and seminary sponsorship from the Potomac Conference. In fact, a few months later when we had the presidential interviews (an annual presentation of graduates to conference presidents in the Columbia Union for this very purpose), not one single offer of employment was made to me.

The campus was abuzz in the weeks before the presidential interviews. Single theology majors became regular callers at the girls' dorm, doing their best to become engaged so they could present themselves as happy couples, ready to enter the field of pastoral ministry. As Religion Department secretary, I was too busy putting their biographical sketches and books together and planning the traditional banquet to even get myself fixed up for the presidential arrivals.

On a particularly stressful day, I was informed it was my turn to join the line of nervously hopeful interviewees. I entered the classroom where a conference president, his ministerial secretary, and, I presumed, the treasurer sat waiting. The president was someone I knew well, so I thought the interview would be comfortable and pleasant. However, for some reason he began the interview in a most officious tone, which annoyed me. For my part, I wasn't too communicative because I did not like the questions I was being asked. Then he asked what my plans for marriage were.

I couldn't help myself. I blurted, "Why? Are you proposing?"

The ministerial secretary doubled over in laughter, but the president was not amused. He spoke through his teeth as he tried to control his rage. "You are an insolent girl—" he began.

"That's it!" I said, and stood up to leave. "I'm almost 39, and that's not a girl!"

"With your attitude, you will never be hired!" he called after me.

Perhaps my attempt at humor was inappropriate, but it certainly did not warrant that response, especially from someone who had previously exchanged lighthearted banter with me. We eventually became good friends again before he retired from office and were able to laugh at the incident.

Although I was through with my college coursework in December 1984, I did not graduate until May 1985. I held my breath up until the very last day, expecting to be hired. But nothing happened. I was offered a position by the college in the adult degree program, but I didn't take it; I wanted to wait for a call to the ministry. Graduation came and went, and I was still unemployed.

A few weeks later, as I was returning from my summer job at the General Conference, Sligo church loomed like a giant before me. I couldn't control the emotions that overwhelmed me and almost ran off the road as I sobbed out loud, "Oh, God, why haven't You found me a job yet? Why do You treat everyone else so well and yet treat me so rotten? You gave calls to some who have no interest in the ministry, yet nothing for me! What do You want me to do?"

As I cried myself to sleep that night something inside began to die.

I really didn't want to go to church. I didn't want to answer the never-ending questions about not being hired. I didn't want to see the "poor Hyveth" faces or hear one more "we told you so; this church will never hire women." How many different ways could I say "Well, they hired Josephine Benton and Jan Dafferen, so why not me?"

But I went to church anyway, driving the 25 long miles to the Pennsylvania Avenue church. Once more my old friend Ralph McClain came up with the answer. He knew I was down in the dumps and took me aside. That entire week, he told me, every time he had his devotions, the Lord impressed him to tell me that He couldn't put me into a church because I was not ready. There were too many rough edges He'd been trying to smooth, too many unlearned lessons. So I had to pray and wait on the Lord.

It made sense. I was struggling with many issues. When we knelt for the pastoral prayer that day I confessed my sins to the Lord and pledged to follow His schedule, not mine. The following Monday I was hired by Dr. Roy Branson as secretary for the Adventist Forum, that produces *Spectrum* magazine.

Sometime during this period I attended the ordination of Maurice Battle, Jr. As I left the sanctuary at the end of the ceremony, Ron Wisbey, the new president of Columbia Union, said, "One day, Hyveth, this too will be yours." He promised to speak to Ralph Martin, the new Potomac Conference president, about hiring me. I was so choked up I couldn't even cry as I drove home.

The next day I decided I would go to the seminary in Michigan and started the registration process. The response to my application was a shock. I was an honor student who had fulfilled all the entrance requirements, but because I was divorced my background was being investigated.

Years before my conversion, I had been divorced. I had not remained in contact with my former husband, but was kept apprised of his whereabouts through relatives. In the summer of 1982 I had been informed of his death, and when the time came for the presidential interviews I told Dr. Stout that I was a divorcee. After we discussed the matter, he explained that according to our church standards and based on the principles outlined in 1 Corinthians 7:15 and Romans 7:1-3, I was free to remarry. And added to this was the fact that all this had happened before I became a Christian. I could have kept my divorce a secret and simply said I was a widow, but I felt obligated before God to tell the whole truth. In the biographical sketch book, Dr. Stout, with my full consent, indicated that I had been divorced but was cleared of responsibility. This same information was included with my application to the seminary.

Imagine my surprise when I received a telephone call from the dean of the seminary, asking me to provide a written explanation of my marriage relationship, its breakdown, and who was at fault in the divorce. I reminded the dean of Dr. Stout's statement, but he insisted on a response to his request or my application couldn't be considered. This, and the fact that at 39 I was considered too old to be hired as a pastor because of a General Conference rule, were used as reasons to discourage me from studying at the seminary.

I was outraged. It wasn't that I was being pressed to revisit an unpleasant past, but the tone in which I was being commanded to do so that really rankled. Had it not been for the support and encouragement of Roy Branson, I wouldn't have followed through and gone to the seminary.

Instead of a warm letter of acceptance to the seminary, on May 27, 1985, I received a letter from the dean that was intended to discourage me. Subsequently, I was accepted as a provisional student, which meant I could be terminated at the whim of those in authority. Thank God, this story didn't end there, though the ending would be another year in the making. Here's how it happened.

In October 1986, just a few months after accepting my first assignment at Sligo church, I returned to the seminary to honor a speaking invitation. I struggled with what to say because I was being impressed by the Spirit to speak on an issue I had always carefully avoided before. Cheating among some seminarians was at an all-time high, and although this group was in the minority, they were becoming more brazen each quarter, even purchasing term papers prepared by former graduates.

During one final exam, monitored by a not-too-observant secretary, I remembered a young man next to me who hid his class notes under his chair and copied the answers. As I passed his desk I pretended to accidentally brush his cheat sheet to the floor, then picked it up and turned it over on the desk I had just vacated.

"Sorry!" I smiled, and walked quickly away.

I should have reported him immediately. Instead, when he caught me on the steps of the library after the exam and began to argue with me for interfering in his business, I followed the Matthew 18 approach. He was so rude, I made up my mind to go to Dean Hasel, but when I thought that I would be ostracized as a tattletale I dropped the idea and kept quiet.

But now, as I struggled with my sermon, the Spirit wouldn't let me rest. It was as though I had committed the crime. Finally, I chose texts from Deuteronomy 27 and 28 and entitled my sermon "Between Gerizim and Ebal." Instead of exposing or excoriating anyone, I simply confessed how weak and emotionally needy for human approval I had been to have overlooked such a terrible deed and kept silent about sin in the camp.

Several weeks later, I learned that a revival had taken place at the seminary. Students confessed to each other and to teachers, sought forgiveness from God, and established prayer groups to help them keep their vows. I received several cards and letters from students and teachers. Elder Roger Coon from the White Estate, who was teaching a class at the seminary for the quarter, sent me a special letter, expressing his gratitude for the prophetic tone of my message. He also shared how he and other professors were changing their method of handling exams to eliminate opportunities for cheating by students.

But the letter that impressed me most came from Dr. Dederen, the dean of the seminary. He wrote:

"Thank you so very much for the powerful and most relevant message which you brought to us this morning. Thank you also for the willingness and courage of sharing your burden with us.

"We all need exhortation, teachers and students. At least, I did, and have reasons to believe that my colleagues' concerns and struggles are not that different from mine.

"God called you to ministry in most challenging times. You were even able to be charitable and loving while delivering your message. May He continue to guide and bless you, making you a source of blessings and encouragement for many."

Through the grace of God and the continuing transforming power of the Holy Spirit, my brother in Christ had come a long way toward accepting me and other women in ministry. So much so that by July 1995, he had come full circle when he stood up at the quinquennial session of the General Conference in Utrecht, Netherlands, and passionately supported the approval of the request of the North American Division to ordain its women pastors.

**Chapter Six**

# The Call!

I arrived at the seminary the fall of 1985 with a big chip on my shoulder. I was ready and eager to take on the administration, academically. I was going to prove that they were wrong about me. I had a call from God to ministry and would show them!

I did not expect the atmosphere would be as harsh as it turned out to be. Orientation was a disaster because I felt so out of place. Even though several of my classmates and their families from Columbia Union College were there, too, it turned out to be one of the loneliest, most emotionally painful periods of my life. However, the discipline that accompanied this experience enabled me to function successfully as a student.

Although I was not a sponsored student (meaning I had not been hired by a conference and sent to the seminary on a stipend as had the majority of my classmates), I had moved to Berrien Springs, Michigan, with more faith than financial resources, hoping that the Lord would open a way for me to finance my education. And even that faith trembled when one of the professors stood up during the "get acquainted" time to testify how fortunate he was to have several thousand dollars salted away in his savings, plus a new house. Now he and his wife were in a real dilemma as to which of two baby grand pianos to select for their new home.

Perhaps he was trying to encourage us to see that there would be light at the end of the tunnel and rich rewards would be ours if we hung in there and finished what we were about to start. But being jobless, with barely enough resources to last a month, I did not find his testimony uplifting.

Rather, it irritated me. I left the program before it was over and went back to my apartment to finish unpacking. It was just as well that I was still unaware of the harsh realities of the cold winters in this one-traffic-light town, sandwiched between Niles and Benton Harbor. I'd had enough to process for one day.

I was one of seven women and 450 men who began classes that fall. My early encounters with the seminary dean, the long, cold, dark winters, and the heavy academic demands didn't get to me so much as the sense of isolation from my peers. That broke my heart. Many of the women, then and later, complained bitterly of tremendous gender prejudice from some teachers and sexual harassment from some students. Some women still complain about being excluded in the male-dominated atmosphere of the seminary, even though the issue of sexual harassment was eventually addressed when a policy was adopted and published in the seminary.

In the early years of my ministry I had difficulty reporting such incidents, because being "the first Black female pastor" in the denomination exacted a different kind of responsibility, and were burdens which I bore privately. I was afraid that if I told of these incidents some of the leaders might take it as a sign that women should not be allowed in the ministry. My fears were not without foundation.

During my first assignment after the seminary, we held a union-wide convocation in Williamsburg, Virginia. One of the presenters from the General Conference expressed the opinion that women should be given a broom, not a pulpit. Although most of the men who heard this raised strong objections, it made us women very vulnerable to some of the wolves in sheep's clothing.

About 11:00 that night there was a knock on my door. It was a pastor, who later became a conference evangelist. He said it was an emergency. Since I knew him, I foolishly opened my door and invited him in. He grabbed me and tried to pull me into his arms and, breathing heavily, told me how his wife didn't understand him and how much he wanted me. I managed to break away from him and stepped back, catching my breath. I was so shocked, the first thing I said was utterly stupid.

"You want me? I'm wearing rollers in my hair!" Then I snapped to my senses and ordered him to leave.

He refused, and began to chase me around the room.

"I swear, I will tell your conference president about this!" I shouted angrily.

"Go right ahead," he answered smugly. "Who's going to take a Black woman's word over the word of a popular White pastor like me?"

I began screaming and threatened to continue to scream until the hotel security came. That frightened him into leaving.

I was weak with fright. What if he was right? What if the brotherhood of believers protected its brothers against the accusations of some of us women? So I kept my mouth shut. But God's Word is true: Whatever we do in the darkness will come to light. This man's misdeeds were exposed and, years later, he was defrocked for sexual misconduct.

Because of this incident, I have been very cautious. But how many horror stories are being kept secret by women who are afraid to come forward, not only fearing their reputations will be ruined, but that their fragile acceptance in the ministry will be jeopardized?

Before I entered the seminary, I decided that I would dress professionally, as though I were going to the office. Some of my classmates teased me, misunderstanding my reasons, but it worked there as it works everywhere. People tend to treat others according to their dress and demeanor. I was treated with dignity and respect.

I also decided that I was not at the seminary to be made into a pastor— I was already a pastor, needing to be better equipped for ministry. Nor was I a Black woman pastor. I was a pastor who happened to be a Black woman.

In spite of these attitudes, the isolation I experienced from my peers, whether by their design or because of my difficult first impression, caused me great despair. I first noticed the detachment when one of my classmates hosted a Sabbath lunch for a conference president. He went to great lengths to invite other classmates, but kept the occasion a secret from me. I found out about it by accident the day of the feast. I was deeply wounded, and when I asked why I was treated that way, was told that I was left out to spare my feelings. Being single, I would have been an oddity at the luncheon.

I discovered that the real truth was that the conference president was against women in ministry. And since these men were vying for employment, they played it safe by temporarily distancing themselves from me. I wasn't making friends with the women either, single or married. In addition to the fact that some may have been put off by my direct, no-nonsense approach, I think we women are programmed to compete with and distrust each other. Where men network and establish a "brotherhood" to look out for each other, we women often undermine each other by gossip, backbiting, and self-righteous attitudes that pit us against one another, instead of uniting our scanty resources to liberate ourselves from the tyranny of misogynism, no matter what form or ritual it takes.

That first year, after several failed attempts to be more than a tutor to some of my peers to gain social acceptance, I buried myself in my books. At every opportunity, I drove the 14 hours to Maryland to stay with Bob and Diane Freeman or Karen Lumb, where I felt accepted and loved. That I did not feel a sense of belonging may have been a reaction to my earlier encounter with the dean of the seminary. Whatever the source, I take full responsibility for my feelings as I try to represent them as authentically as they were experienced. A major part was my own emotional brokenness, the healing of which didn't occur until a few years later.

All seminarians are assigned to intern in a local church. I chose to affiliate myself with the Berrien Springs Village church, primarily because I had met the senior pastor, Larry Lichtenwalter, while he was in the Potomac Conference. I decided to work with the youth.

We started with about three or four young people, who were there because their parents made them attend, but by the end of the first quarter there were at least 30 attending our programs. This was due to the support of Bill Knott, the new youth pastor. We introduced some innovative ideas, such as serving a snack on a beautiful, candlelit table, making the Sabbath school lessons relevant, and by sometimes taking them to the beach or on cookouts.

I grew, too, under the nurturing influence of Bill and his wife. One Sabbath they invited me to lunch. I met one of their friends, a pastor who had just been assigned to a district in St. Joseph, a town about 10 miles north of Berrien Springs. He was a very pleasant person, although some of his idiosyncrasies took a little getting used to.Unfortunately, he was looking for a wife, and before I knew it he had decided that I was the one. I had never met anyone so persistent, and I made the mistake of spending too much time with him. Soon he was calling me and making plans, not just for an evening, but for the rest of my life, insisting that God had told him I was to be his wife. When I rejected his offer of matrimony, he began to come to the seminary and watch me from his car. He would call me at home in the evenings to tell me what I had done during the day. He left food and cards at my door, expressing his love. In general, he made such a nuisance of himself that I had to threaten to report him to his conference president or call the police. He eventually got the message, and three weeks after his last love note to me was married to a member of his church.

That marriage was not to last long, but I recount this incident because he was so sure "God told" him I was the one. Had I been an inexperienced young woman I would have fallen for that sort of talk, and I have seen many who have. The heartache and long hours of counseling spent trying to help some of the victims of these "spiritual attractions" has often consumed my ministry. I know this is a two-way street. That's why I wish some men and women who read this will stop using that tired, old line. And those on whom it is used should wake up and realize this is another demonstration that for some misguided people Jesus "sells" more than He "saves."

When Bill was ordained he received approval for me to be among those who laid hands on him. This was my first such experience, and it brought tears to my eyes. I felt that I would never have the opportunity to be so affirmed by my church, no matter how magnificent my ministry. It took some determined self-talk not to get morose about it. As we prayed, I made up my mind that I would never allow myself to be engaged in this issue on that emotional level again.

However, during the discussion on the floor of the 1985 General Conference session in Indianapolis, it almost broke my heart when some of my seminary classmates spoke out against the ordination of women. The language used in the approved resolution stated the action was taken "in view of the possible risk of disunity, dissension, and diversion from the mission of the church." I refer to these as "The Three Big Ds," which, I fear, are still very much evident in our denomination, in spite of the decision to not ordain women.

I don't know whether it was the Holy Spirit or the look of defeat on my face, but something happened in my conference president's heart that day in Indianapolis that brought about a dramatic change in his attitude toward me. At the end of the debate, Elder Steiner came to me and hugged me and apologized for his past insensitivity toward women in ministry. He explained that it had never occurred to him that I faced prejudice, and how sad he was that he had in any way contributed to it. A few weeks later, he invited me into his office and affirmed my ministry. He had not yet visited my church, but made arrangements to do so. Unfortunately, his change of heart came a little too late to change the attitude of some pastors in our conference. It would take the arrival of a new president, Charles Case, and his attitude of collegiality toward me, to bring about changes in the way some of the Southern New England Conference pastors related to me.

When I left the General Conference session in Indianapolis I remember feeling numb as I sat in the airplane for the long flight home. I began to write a searing sermon that would communicate my disappointment and pain to my congregation and incite them to take action. But early Sabbath morning the peace of God came over me, and I decided that if He wanted me to be ordained, no height nor depth, no man or woman, and no church organization could prevent it. In my sermon I called for reconciliation with Christ, instead of anger with the church. I shared the results of the General Conference as objectively as possible. I urged my congregation to accept the decision of the denomination and not withdraw support, to commit themselves fully to Christ so that together we could bring about changes inspired by the Holy Spirit. This was especially important for my congregation, because the majority were former Adventists who believed they had been mistreated by one or another of our institutions or leaders, and had only reluctantly returned to the church, hoping that their decade or more of absence had brought about changes that could initiate healing.

A discussion of the Indianapolis action at the end of the worship service was a turning point in my relationship with my members. They cried and prayed with me, supporting me in every way possible. As I was greeting people at the door, a visitor spoke to me. I knew something was amiss the moment he invaded my space and stuck his nose almost on mine, his blue eyes as cold as steel.

"I'm glad they voted against women's ordination" he snarled. "You are an aberration! The leaders should shut this church down!"

"Thank you for your thoughts," I replied, forcing a smile and trying to pull my hand out of his grip. He was crushing my fingers. "Sir, you are hurting me," I said loudly enough to attract the attention of people milling about the foyer.

Frank DeCampo, our current church clerk, came and put his hand on the man's arm, asking, "Is everything all right, pastor?"

"I'll be OK, Frank, thanks," I said.

Then the visitor pulled me by the arm away from the door. "You don't seem to have heard what I said." His face twisted with anger. "You women ought to be kicked out of the church; you're turning it into a farce!"

That day I knew I was a Christian, because instead of allowing myself to be caught up in the contemptuous attitude that man displayed, I simply wished him God's blessing and watched him leave, threatening to return to "settle things later." Strange, but something about that encounter filled me with a confidence I had not experienced before. We women are called, and we'll keep on coming till Jesus comes!

~

At the seminary I was hired as a graduate assistant by Ron Dupreez, who was working on his Ph.D. I was to help tutor and administer the study lab. I also worked with Janice Watson in the new learning center on campus. Even though mine was a prestigious job on campus, my weekly income was nowhere near what I needed to survive. So I developed several seminars and began to accept off-campus appointments to augment my meager income.

One depressing Tuesday evening, as I sat curled up on my sofa preparing for an exam, I knew I was at the end of my rope. Weary from too much traveling and the inconvenience of living out of a suitcase, I was exhausted from too much work and too little play. Maybe the dean of the seminary was right—I would never be employed in this church I had grown to love so much. I began to doubt God's promises and His call to the ministry. I couldn't focus on the material I had to review for the exam for worrying about my future. I completely forgot the many miracles God had used to wean me from the world and restore my dignity and self-respect. I began to think of the various disciplinary experiences He'd given me as punishments that did not fit the crime, and sank deeper into depression until I became hardened in my heart against God. Like the children of Israel at Kadesh when there was no water for the congregation, I railed at God. *Why? Why? Why?*

I slumped over my books, unable to study, cry, or pray, consumed with self-pity and numbed by fear. I'd drop out of the Master of Divinity program and, perhaps, even the church, and disappear among the multitudes trapped in the abyss of deferred dreams with no way out of a bleak situation. I even flirted with the idea of ending my life to stop the pain.

I really don't know how long I remained in that position, but I know I dropped into an empty, dreamless, sleep. The distant sound of bells brought me back to reality. As I opened my eyes and tried to orient myself, the telephone on the wall in my small kitchen rang again. I snatched up the receiver, hoping the caller would hear the crankiness in my voice and be brief or hang up.

A voice I didn't recognize asked, "May I speak to Hyveth Williams?"

"This is she," I muttered. I hoped it wasn't a certain seminarian who often called, pretending he was a conference president, to offer me a job as pastor. I was in no mood to joke.

Sure enough, the caller said he'd like me to consider a job opportunity. I'd fallen for that three times too often. As soon as the words were out of his mouth I slammed the phone down. But before I could cross the room, the phone rang again.

Speaking quickly, the same voice said, "My name is Charles Scriven, and I'm the new senior pastor at Sligo church. Would you consider coming to Sligo as an associate pastor?"

I was dumbfounded.

"Hello? Are you there?"

I heard myself screaming, then began demanding that he prove his identity before I dropped dead of shock. "If you are who you say you are, call me again tomorrow!" He agreed, after I promised not to die when he hung up!

I ran across the hall and burst into the Mulzacs' apartment, sobbing hysterically. They thought my mother must have died, or some other horrible disaster. I finally got my good news out, then ran back to my apartment and cried across the ocean to my mother and sister in England. For the next several days, I cried in the shower and I cried in class. I cried while driving, I cried while sitting in church. I cried when I shared the good news and I cried when I didn't. I cried when I laughed and I cried when I cried. I washed my dishes in saline solution and greeted visitors with tears. No matter what anyone said to me that week, I cried because I was overwhelmed by God's wonderful timing, in spite of my wavering faith in Him.

I arrived for my interview at Sligo, the college church for Columbia Union College, as nervous as a frightened kitten. The vacancy had been created by the departure of Pastor Jan Daffern, who had been such a source of encouragement while I attended the college. I met the pastoral staff, who did their best to put me at ease during the interview, but I was too keyed up and anxious to make the right impression as they fired questions at me. I left, not knowing whether I was hired or not.

A few days later, I received a letter from Elder Ralph Martin, Potomac Conference president, inviting me to join the Potomac team. I returned to the seminary to complete the quarter, after which I would assume the responsibilities of associate pastor for evangelism at Sligo church. I still had a year and a half more before I would finish the seminary, but that would wait. This was the second fulfillment of my "grapefruit" dream.

My mother came to help me make the transition to Sligo. We were both invited to Bill Knott's ordination celebration luncheon. As we sat next to his conference president, I started to introduce my mother, but she quickly said, "My name is Margaret Page and I'm a Baptist."

I was quite embarrassed, especially since I wanted to make a good impression so that he would one day consider me for a job. After that, my mother insisted on telling everyone she met that she was a Baptist. I realized she was fighting for her identity, and it must be tough being a quiet, soft-spoken person with a daughter like me who had a last word on everything. So I decided to join her, and began introducing her as "my mother, the Baptist."

As the weeks passed, she stopped going to church on Sunday and began to accompany me on Sabbath. She enjoyed the Friday evening vespers which were held at various times by myself and other seminarians who lived in our apartment complex. When she asked me questions about my beliefs I would say in the most affectionate manner, "I'm sorry, Ma, but you're a Baptist and I don't want to offend you." I refused to share anything with her in the hopes that reverse psychology and the testimony of my transformed life would win her. I knew it would take more than a witness of words to win this woman. She still had vivid memories of running out into the London snow without a coat or shoes just to escape my temper and profane language.

Nothing I could say would show her my love for Jesus and the incredible way He had changed my life. But I made sure that Bible studies, devotional books, and other interesting materials were left where she could have easy access to them. While I was in class, she read everything.

My mother stayed with me for six months. She was with me when I was introduced at Sligo, and she helped me settle into my new home in Laurel, Maryland. By the end of her stay she no longer said she was a Baptist, but then she never gave any indication that she wanted to join *my* church, either.

I was invited to speak at the seminary on her last day in America, so I arranged for us to drive to Michigan. I would take her to Chicago's O'Hare airport after my talk. We left Washington, D.C., very early in the morning, and on the long drive to Berrien Springs my mother asked a variety of questions. I could tell she was seriously contemplating becoming an Adventist. Since Jesus called His disciples to be fishers of men, I had read a few books about fishing and learned that when a big one is on the line, you don't reel it in quickly or else it might thrash about until it tears itself off the line. This, and other tips, would come in handy if I were to land my mother, my biggest fish to date.

So when she asked, out of the blue, as we drove along, "So this means that I will have to become a vegetarian if I became an Adventist?" I smiled, letting the line play out a little.

"No, Mother, you will not become an Adventist. You are a Baptist, and we don't want Baptists in our church!"

She nudged me with an elbow and complained that she would never consider breaking her family's tradition by becoming an Adventist. But an hour or so later she asked, "Are you sure the Sabbath is from sunset Friday to sunset Saturday?"

All the way to Berrien Springs we played this we-don't-want-a-Baptist-in-our-church game. By the time we arrived, I knew I had her, but, of course, I said nothing.

Mother arrived in London on Thursday. The following Sabbath she was worshiping in an Adventist church. After church she called to wish me a happy Sabbath.

"But you're a Baptist," I reminded her.

"I used to be one," she corrected me, as though she had just discovered the pearl of great price. "I joined the Adventist Church this morning," she said happily.

I can't remember when I heard my mother laugh with such joy as she expressed ownership of this wonderful experience she was having. I wanted to clap my hands and shout! So I did! "How did it happen?" I asked, catching my breath.

She had gone to the pastor, a winsome Irishman whose brogue, mingled with a London accent, made his sermons sound like poetry. After church, when she asked about becoming a member, he wanted to know how she had heard of the Adventist Church.

"I was introduced to it during my stay in America," she told him.

He looked concerned. "I'm so glad you didn't join the church over there. I'm afraid they are losing the essence of what it means to be a real Seventh-day Adventist."

"What do you mean?" asked my mother, as the old memories began to rear their ugly head and the thought that she might be making a misstep darkened her happiness.

"Well, they are allowing women to become pastors. For instance, I just received this article." He pulled out a copy of an *Adventist Review* that included my photo, announcing that I had been appointed as associate pastor at Sligo. Not noticing the look on my mother's face, he continued, "Believe it or not, they have appointed this Jamaican woman as pastor!" He shook his head in dismay. "I don't know what the American church is coming to these days."

"Well, pastor," Mother said, speaking deliberately, "that woman is my daughter. I learned about the Adventist Church from her while I was there for her appointment. And in spite of what you say, God has chosen her to do this work. Now, are you going to let me join your church, or not?"

We laughed together as she described how the crimson-faced pastor tried to apologize profusely, but the words, like arrows, had been spent and couldn't be retrieved. My mother would be the first of many of my family members to break with family tradition and join the Adventist Church.

~

My first assignment at Sligo was to develop an evangelism strategy for the church. I presented a detailed proposal for an old-fashioned tent meeting on the college commons, across the street from the church. I called it the Festival of Faith. At first, some members were skeptical of the idea, but when they read the proposal the church gave its full support to what became the defining deed in my ministry at Sligo.

We invited Dr. John Brunt, a professor at Walla Walla College, to be the main speaker, and Dr. Darold Bigger from the Walla Walla College church presented health messages. The plan was to set up a large tent that would accommodate 2,000 people. A smaller tent would be pitched for a family festival, featuring clowns, animal shows, demonstrations by the fire and police departments, an international day for food and art, and a grandparents-are-special day. Chuck recommended that I invite Karen Lumb, then vice president for nursing at Leland Hospital, to chair the family festival committee. Karen is a tall redhead who exudes strength, confidence, and success. I was a little intimidated by her no-nonsense reputation. We still laugh about our first meeting in the hospital cafeteria as we tried to out-impress each other. However, by the end of the meal Karen had agreed to chair the family festival committee. As the days passed into weeks and Karen and I worked together, we became close, lasting friends.

Though we got rained out the last week, the Festival of Faith was successful on two fronts. First, it renewed commitment to evangelism so that every year thereafter members would ask to have the event repeated. Second, it accomplished the following goals, voted by the congregation in the proposal:

1. To attract and bring to Christ the unconverted and/or unchurched. One hundred and thirty non-Adventists attended most of the 16 meetings. While we cannot account for everyone who joined the various churches in the area, 23 requested baptism, two joined on profession of faith, and 14 former members indicated their decisions to come back.

2. To bring spiritual renewal into the experience of our members. The fine preaching and stimulating presentations by the team of Brunt and Bigger, plus the work of the executive committee, composed of the pastors and lay participants who met once a month to plan the Festival of Faith, ensured the achievement of this goal. More than 100 members showed up to help set up and take down the tents. They donated materials to construct platforms, time to operate the sound system, and some operated a child care program and provided assistance in the parking lots. The city of Takoma Park worked closely with us in providing police security and other administrative support to meet their codes. The mayor, who proclaimed each Sunday as Family Festival Day, was on hand to open the festivities on Kids' Day.

Sligo church was like a classroom where I learned unlimited lessons. I tried not to miss any of them. I'm grateful for the head knowledge provided by the seminary, but it was the lessons learned at the feet of the rich mix of pastors who served during my tenure at Sligo, plus the invaluable insights of the support staff, that really gave me the tools for successful parish ministry. Dr. Ken Stout and Bertram Melbourne at the college were also my mentors, helping me hone my preaching skills.

During my first month, Dr. Jim Londis, the former senior pastor, invited me to lunch. I had always addressed him as "Dr. Londis," but as soon as we were seated at the table he said, "Hyveth, you can drop the 'Dr.' stuff now. We are both colleagues in ministry; call me Jim." He suggested that if I wanted to be taken seriously in this church I should "write as much as you can and get yourself published as often as you are able to." I have followed his advice and found it to be sound indeed.

Jim was used by God a second time to give me advice that would help reform my attitude toward ministry. In 1993, while I was recovering from a serious illness, he visited me in the New England Memorial Hospital where he also worked as public relations director.

During our conversation, he said, "Hyveth, you don't have to prove yourself to anyone anymore. Everyone in this denomination knows that you are a good minister, so stop driving yourself so hard, trying to prove yourself."

I took that to heart. During the three months I stayed at home recuperating it became my new self-message. When I returned to work it helped me plan my schedule and gave me the willpower to say no to some speaking engagements. I had been so desperate for approval and acceptance that I said yes to every invitation. I was afraid that if I said no people would permanently reject me.

While we prepared for the Festival of Faith in Takoma Park, I held a prophecy seminar to generate interest so that we could have a good baptism at the end of the tent meetings. That seminar was a smashing success—the attendance was great and many souls were won to the Lord. I was now feeling confident in my work as I conducted weeks of prayer in our North American colleges, universities, and academies, as well as in Trinidad and my home church in Deptford, England.

I also performed my first baptism at Sligo. The Friday night before, Pastor Norma Osborn, who was also doing her first baptism, and I practiced on Pastor Warren Zork, a man of no small stature. What an incredible man Warren is! He stayed in that water until his skin was like a prune, but he never complained. He believed in us and wanted us to be ready. I took him under at least 17 times before I thought I could do this rite properly in public. Because of what he taught us that night, I have been able to baptize men and women three and four times my size.

I had three candidates to baptize. One of them, Ron Warren, is currently the organist at Sligo church and a music teacher at Columbia Union College. Performing those baptisms was incredible! It was only after this experience that I really began to understand what was being withheld from women pastors in our church, especially when they are hired as pastors. I had seen evangelists give male students, in their sophomore year of college, permission to baptize candidates at the end of a crusade, but women pastors were being denied this privilege. These inconsistencies in practice only belittle the whole process and fuel the pain of rejection women feel toward the entire issue of our assimilation into the pastoral profession as respected, ordained members. Sometimes I think that my church would sooner ordain a male with only a high school diploma and no pastoral training (and, indeed, has done so), than a qualified, committed Christian woman whose highest desire is to serve the Lord and help accomplish the assignment He has given His church.

During the first few weeks I was at Sligo I had a recurring nightmare. I dreamed that I stood before the congregation to preach my first sermon. The place was packed. Standing room only. As I put my notes and Bible on the podium, I looked down to discover that I was naked to my waist. At this point, I would wake up in a cold sweat, sometimes totally disoriented, unable to determine the day or place. Not until I stood in the pulpit for a practice run the Friday before my first sermon did I realize the preacher is visible to the congregation only from the waist up. My nightmares were evidently related to a fear of being exposed as a failure in these new surroundings.

My first sermon was well-received by the congregation, and 16 people responded to an appeal to give their lives to the Lord and be prepared for baptism. I never had those nightmares again.

It would be incorrect if I gave the impression that everyone was happy with my preaching. Some objected to my evangelistic style and use of appeals which "broke with the long-standing tradition of Sligo church." Although their comments hurt, they were not as surprising as the response I got to my hats.

As people have come to know me, they realize that I wear a hat every Sabbath to the 11:00 service. Let me briefly explain why. When I was first converted, the Lord instructed me that He wanted me to tell the world what He had done for me, even though I did not understand it then as the call to ministry. I was also to study 1 Corinthians 11:1-11. (I agree that the instruction in verse five about a woman having her head covered is related to the culture to whom this letter was written, but the Lord used it to call *me* into a special covenant relationship with Him as *I* officiate in the role of pastor.) I promised God that to demonstrate my submission to Him as He used me to do a strange and new thing, whenever I was His mouthpiece in public I would cover my head.

At first, I hated wearing hats because I was so afraid of criticism. But over the years I have come to love them and am now known for my hats, which often go well with my hair eccentricities.

I'm not a legalist about hats, but when I wore my hat that first Sabbath at Sligo, I caused an unexpected reaction from some members. Even my senior pastor wanted me to assure him that I would not be preaching, teaching, or insisting that our women also had to wear hats. I had no such intention, but I realized how strong their fears were when one lady took me to lunch and told me that she was speaking for a large segment of the women in the congregation who were uncomfortable with my wearing hats and wanted me to not do it again.

"Jan Daffern never wore hats in all the years she served us," she insisted earnestly, "so I don't see why you have to!"

I thanked her for her concern and continued to wear my hats. Within a few months, hats became the trend as some even tried to outdo my flamboyance. I knew I was accepted when Dr. Elmer Careno, who had said very little to me before, told me that he almost bought me a most exquisite hat while he was shopping in the mall one day.

Chuck gave me freedom to carve out a place among the staff and in the congregation, but he sometimes shared in the matchmaking ministry some of the members seemed compelled to undertake. With a smile and a wink, he would sometimes suggest eligible bachelors that I might want to check out. He soon learned that I was not ready for that scene and dropped it. But the members didn't. I used to dread invitations to lunch because invariably there would be someone I "just had to meet." I even wrote an article on this topic in the Adventist Singles newsletter, but nothing deterred these wonderful saints. I count it something of a miracle that I escaped Sligo unmarried.

I was smart enough to begin my ministry in my next parish by declaring that I was single by choice and would make a change only with God's help. That brought an unusual response from a visiting physician. He made sure he had the full attention of the potluck crowd after the service, because he was about to share a juicy piece of gossip.

"Well, pastor," he said, "you probably can't get married again anyway. The word is that you've already gone through three husbands."

I nearly swallowed my tongue, but replied, "Well, I know where one husband is buried, but you better take me to the other two before I start some malicious gossip that you, a married man, are trying to make a pass at the pastor!" That silenced him, and I have not heard a word of that story since.

~

The issue of women pastors baptizing the candidates they had nurtured into the church was a raging controversy when I arrived at Sligo. I observed its effects on Pastor Jan Daffern and couldn't understand how church leaders could knowingly pierce the heart of women. Jan and two other women in the Potomac Conference spent an exorbitant amount of time in meetings at the General Conference from which they invariably emerged disappointed and often in turmoil.

I had to make a decision what to do about this and the growing debate about ordination of women. I felt then, and even more so today, that it was the moral duty of our denomination to ordain the women it had allowed to respond to the call of God and encouraged to study at the seminary with the promise that if we followed the principles for ministry we would be likewise affirmed. The church's *Manual for Ministers* states that "ordination was not instituted to build up a religious hierarchy," stipulating the criteria which must include, among other things, the candidate's evidence of being divinely called to ministry and past success in soul winning since entering the gospel ministry. I have witnessed the ordination of many men who had never won a soul, but were ordained simply because they were men, or the sons of pastors who have a heritage and history in the church. I believe that God's intervention and command to Moses in the story about the law of inheritance reported in Numbers 27:1-14, as well as 1 Corinthians 11:5, gives good ground on which the church can base its theology on the ordination of women. I have concluded, as have other leaders, that while there is no specific text approving the ordination of women, the decision of the counsel in Jerusalem, when it had no clear, biblical basis for Paul's ministry to the Gentiles, allowed the Holy Spirit to lead them into uncharted waters. We also should allow the Holy Spirit, who anoints women to the pastoral ministry, to lead us.

This debate was taking an enormous toll on the women in ministry. Some were leaving to accept other professional opportunities in the church, and others were leaving the church altogether. I decided two things. First, I would not allow myself to be engaged in the emotional battle because the price was too high. This was confirmed at my first Association of Adventist Women Conference at Sligo church during a meeting for pastors and chaplains. The conference was called by Elizabeth Sterndale, under the instruction of Elder Bill Scales. I had not seen so much pain and anguish as woman after woman shared her frustration with the church. We all wept bitterly for ourselves and for our denomination. Second, I knew that I had been called by God. I was not encouraged by some good men and women in our church. I had not been urged by the desire to prove that women can do just as well as men in this profession. I had been handpicked and ordained by God for the ministry, and I would not seek human permission to function as a minister. This would require that I also not become involved as a spokesperson for ordination. However, my very life and ministry would demonstrate the disparity between myself and certain men who graduated from the seminary and were ordained quickly, against clear instructions in the *Ministers' Manual,* some to be dismissed only within a few years for sexual misconduct and other perverse behavior.

While there are those who are called by God to make verbal protest against this injustice, I am not. My role is to support them with tangible evidence in pastoral ministry so they can point to those accomplishments and say, "What do you do with this, then?" This does not mean that I avoid opportunities to call my church back to a just and responsible attitude toward women pastors, only that I will not be engaged in the front line of battle so that I can focus on my part in the greater great controversy to which God has called me.

In 1988 I received a leave of absence to complete my Master of Divinity degree at the seminary. I returned to Berrien Springs for a second time, but this time I was not unemployed. The authority of the parish that I enjoyed at Sligo accompanied me to the seminary—along with a bad case of pneumonia. Instead of seeing a doctor, however, I allowed my illness to get worse until I could no longer attend classes. When I finally went to the doctor, he gave me medication and told me to stay in bed or I would be hospitalized.

I went to bed about 2:00 in the afternoon, drifting to sleep to the sound of children playing outside my window. A few hours later, I snapped awake to total stillness. There were no children outside. I couldn't remember where I was or what day it was. Why was I in an unfamiliar apartment? What had happened? When I eventually remembered that I was at the seminary, I panicked, thinking that I had slept for days, missing my important classes. The sun had almost set, but I thought it was dawn. My watch read 9:00. I thought it was a.m., not p.m. I jumped into the shower, got dressed quickly, and ran out the door. I bumped into the upstairs neighbor and asked, "What's today?"

She looked at me quizzically, but answered.

I slowly returned to my apartment thinking, *If this is how this quarter is beginning, God help me!*

But the quarter was great! Again, there were seven women among more than 400 men. Sali Jo Hand and her children, Lucian (Luke), Steven, and Andrew, would become my very good friends. By the second quarter, tension was rising about the treatment of women in the seminary. The outcome was the beginning of recognition and establishment of rules against sexual harassment. But, according to some of the women, nothing was really accomplished in terms of helping women, who felt excluded because of their gender, to have a greater sense of belonging, even though hours were spent in meetings to discuss ways in which to create this kind of atmosphere.

At the same time, attendance at the weekly chapel worship was at an all-time low. Dr. Raymond Holmes asked Sali and me to take over planning these weekly convocations. We formed a worship committee, composed of several seminarians, and by the end of the quarter we had standing room only at these weekly worships. Students from other departments began to attend, and the wives of seminarians came with their husbands as we worshiped God.

We introduced litanies and visual symbols, and involved the rich diversity of cultures and languages represented in the student body to heighten the worship experience and make God more real to us. How thrilling to hear prayers offered in a variety of languages and allow the congregation to be more than passive participants! Not only do I continue this practice in my church, but I encourage every pastor to establish an active worship committee, no matter the size of the congregation. The members will exercise ownership and model a deep commitment to Christ and His church. It will bring about renewal and revival in the regular liturgy. Gone are the days when ministers can impose their worship ideas on a congregation. You can tell the ones who still do because they oversee a dwindling membership or a community divided by a myriad of internal problems and disaffection.

One of the defining moments of my life occurred during this period at the seminary. To explain it, I must take you back to my past in Hartford, Connecticut, before I was converted.

I had fallen in love with a wonderful man. Ted Driscoll was a reporter at the Hartford *Courant* and a fellow atheist with whom I had some of the most intellectually stimulating conversations about our belief in evolution. He was a married man and, being a principled person, would not encourage a relationship between us. So we became best friends. He saw me through those crazy, rough days when my life was being threatened as the Lord pulled me out of that world of darkness. He helped me find safe hideouts, and I repaid his thoughtfulness by leaking incriminating information to him about corruption at city hall. When I told him that I had accepted Jesus Christ as my personal Saviour, during what I called our last supper, he was very skeptical, but respected my opinion as he wished me luck on what he called my "wild leap into the unknown." We said goodbye, and I went on with my life.

When it became known that I would challenge the mayor by running for office against him, Ted was assigned to do a story about my plans and strategy. That would be our last conversation for several years. I will never forget him sitting in my living room, asking questions about my political quest, while I daydreamed about how great it would be if he also became a Christian and we lived happily ever after. The dream would not last too long, because soon the "voices" began interrupting my concentration, and I began rambling about the conspiracy to use our city as a pilot program to test materials for space stations which the government was planning to build in the near future. He was very concerned that I was losing it. But when I shared what tremendous pressures I was under, and the threats to my son's life, he decided to help me. If it had not been for Ted I would have either gone completely insane or ended up murdered and stuffed in the trunk of a car in a hotel parking lot, framed as a prostitute. (That's what happened to another ambitious woman during this same period.) Ted helped to hide and protect me until I left Hartford. He never forgot the stories and materials I shared with him.

In 1986 I visited Hartford again. A reporter from the *Courant* informed me that Ted Driscoll was dying from cancer. He gave me Ted's telephone number and I immediately contacted him. When we met that evening it was as though time had stood still and we had never been separated. As we hugged, I felt as though he had given me his soul. I was disappointed to learn that he was still an atheist, and I was reluctant, at first, to share my passion for Christ and deep faith in God. It took several visits and letters before I could pluck up the nerve to give him sermon tapes and books or disagree with his positive thinking theories and humanistic philosophies to which he clung in a desperate search for healing.

He was by then divorced, but was living with someone. I found his honesty very refreshing (when compared to the games some of the Adventist men I knew had tried to play) as he explained how he had searched for me in London in 1980, only to learn that I had returned to the United States shortly before his arrival. He had never followed up on locating me, but went on with his life. I wondered why it wasn't God's will that we should become one in marriage. The reunion was bittersweet as we both reminisced about what could have been, but would never be because of the divergent paths our lives had taken. I thought that all the emotions that then sprang to the surface had long since been taken care of through conversion. For a while I toyed with the idea of resurrecting our past relationship, but in the end could not be a hypocrite, preaching from the Bible the importance of obedience, while yielding to my desire to be unequally yoked with an atheist, no matter how principled a man he was.

There were other mitigating circumstances. Corrine, for instance, with whom he had been living for several years. It is painful to describe the nights of weeping and days of soul-searching before I came to the place where I could let go and let God have victory in my life. I was lonely and longed for someone of the opposite sex to trust.

One day we exchanged strong words when he echoed a variation on a sentiment from the past. He declared angrily, "I don't want to be Mr. Hyveth Williams, sitting in some empty church hall, waiting for you to be ready to come home!" Years before he used to say he didn't want to be "Mr. Hyveth Williams, married to a political hack." This conversation upset me to the point where I had to go to London for several weeks to sort out the conflicting emotions.

In the end, we stayed friends, and as his illness became worse he turned to me as his minister. It was a thrilling reward to share my faith and watch him develop a yearning for spiritual things. He called often for me to pray for him, even though he never said to me that he had accepted Christ as his personal Saviour.

On one of my visits to Hartford, Ted invited me to lunch with his lawyer. Imagine my surprise when I discovered it was Attorney Glen Coe, an outstanding Seventh-day Adventist leader in Southern New England and a former counsel in the state attorney general's office. I was even more surprised to learn that one of Glen's partners was Barry Zitzer, the former assistant corporation counsel in Hartford with whom I'd had a brief, torrid affair before becoming a Christian. I tried to talk to Barry, but he had no time for me. But when he discovered that I was with Ted and Glen, he showed up for lunch, uninvited.

In typical Zitzer fashion, he monopolized the conversation by regaling us with intimate details of his and my past relationship in an effort to ridicule my religious faith. I was more than embarrassed, wishing I could crawl under the table. Instead, I sat and watched Glen's discomfort and the mild amusement of Ted, who did nothing to stop the Zitzer monologue.

At one point, Glen looked at me and innocently asked, "Does Chuck Scriven know these things about you, Hyveth?"

"Everything Barry says is true," I replied. "But the woman who did them died when I became a converted Christian, and 'Alice doesn't live here anymore!'" I looked Barry Zitzer directly in the eye as I spoke.

"I assume you're going to tell me that I'm a lost sinner and I'm going to burn in hell unless I turn to Jesus. You're now going to try to convert me?" he mocked.

"Absolutely not!" I answered, smiling sweetly. I reached over and placed my hand on top of his in a matronly manner as our eyes locked. "Barry, I have sacrificed everything to have Jesus. And for that He has given me salvation, joy, and peace. He promises that if I hold on to the end I will also have a place with Him in eternity." He pulled his hand away and tried to turn his gaze aside, but I defiantly held his eyes. "You've worked hard for your reward, which is waiting for you in the fires of hell. And just as I won't allow you to steal my joy, I will do nothing to rob you of your reward!"

He quickly excused himself and left the table.

Glen turned to me. "Hyveth, you are an incredible woman! I don't know how many people would have accepted responsibility in such an embarrassing situation, but I admire you! You are indeed called by God."

I expected rejection; I received affirmation. Too often we allow our past to hold us hostage so that we cannot enjoy freedom in Jesus Christ. If there is one thing forgiveness has done for me it is to make me free in Christ, emotionally, mentally, physically, and spiritually. It is a freedom that is available to all the instant we believe in Jesus Christ, but it takes a while, through sanctification, to work out the practical issues of our lives. And sometimes it seizes embarrassing moments to express its regenerating power.

When we left the restaurant Ted told me how proud he was of me and encouraged me to never allow my "checkered past," which all of us bring to the table of humanity, to determine how I would function in this broken world.

One cold Michigan evening, I received word that I had lost my friend. His new wife, Corrine, had called me the day before, telling me Ted was ailing and wanted to talk to me one last time. She held the phone to his ear as he asked me to get a mirror and describe my face, not leaving out a single detail. Then he asked me to pray for him. Somehow I knew this was goodbye. All through the night I was haunted by an impression I should call him back and invite him to accept Jesus Christ as his personal Saviour, but I didn't. The next morning Corrine called to say Ted had passed away in his sleep. It had been a long time since I had mourned the loss of a loved one, probably the first time since my friend Maurine passed away.

When I was a teenager in one of my first jobs, Maurine was my supervisor at a window cleaning company in Kings Cross, England. I had resigned to pursue a career in modeling and television and, like many who suffer from separation anxiety, she created a quarrel so she wouldn't have to deal with my leaving. Because I did not know about these intricacies of human behavior at the time, I met her anxiety with anger and walked away, swearing I would never speak to her again.

But at Christmas I visited Maurine to make up. I missed our friendship so much. We reminisced about our search for spiritual meaning, how we had explored everything from séances to Buddhism to atheism. Shortly after Maurine returned to her office, she complained of increasing numbness in her right arm. Within minutes, she had fainted and fallen into unconsciousness, never to wake up again. She died three weeks later from an aneurysm in her brain that her doctors believe was caused by the diet pills she took as a human guinea pig to make extra money.

Her death was devastating to me. It brought up childhood issues that I was neither emotionally nor spiritually able to cope with. I attempted suicide a week later because of the deep depression that came over me. Renita, my sister, discovered me in my flat and took me to see Dr. Rubra. He advised me to leave England and start a new life elsewhere. This ultimately led to my coming to America to seek fame and fortune, but where I continued my negative, destructive behavior.

So when I heard of Ted's death, all these forgotten memories came flooding back. I couldn't focus on work or studies. I walked around the campus like a zombie. I was sitting on the steps of Pioneer Memorial church, feeling lonely and depressed, when Viviane Haenni, a pastor from Switzerland, who was working on her Ph.D., came along. She simply sat with me and said nothing. She allowed me to unburden my heart, to share my sorrow, to rue missed opportunities, never reacting in a surprised or judgmental manner, even when I shared some pretty gory details about my past. She laughed and cried with me, and when I had emptied my soul, she prayed powerfully on my behalf. Viviane skipped her classes to stay with me and see me through that day. I am eternally grateful.

~

Elder Ralph Martin, then Potomac Conference president, had promised to assign me to my own church when I returned to Sligo after getting my degree at the seminary. But in December 1988, Dr. Walter Douglas mentioned that he had proposed my name for a church in Boston. I was also being asked to consider a teaching position at the seminary. I was offered the opportunity to study for my Ph.D., then return to the seminary to take the place of Dr. Holmes, who would be retiring soon. Dr. Holmes was the driving force behind the plan to have me take his place and one day teach preaching and worship. This surprised me since he was also at the forefront of the opposition against the ordination of women.

But then, our relationship was always a paradox. While preparing the manuscript for his book, *The Tip of the Iceberg,* he asked me to write the preface, even though the theme was against the ordination of women. The truth is, Dr. Holmes and his wife have always been among my strongest supporters. In fact, he has made me something of a legend in his homiletics classes. When I travel, I invariably meet one of his former students who will embarrass me with one of Dr. Holmes' statements about my preaching.

I had only one contrary experience with Dr. Holmes. I was invited to conduct a Week of Prayer for Andrews University a few years ago. Pastor Dwight Nelson, senior pastor of Pioneer Memorial church, where the services were held, invited me to conduct the Communion service which traditionally concluded the week. At the time, I hadn't yet received my ministerial license, and Dr. Holmes wanted me to adhere strictly to the letter of the policy which said that local elders can perform these duties only in their own local churches. What he did not consider was that my own conference had already surpassed this rule when they gave me a second church, 30 miles away from my main parish.

Dr. Holmes talked with me and asked me to not participate in the Communion service. While I understood his concern, I was not personally convicted by the Holy Spirit that this was wrong. However, when he threatened to boycott the service if I conducted it, both Dwight and I decided to take the high ground and not allow ourselves to become embroiled in a controversy that might dilute the powerful outpouring of the Holy Spirit on Friday evening when dozens of students committed and reconsecrated themselves to Christ. So Dwight quietly contacted his conference president, who then called the union president. As a result, for the first time in my life I had the privilege of officiating at a Communion service, blessed by the Holy Spirit and the presence of these men of God who stood solidly behind me. Dr. Holmes did not attend, and we never spoke of it again.

A few years later, while he was at Atlantic Union College to teach a Master's program, I invited Dr. Holmes to speak at my church. He did a magnificent job; no one would have guessed his opinions about women in ministry. In a rare light moment he once said to me, "Hyveth, you make a liar out of me because I am fully supportive of your ministry!" Like I said, we enjoy an unusual relationship!

It was difficult to make a decision about the offer from the Church Ministries Department of the seminary. Dr. Miles, the department chairman, and Dr. Holmes were trying to convince me of the merits of accepting, while the late Dr. Gerhard Hasel was trying to convince me not to. Other friends urged me to stay in parish ministry, which was what I sensed the Lord wanted me to do. But it was difficult to say no to my supportive teachers. Dr. Ken Stout eventually accepted the position after I declined, and is now professor of preaching at the seminary. I think it is a great compliment that I was offered the same position as the man who taught me preaching. He is the better addition to the seminary, bringing a breadth and depth of experience that I hope I will develop after a few more years of being seasoned in the pot of parish ministry. We are good friends, and he knows, as I do, that it was the will of God that he go to Michigan and I go to Massachusetts.

In the meantime, Dr. Douglas was relentless in his appeals for me to consider the Boston Temple position. But it wasn't until a visit in the home of Dr. Larry and Gillian Geraty, while he was president of Atlantic Union College, that I began to consider this as an opportunity.

I had returned to Sligo after graduation from the seminary. The members seemed genuinely happy to see me, and I was indeed glad to be back. I was also eager to see what church Elder Martin might have in mind for me, so I wasn't really interested in Boston. Then Dr. Geraty invited me to speak at the graduation baccalaureate, and in that brief weekend I had two life-changing experiences.

The first occurred during the Sabbath service. Worship had already begun, and from my vantage point on the platform I had a good view of the congregation. As I watched the worshipers greet their families and friends who had packed the sanctuary for the graduation worship, a man strolled in wearing the most incredibly wrinkled beige-and-brown checkered suit. It was easy to tell that he thought he was the cat's meow by the way he sauntered up and down every aisle in the church. I couldn't wait to discover what on earth that little display was all about. And I didn't have to wait long, because as soon as the congregation began to file out after the worship service he almost blocked one of the exits, explaining earnestly that he wanted the entire congregation to see that he had not, and would not, break the Sabbath by ironing his suit. He had traveled a long distance to get there and the suit had become wrinkled in his suitcase. But this legalist, like the Pharisee of old, stood beating his chest, proclaiming what a great Adventist he was, even to the precision with which he guarded the edges of the Sabbath.

The incident impressed me with the importance of conducting regular self-examination of my motives regarding the fourth commandment. At first I rejected that man out of hand as a fanatic legalist and congratulated myself for being such a radically responsible Adventist. Upon closer examination, however, I found so many skeletons in my own closet that I had to throw myself on the mercy of God with renewed appeals for His strength and the ability to seek first the kingdom of God and His righteousness.

The second event unfolded throughout the course of the weekend. On the way from the airport, I asked Larry about the Boston Temple. He encouraged me to consider it because it was a church with a distinguished past and great potential for the future. During one of our after-dinner talks, he and Gillian asked me to describe the profile of my dream church, the one I would be most eager to pastor. When I shared the burden the Lord had placed on my heart to revive a dying congregation, they looked at each other and said in unison, "We've got the church for you!"

Within minutes, Gillian was on the phone to Dr. Paul Robb, then the local overseer of a congregation that had not had a pastor for more than 18 months. "Dr. Robb, I have a pastor with me who's looking for a dead church, and I recommended the Boston Temple. Are you still searching for a pastor?"

We had to laugh at how she phrased her introduction, hoping that Dr. Robb would not get the wrong impression.

Sunday morning Gillian drove me to Boston to look at the church. I know exactly how Elizabeth felt when she saw Mary coming. When I saw that old dowager of a building, the baby of hope leaped in my bosom and I was filled with the Holy Spirit. I could just see what He wanted to do with this grand church, located in the heart of Boston. I prayed silently, afraid to speak for fear I might gush. To our great delight the doors near the parking lot were open, but when we entered the foyer our senses were assaulted by an overpowering blast of incense. An Indian congregation was at worship in the sanctuary. When we crept up to the balcony my initial joy dimmed a little when I saw the condition of the church.

As we drove back to Lancaster, Gillian tried to allay my fears by pointing out that the building had been exceptionally dark, so I should not make my decisions based on such a quick glance, that I should wait for an opportunity to see it on a Sabbath.

I left Massachusetts more confused than when I came. I decided not to accept the call to the seminary. One decision down, two more to go. Nothing about the ensuing weeks gave me the vaguest impression that God was working behind the scenes to bring about what would be the greatest gift in my ministry.

A few weeks later I was invited to be a speaker at the Greater Boston Chapter of the Adventist Forum. I learned later this invitation came about because Stanley Steiner, the Southern New England Conference president, had refused to allow the Boston Temple congregation to invite me to speak so that they could get acquainted with me. So being a group who, when confronted by an obstacle, finds a creative way around it, they invited me as a guest of the Adventist Forum. At that meeting I met Richard "Dick" Lewis. He said to me afterwards, "If you come to Boston, I will support you. I will come to your church and help you." And he kept his promise. Until he returned to California where he died unexpectedly, Dick was the person I relied on when I needed a shoulder. His advice and help, especially in establishing a liturgy unique to the Boston Temple, would take another entire volume to tell about.

The members and participants in the forum liked me, but when they recommended me to the conference president he flatly rejected their request. So they began a letter-writing campaign, urging him to change his mind. At the same time, Larry Geraty was lobbying the conference executive committee. A few years later, I was invited to speak at the College church in South Lancaster. With Dr. Geraty sitting right in the audience, a former pastor, who had earlier indicated to me that he did not support my coming to Boston, introduced me by saying, "Some of you may not know this, but I was the one who was instrumental in bringing Pastor Williams to Southern New England." I have it on video tape! I sat there thinking, *It's a good thing we aren't in ancient Israel, because the fire of God would have consumed this man for not speaking the truth.* Oh, well. Someone once told me that success has many mothers, or something to that effect.

That first Sabbath back at Sligo people lined up all around the sanctuary, waiting their turn to welcome me back home. In Sligo, I had found a place to belong. Maybe I wouldn't leave. But at camp meeting a few weeks later, Elder Martin suggested that the time had come for me to pastor a church on my own. He had a location in mind, he said. Maybe I would leave Sligo.

Then a telephone call came for me, inviting me to Southern New England Conference for an interview. The letter-writing campaign had prevailed, and the executive committee had voted with the members of the Boston Temple to interview me for the position of pastor of their church.

I was confused again. I could stay at Sligo. I could accept a church in Potomac Conference as solo pastor. Or I could go to New England and become senior pastor of the Boston Temple. I went looking for Ralph Martin. He gave me the fatherly advice I needed.

He said, "Hyveth, go for the interview. If you are offered the call, accept it. I can always call you back to Potomac, but right now you need the opportunity to pastor on your own. A male pastor with your experience would have had two, or more, parishes already. Don't let your loyalty to Sligo or the Potomac Conference blind you to the opportunities God may be opening to you."

This is the same advice I now give my associate pastors when they receive calls, and it never fails to produce deeds which glorify our Father in heaven.

At the Southern New England Conference office, I was immediately ushered into the interview with the president, the ministerial director, and the treasurer. I was given a chair that put my back to the president's desk, and the ministerial director and the treasurer sat on a sofa in front of me. The president took a chair to my right, with his back partially turned toward me. At no time during the interview do I remember him looking me in the face. There were no preliminary pleasantries before the president opened the meeting with a brief prayer. He did not look at my résumé, but began by saying that he was interviewing me under duress, because he was against women in ministry. However, his executive committee was forcing him to do this. It was a disturbing encounter. The president informed me that the

Boston Temple was a dying congregation; they had plans to sell the building and move the few remaining members to a suburban location somewhere off I-495 and use the majority of the funds for a big Boston evangelism program. He said the congregation already had an offer for approximately $1.5 million, which they were seriously considering. If I were to be hired, he was sure there could be only two results which would work in his favor.

"One, you will turn the church into a Black congregation and we will give it to Northeastern Conference. And two, you will finish killing off the already-dying congregation and we'll just carry on with the plans we have for the building."

I was flabbergasted. "Why aren't you concerned that I will turn it into a women's church?" I asked. I'm sure I said much more, but I was too impacted by the impression they were making on me to worry about the one I was making on them.

I returned to Sligo to announce to the staff that I was sure I wouldn't get the call, because I knew some of my responses would not have been received favorably. Moreover, I concluded, even if they asked me to come, I wouldn't go. "I don't see why I should leave Potomac, where my ministry is accepted and I'm treated with respect, to go to that cold, crazy conference," I sputtered.

To my surprise, a few days later I received a telephone call from the Southern New England president, inviting me to come to the Boston Temple. I thought about it, then rejected the offer. I was intrigued by its past. Some of the founders of the Adventist Church had stood in its pulpit, and contemporary leaders had served as pastors. I was challenged by its present needs, but I was seriously put off by that interview.

By then I had also had an opportunity to look at the church. The original carpet from 1904 was tattered and patched with orange duct tape. Most of the pews were broken down, some carelessly stacked in the balcony. The roof leaked; the entire building was dilapidated and in need of complete renovation. I had seen a proposal by another pastor, outlining the tremendous cost and effort it would take to renovate the building and revive the dying congregation. I decided to write a letter outlining my stipulations for employment. I knew the president would reject it, in spite of Dr. Paul Robb's calls, day and night, to persuade me to accept the call.

On July 17 my former roommate, Helen Hawley, and her husband, Leonard, with whom I had been at the seminary, held a birthday party for me. Knowing I had not seen former members of the Pennsylvania Avenue church for a long time, they also invited them. I went to this event with a heavy, indecisive heart. I had reached the point where I now felt like I should leave Sligo for a place where I could experience more personal and spiritual growth. The church to which Elder Martin was planning to assign me was no longer available—the pastor had changed his mind about accepting a call to another parish.

So now I had only two choices: remain at Sligo, or go to Boston. The fact that the dilapidated church had formerly had 500 members and been a gateway to Adventism no longer excited me. The novelty was gone and I was scared of the challenge, especially when some of my pastor friends and former teachers were telling me that it was an impossible situation. Other pastors had rejected it, they cautioned, and if it was being offered to me I should consider that those who are against women ministers might be using it to accomplish their sinister goals of placing me in an undoable situation. Thus, when I failed they might well say, "See? We told you women couldn't do it!"

I went to the party with all these negative messages swirling around in my head. As we brought each other up-to-date on our lives, I shared my dilemma. Wouldn't you know it, it was Ralph McClain whom God used again to show me the light! He began by asking me pointed questions.

"What are the advantages and disadvantages of staying, or leaving, Sligo?"

I listed the fact that I had just returned from the seminary, I had a new house and wouldn't be able to sell it at a profit, I had only just begun to feel a sense of belonging and was settling into the community, I was approved for a budget of $10,000 for evangelism, I no longer had to prove myself . . .

He looked at me and asked, "Where is God in all of this, Hyveth? I believe God is sending you to the Boston Temple to save you."

I objected, but knew instantly what he meant.

"Well, Hyveth," Ralph said, "you sound like the rich, young ruler who encountered Jesus. Everything you've said about the advantages of staying are pragmatic, but self-centered. If that's where you are spiritually, if you are feeling comfortable and rich at Sligo, even if you aren't breaking God's laws to the best of your knowledge, you seem out of touch with His will. He is calling you back to that primitive Christianity and faith which made your ministry so dynamic!"

I left the party that evening, knowing I was going to Boston.

# Chapter Seven

# Be Part of a Miracle!

The Boston Temple Seventh-day Adventist Church is strategically located in the heart of historic downtown Boston, almost across the street from Fenway Ballpark, home of the Boston Red Sox. The congregation was founded by M. E. Cornell in May 1870, and at its peak in the 1930s had about 1,200 members. By 1940 its membership had declined significantly, so they purchased the present 500-seat building from the Unitarian Universalist church and retained the name, Boston Temple. A school, Greater Boston Academy, was also housed in the facility, but when the socioeconomic changes of the 1960s and 1970s impacted the region, the effect on that once-flourishing congregation was devastating. The move of the academy to the New England Memorial Hospital grounds, accompanied by White flight to the suburbs, contributed to the membership decline until no more than 50 people attended on a given week.

In spite of creative ministries, such as The Gate in the 1960s, revival came only in temporary spurts caused by the ebb and flow of students. In the mid 1970s, Massachusetts received international notoriety when a court order enforced desegregation in the school system. Boston became racially polarized and a hotbed of riots and unrest, instigating further White flight to the suburbs. All of this also affected the Boston Temple.

When I arrived in August 1989, the congregation was almost 120 years old, and the old church was only a shadow of its past glory. It was a dark, gloomy, foreboding sanctuary in a broken-down building, but there was life in the 27 members, even though they were on the brink of despair, having been without a pastor for more than 18 months. I was immediately touched by the physical decay of the sanctuary, especially when one of the members appealed for funds to replace the old, tattered, red carpet.

Like Nehemiah, I told no one what my God was putting into my mind to do for the renovation and revival of the Boston Temple. After the worship service I asked Elder Charles Klatt, the conference ministerial secretary who had introduced me to the congregation that day, to tell the conference president and treasurer that I was requesting the salary that had been saved by not providing pastoral care to the church for more than 18 months. He quickly reminded me that such a thing "has never been done before," and based on his knowledge of the conference leadership, it would not be done now, either.

"Well," I responded confidently, "that may be so, but I'm here to change the record. Please take my request to your leader." When someone says it can't be done, I say, "Just let it go through the system and come to its natural conclusion, and I will accept the results."

That's how I received my ministerial license. I was reading through the policy book and noted that it said "a person (it doesn't say a "male," although that is usually the case) who functions as the sole pastor of a church must be given a ministerial license while awaiting ordination." So I wrote a letter to the ministerial secretary, requesting my license, enclosing a copy of the policy. He interpreted the policy to mean that since I was a woman, and the General Conference had not approved ordination for us, then I didn't fall under the category of "those awaiting ordination." I urged him to put my request through, anyway. He sent it to Elder Scales at the General Conference who placed it on one of his departmental agendas. The matter was discussed, then passed on to Gary Patterson at North American Division, since Elder Bradford was retiring and the new NAD president had not yet been elected. When Gary told me he doubted it would go through, I urged him also to let the request follow its natural course, and I would accept the results. As I sat in his office at the General Conference, I hoped he wouldn't notice how nervous I was as I tried to exude an air of confidence.

When Elder McClure became the new NAD president, Gary, a strong affirmer of women in ministry, passed on my request to him. Both of them agreed that my reading of the policy was correct. A letter of approval was sent to me and my conference. With it came permission to break down the last barrier, that of allowing me to ordain local officers. Until that time, I had to depend on an ordained pastor to ordain my local leaders. I was grateful for the approval of the North American Division because now if a conference president who disapproved of women pastors should come, he would not be able to withdraw my license. Even though it is issued by a local conference, the approval came from the North American Division.

As I tried to show the benefits of having the funds I was requesting from the conference, Elder Klatt agreed. "This could be the something you need to motivate and inspire this congregation," he said thoughtfully. I could see the wheels of his mind turning and knew that he would figure out a way to help secure approval of my request.

The members, however, didn't share my optimism when I told them what I had done. Some laughed. They thought it was a ludicrous idea and echoed Elder Klatt's initial sentiments that the request wouldn't be approved. I met with the church leaders in my office. As I talked about renovating the church and the growth I expected, every idea was shot down by Mabel Arrington, the head deaconess, who was very grumpy and very quick to say, "It can't be done; it won't work!" At the time, I didn't know she was one of the strongest opponents to my appointment as pastor of her church. In one of my seminary classes, Dr. Norman Miles had cautioned us that if we were not able to win the "mothers in Israel," we would never have a successful ministry in that church. And here I was starting off on the wrong foot with the one in front of whom all knees seemed to knock.

But when the conference sent a check to the Boston Temple for $11,000 in response to my request, I gained new stature in the eyes of the skeptical, who began to look at me as a mover and a shaker. The next time I met with the leaders, they were almost unanimous in their support, and those who still felt as they had before kept silent.

While trying to find an apartment, I was commuting between Takoma Park and Boston. Since I was pressing the conference for funds, I decided to save money by hiring someone to find an apartment for me. Ursula Hess, one of the Temple members, discovered an exquisite place in the home of Wendy and Bahman Barahmian in West Roxbury.

The moving van pulled up to my new apartment the last Sunday in August. When Wendy came to the door to show me the apartment I had rented sight unseen, I knew from her accent that she was from England. I began to question her about her employment history. She said she was a nurse, but was doing temporary office work. I felt impressed it was God's will that I ask her to be my secretary. She was not an Adventist Christian, and I knew I would be taking a big risk, especially if the members rejected my idea, but I concluded that if it was really God's will, He would impress them to approve. So I asked her if she would be my secretary and help me write a book about my life. She agreed, and a few weeks later we were a team, traveling to and from work together as I dreamed about the renewal of the congregation. It took six years, but Wendy is now very involved in our church.

When I arrived at the office that first Monday morning, a huge construction project was going on next door where a luxury apartment building was going up. I parked my car and immediately introduced myself to the workers and the police officer on duty. After that, every morning when I arrived they would wave and shout, "Mornin', pastor!" It felt really good. I immediately saw the benefit of making myself known in the neighborhood, which I soon discovered was one of the largest homosexual enclaves in the Greater Boston metropolitan area. As the weather improved from the winter doldrums to spring and summer, I discovered that it was an anomaly to see a heterosexual couple.

Wendy and I opened the door to the room that would later become her office and looked at each other in despair. Ella Taylor, the church treasurer, had spackled and painted my office and had been diligently raising money to replace the old sanctuary carpet. At nights she brought her ladder and tools and redid the ceiling in my office so that her new pastor would have a pleasant place to work. But Wendy's office was nothing more than a filthy junk room of a closet. Being a perennial optimist, however, I encouraged her to help me clear a path into the room, and something about the entire situation caught her imagination as we stood surrounded by rubble. Wendy signed on to the dream, and today she works in a state-of-the-art office with the latest equipment at her fingertips, much of which was provided through generous donations of members and friends. That first day, we found an old desk, and I brought in my computer and set up shop. There was already a telephone and copying machine, so in spite of the modest beginning, we laughed a lot and comforted each other by repeating the dream we had of totally renovating the building and reviving the congregation.

Wendy was a tremendous asset with the elderly members. Being a nurse, she was able to communicate with them in a way none of us have been able to duplicate. She sometimes even paid them visits on weekends to give a back rub and friendly encouragement.

All the while I was attempting to motivate Wendy and the members to capture the vision I was preaching about, I was being the biggest hypocrite. I would show up each Sabbath and preach a rousing sermon to encourage the congregation, telling them that they were not chickens, but eagles. I exhorted them to dream big. "One day soon the angels who are occupying these empty pews will be displaced by hordes of people seeking spiritual renewal as this congregation bounces back and begins to grow and glorify God," I preached confidently. My congregation didn't know that after two months in Massachusetts I still hadn't unpacked my bags, and that immediately after church I would jump in my car and drive eight hours to Maryland, where I spent the time crying and complaining about the rotten luck that had landed me in that no-win situation.

I felt especially discouraged one Sabbath. As I was preaching, someone in the back of the dark sanctuary yelled, "Watch out!" As that's an African-American response to good preaching, I preached even harder. Only when the balcony ceiling came crashing to the floor seconds later did I realize that a congregant was simply yelling out a warning so people could escape injury.

I drove to Maryland in a particularly bad mood that Sabbath, turning my mind inside out for a way to get out of this situation without losing face. I remembered Ralph Martin's promise to call me back to Potomac and thought this would be as good a time as any. But I needed to talk to him when I was more upbeat, so he wouldn't think I was really defeated and running away, rather just terribly homesick for Potomac.

I had a terrible weekend. I found no peace in Takoma Park where I stayed with Karen Lumb, in spite of her hospitality. My house there, now rented, was also a big source of worry as it was being vandalized by the tenants who hadn't paid rent for several months. As I made the long trip back to Boston, I began to cry and complain to God. "Why do You treat me worse than everyone else? You give others good churches." (Never mind that when I thought I was getting a 500-member church, pride reared its ugly head and I stuck out my chest and gloated as I told and retold the story of how I was going to be "senior pastor" in Boston.) "You provide other women pastors with husbands to help them through tough times like these; You give them everything to make them happy. But me? You give me the Boston Temple, a broken-down old church that's going nowhere!" I whined.

Then the Spirit began to minister to me. He broke through my despair, and in a still, small voice heard only in my soul said, "Hyveth, Hyveth, if you would only decide where you live, then I would be able to use you."

Decide where I live! It was like a light being switched on. He didn't have to explain the rest to me. I couldn't wait to get back to West Roxbury. I quickly unpacked my boxes, hung my pictures, and settled into my apartment. Whenever I hang my pictures, you can take that as a sign that I'm staying awhile.

As Wendy and I drove to the office on Monday morning she could tell something had happened to me. The old attitude of whining had been replaced by a confidence that scared even me. We were going to turn this church around! The first thing I did was to draw up a proposal for the renovation of the building and call a board meeting to share the dream with them. I proposed that we begin with the sanctuary and have a rededication service at the beginning of the year. Although they caught the vision, the board did not agree that we could accomplish such a major task in three months. When I told them that I expected at least 500 people to attend the rededication service, they thought I was totally crazy.

Frank DeCampo, a church elder at the time, stood up. With tears in his eyes he shared his dream that not only would we renovate and revive the congregation, but we would grow so large that one day we would have to rent the Hynes auditorium!

The fire of renewal was lit.

When the meeting was over, Ella Taylor said, "So, pastor, I see you've decided to stay with us."

"What makes you so sure?" I asked suspiciously, almost expecting her to tell me that God had revealed it to her, since that's what He seemed to do to me over and over again.

"Your fingernails," she said, pointing at my hands. "I see you've cut them off, and that can mean only one thing—you've decided to stay and rebuild this church and, I hope, the congregation, also."

It's amazing how people pick up on such little things. I have a thing about beautiful, long fingernails. I used to keep mine about an inch long. Because I wasn't doing any manual labor at Sligo, it was a luxury I could easily afford. When I decided to stay in Boston and invest myself in the vision God had given me to renovate the building and bring about spiritual renewal in the congregation, I cut them off. Just my personal sign of a renewed covenant.

Later, after Ella and I became best friends, we talked about those uncertain beginnings. She confessed that although she had been impressed on my first Sabbath when I prepared and served a prayer breakfast to make the statement that my ministry was to be one of service in an atmosphere of a healthy, loving, growing family in Christ, it wasn't until I cut off my fingernails that she believed I was committed to the congregation and my words began to have meaning. I had to do more than articulate a vision—I had to live it, even in the simplest areas of my life.

Our tithe was less than $24,000 in 1989. Today it is five times that amount and increasing, and our local giving nearly equals the tithe. Then we had $23,000 in our account, including the $11,000 that came from the conference. The best cost estimate to renovate the building was well over $250,000, with the sanctuary alone costing about $80,000. When we looked at our finances we realized that although the attendance had increased to 60 people, most of them were just curiosity seekers who had not committed themselves to our cause.

The 27 members would not be able to raise that much money. I asked for a few days to fast and pray to seek the Lord's directions. His directions came in the form of human intervention when the Paul Perkens family, the David Mee Lee family, and many others began to personally encourage me. I also began to read the passages in the Bible that dealt with the construction of the sanctuary. As I reviewed these stories, a common theme kept attracting my attention. In every instance God gifted people in a special way to do the various tasks so that it was not necessary to hire professionals who, even if they were available, would have charged a great deal for their services. What was good for Moses and Solomon would work for the Boston Temple!

I convened a board/church business meeting at which I shared my conviction that God wanted us to use unskilled labor and trust Him to give us special talents for the task. I asked for the names of local builders I could contact and again shared my dream for a completed renovation by January 1990, only three months away. I also solicited from everyone the names of five people they knew who had once been members but were no longer attending church. We placed those names in a basket and prayed over them. I wasn't yet quite sure why the Lord wanted me to do this, but I would soon find out.

It was Val Cargil, the chief cook of the church, who recommended Herman Frois, a house painter in her Portuguese community. When

Herman came to look at the sanctuary, he laughed at me.

"Are you crazy, lady? You need scaffolding and a lot more than I'm able to do. I've never worked on a job this big. I'll have to think about it, but I can tell you right away, I don't think I'll do it."

I told him to just think about it, but if he took the job God would bless him with the knowledge and skills he needed.

He looked at me in complete puzzlement. "Pastor," he said, "I'm just a simple house painter. You need a builder with the right equipment and people to do this job."

I would not be put off by his skepticism. A few weeks later he called to say that even though it didn't make sense to him, he would do the sanctuary for $28,000. We had the letter of agreement from the conference pledging to match whatever funds we raised. We had already made up our minds not to spend what we didn't have, but with that low bid we realized we could begin the task. Not only did God give Herman the skills to do this church, but he has done several sanctuaries since and in the process built a respectable company, hiring several people to work with him.

To fully appreciate the incredible renovation job that was done one would have had to visit our church before. When Elder Neal Wilson spoke at the Temple later the following year, he exclaimed in his opening remarks, "I have spoken in this sanctuary before, and friends, I must tell you, this is not just a renovation, it is a resurrection!" He recalled how dilapidated the building had seemed to him when he last had visited several years earlier.

Mabel Arrington became the Temple's "cover girl" when she was photographed with Elder Wilson and the picture was used on the cover of the March 1, 1990, *Gleaner*. The accompanying article stated that she had attended the Boston Temple longer than any other member. This comment raised the ire of another "old-timer," who no longer attended because she was sure God would never call a woman to be pastor. She called my friend Ella, the treasurer, then followed up with a terse letter stating that she, not Mabel, was the one with the longest attendance record, and because she was not so recognized she would not share her recent large inheritance with us. She was as good as her word, and sent several thousand dollars to the church every month, with instructions that it be sent on to the conference.

To prepare ourselves for Herman and his crew, we removed all the pews and old carpet out of the sanctuary and stripped away all the old asbestos tiles that covered some of the floors. On several Sundays, a work crew of church members helped with this work. We climbed ladders and cleaned all the woodwork in the high ceilings. We washed the walls and cleaned the chandeliers.

While the sanctuary was being renovated, we worshiped in Powery Hall, a large room next to the sanctuary. As the work progressed and we realized we would have to do the adjoining rooms, we sought the Lord's guidance in raising more funds.

In the meantime, the visual arts committee, chaired by Florence Robb, evaluated the pews and reported that they not only needed to be replaced or rebuilt, they also needed new cushions that would fit in with the renovated sanctuary. We voted to rebuild the pews to keep the historical authenticity of the building, and hired Manley Evelyn, a carpenter from the neighboring Berea church, to do the job. Florence's committee chose a rich purple carpet and matching pew cushions that highlighted the colors in the stained-glass windows. Our old dowager was beginning to smile with every touch of makeup we applied.

Prior to my arrival, the church had rented the facilities to the Boston Church of Christ. Through some oversight, the rent had never been collected, and they owed us $14,000. I suggested to our board that we should ask them to pay it at once. Some of the board members protested vigorously, saying that if I pressured the Church of Christ people it would drive them away. I pointed out that we were already paying for them to use our facilities, so if we drove them away we wouldn't be losing anything. Moreover, they were a very Pentecostal group. When they sang and got in the spirit they would jump all over the pews, breaking them and ripping the already tattered cushions. Baptism was also an important part of their worship. Every week when a new person was brought to the meeting, they would brainwash him or her into being baptized, and often filled the baptistry until it overflowed into the basement. They would leave without mopping up.

I finally convinced the board that it was in our best interest that we demand our rent and wrote a letter so stating. Within two weeks we had the check for $14,000 and a signed lease for a monthly payment of $400.

I happened to be working late one night when the Boston Church of Christ were holding their meeting. As I walked upstairs to my office, I passed a closet where old choir robes were kept. Hearing a deep moaning sound coming from inside, and thinking someone must be ill, I opened the door to find three BC members with their hands firmly planted on the head of a moaning visitor, exhorting her to accept Jesus Christ and pledging not to stop until she did.

On another occasion, a student from Boston University escaped into my office and begged me to help her get away because she was being forced against her will to move out of the dorm into one of the BC houses and the control of this group.

Articles written by a Harvard professor about the cultist, mind-altering behavior of the Boston Church of Christ eventually led our board to vote not to rent to them anymore. Today our church is used as a center of change for the community who hold their meetings in our facilities. Every day something is happening in our building, but our sanctuary is used only for our worship, weddings, and organ recitals. Incidentally, our organ is one of the oldest, continuously used organs in the Boston area.

When the funds began to flow into our coffers, our members were elated. Even the gainsayers joined in the celebration. I appealed for members to adopt a pew and raised $4,000 for that project. The members were so motivated by this that they gave even more sacrificially. I was sitting in my office one day when I felt compelled to go for a walk in the neighborhood. I was really reluctant to obey, but the Lord kept pressing me. Rather than wander aimlessly, I took mail to the box at the corner. I returned to my office, but still felt the Spirit urging me to walk around the neighborhood. I found myself walking into a school building, located almost diagonally from our church. I had heard it was a school for juvenile delinquents. After passing through a metal detector and being checked by two armed police officers, I still wasn't sure what I was doing there. When introduced to the director, I found myself volunteering to speak to the teenagers about a variety of topics that would help improve their self-image. The director reciprocated by offering the services of their carpentry class to work on our church. She said they needed a project where the class could gain practical experience. We were able to get several of the rooms prepared for painting with this free labor.

As we talked, I mentioned our parking problem and our expectation that a large number of people would be coming for the rededication service. She offered us the use of their parking lot, recommending that I secure it by speaking to someone in the mayor's office. Through the generous efforts of Ed Burke, neighborhood coordinator in the mayor's office, we received permission from the police department to use the school lot. He also helped us secure street signs to our church, and even arranged an invitation for us to help turn on the Christmas lights in the Fenway community. Later, we secured more than 200 spaces on a permanent basis from Sy Gotleib, who operated the Fenway Ballpark lot across the street from our church. (The school lot came in handy on game days!) Sy still sends an annual donation to our church, even though he no longer operates the parking lot. Pilgrim Parking, who now runs the lot, continue to extend parking privileges to us. I returned from my visit with the school director marveling about the wisdom and grace of God.

The Spirit began compelling me to immediately develop a newsletter and send it to the people whose names and addresses I had secured a few weeks earlier. Wendy and I worked feverishly to produce our first newsletter that was mailed to fewer than 100 people. (The list is close to 1,000 today.) The response was overwhelming! We had not asked for funds, but we received $8,000 in gifts. We were able to expand our renovation efforts to include the entire first floor and the old bell tower in front of the building that was about to collapse.

My original plan had been to just put new carpet in the sanctuary. But the following summary of renovations and expenditures so far (through 1995) outlines what I began to call the miracle of the Boston Temple.

1989:  Sanctuary Renovation: $40,000.

     a.  Painting, carpet, refurbishing hardwood floors and woodwork. (This doesn't include hundreds of member hours cleaning windows, woodwork, and light fixtures.)

     b.  Pew Restoration/New Cushions: $16,750.

1990:

     a.  Restoration of Powery Hall and Gold Room: $7,000.

     b.  Renovation funds for the children's division: $14,000. Donated by Ruth Fagel and named, in honor of her parents, The Alexander and Esther Smith Division.

     c.  Bell Tower, repainting and the external facade of the building: $12,988.

     d.  Patching the leaking roof: $4,000.

1991:  Replacing the old concrete steps around the church: $6,500.

1992:  Replacing the roof: $30,000.

1993:  Renovating associate pastor's apartment, Fellowship Hall, and the kitchen: $10,000. (All done by members.)

1995:  Erecting wrought iron fence around the building: $20,000.
       Installing crash bars: $5,500.
       Total improvements: $165,738.

By the grace of God, we were able to do all this work, paying as we went. We are still faced with replacing a deteriorating smokestack ($20,000), and kitchen renovation ($50,000).

While all the renovation work was being done, I encountered some severe leadership problems. When I was unable to secure the membership list from the church clerk, with whom I was locked in an indescribable power struggle, I turned to Mabel Arrington, who often boasted that she could remember the name of every member from the last 10 years.

Born and raised in New England, in her entire life Mabel had lived in only two homes, held only one job, and been part of only two denominations. By then in her mid-80s, she had been a member of the Boston Temple for more than 45 years "without missing a Sabbath." Until I arrived. She later confided to me that the only Sabbath she did not worship at the Temple was the one she spent visiting another congregation when she planned to leave during my first few months there. But then the $11,000 check came from the conference, and she began to see that I was organized and trying to do my best. She decided to wait and see what the outcome would be.

So I called Mabel and asked if I could visit her to secure the church list information I needed, and she agreed. When I arrived, she immediately escorted me to sit on her balcony, although it was cold and dark. She began our meeting with a terse statement.

"I suppose you're here to tell me about all the changes you're going to make in our church."

Before I came, I had decided to play this one by the book. At the seminary I had learned that a pastor must never make changes until the congregation signals its approval. And at that time, I did not have the congregation's acceptance, much less approval. One of the other "old-timers" had sworn never to set foot in the church again until I left. She has since changed her mind, but it wasn't easy. I had to suffer through having the phone slammed in my ear several times before she returned, after almost two years. And then when she did start attending again she offered nothing more than a grunt in response to my greetings.

Mabel sat stiffly upright, staring straight ahead, her hands balled into tight fists in her lap,

"Mabel, I need your help," I said finally.

"You need *my* help?" she asked incredulously.

"Yes," I said, with all the humility I could summon. "I've never pastored a church on my own before," I admitted honestly. "And, frankly, I don't know what to do right now."

Even in the poor light, I could see her eyes begin to twinkle and her body language change from defensive to almost pushy. I had surrendered at the feet of the tower of power and she was delighted.

"Well, get a paper and pencil," she ordered. And while I wrote just as fast as I could, she listed, from memory, all the names, addresses, zip codes, and telephone numbers of all the members, if they had moved, where they had gone, who had died, and who was missing. From that evening, Mabel became one of my most staunch supporters, and a dear friend.

One day she called to say, "You know, pastor, your enthusiasm is very infectious, and I want to thank you for giving me a new reason to live."

When she died a few years later I took care of her to the very end, sleeping at her home, caring for her personal needs, and performing her funeral.

Another challenge was Mel Conners, who was the adult Sabbath school teacher, superintendent, and elder. One Sabbath he told me he was planning to leave the church because he did not believe women should be ministers. I knew that if he left it would cause a White flight, and the revitalization which was but a flickering flame would be doused by his actions. Rather than appeal to his sense of justice, I thought I would challenge his faith.

"Mel, I have observed that you are a committed Christian man and that you would do this thing only out of a deep conviction. I would like to make an agreement with you: Give me three months, and if you do not see the attendance increasing and visible signs of renewal, I will resign and admit publicly that I am not being led by God to be a pastor. But if it's working, you will stay and support me."

He was happy to accept the challenge, stating that he knew he was right and that God would affirm his position. I have learned that God loves these kinds of odds and is always seeking opportunities to reveal His power and teach His people that He doesn't always have to do things the same way in every situation. Because He is God, He can always do a new thing (Isaiah 43:19). Well, Mel is still a member of our church. He's now homebound as the result of a series of strokes and cardiac problems, and I hold his power of attorney.

I try to follow the Lord's instructions regarding personal relationships as outlined in Matthew 5:21-26. I believe it is my responsibility as a leader to model this behavior before my congregation and will quickly call and visit the person(s) whom I discover is angry with me, even if I feel that I'm the victim. Some do not respond to my overtures, and that's all right. I still have to do what my Lord says.

Over the years, many disaffected members have returned and we have become better friends. Because I have been healed emotionally, I find that I have a growing, healthy congregation. We have not had problems with divisiveness or gossiping because I will not tolerate it. When I first came, some members were quick to tell me the details of missteps by former pastors. I would stop them before they got into their story by saying, "I'm really not very good at keeping these kinds of secrets. In fact, I repeat them, mentioning who said what, when, where, and how. And I normally repeat them to the person being gossiped about." I didn't have to make that speech too often before the news swept through the congregation that the pastor did not like to hear bad things about people. One day I will be their former pastor, and God knows I've made enough mistakes to fill volumes. I hope they will remember me kindly; that's what I want and need. I'm sowing so that I can reap a rich harvest!

~

The rededication service was scheduled for January 6, 1990. We all worked night and day to meet that deadline, and invited people to come and be part of the miracle. Seven hundred people heard Dr. William G. Johnsson and wife, Noelene, guest speakers at the 11:00 worship service. At the afternoon program, Pastor Wintley Phipps performed before a crowd of more than 1,000. Dr. Johnsson described what he saw and experienced in his March 22, 1990, *Adventist Review* editorial:

"Several Sabbaths ago I witnessed a resurrection. A church that six months before was in its death throes was now packed with people . . . the Boston Temple, located downtown, two blocks from Fenway Park, had fallen on hard times. The church needed renovation; membership had dwindled; parking was impossible. Conference leaders contemplated the sale of this property.

"They decided to make a last-ditch effort to save the church. Calling a new pastor, they pledged their support for a program of renovations . . . After only four months [from the time the new pastor arrived] the sanctuary was ready for rededication. I looked out over a church crowded to the gunwales. How I loved to see the deacons filling the aisles with extra chairs! Perhaps 600 to 700 people jammed into the church that morning. The offering plates overflowed—money fluttered to the floor when the deacons brought them forward. And the mood? Thanksgiving, rejoicing, wonder, a sense of being part of a miracle."

The congregation grew quickly from 27 to more than 150 the first year. At the end of six years we are at 250, with approximately 350 attending. Our congregation is composed of 33 different nationalities. Ethnically, it's 60 percent Caucasian, 30 percent Black, and 10 percent Spanish and Oriental, a wonderful blend of people who demonstrate what the kingdom of God on earth should be like.

As I write I am a guest in the home of Dorothy Aycock, one of the most gentle, nonracial souls I know. She invited me to speak at her seventh annual women's ministry retreat in the Arizona Conference, which has turned out to be a high spiritual experience. As we drove from the airport she asked about my associate pastor. I told her he is a married White male. Since I am a single Black female, I explained, we felt we should have some balance.

Her mouth dropped open. "You have a White male associate?"

"Yes," I answered, "because the majority of our members are White."

She was incredulous. "Your congregation is almost all White?"

Then came the questions, one after the other, about a White male accepting my ministry and leadership. Isn't it amazing that when I, a woman who happens to be Black, talk about my congregation, people automatically assume that they are all Black, but they never assume they are all women? My experience is that people, even in a racially divided city like Boston, are seeking the truth. When they find it they are not too particular about the complexion or the gender of the one delivering the message.

I was so excited about our dramatic growth that I thought it must be the big-name speakers and singers we brought in who were drawing the crowd. So I planned a whole year of exciting programs. Every week we tried to make each Sabbath event bigger than the last. Then I began to notice that though attendance increased, there was not a corresponding commitment to the church—only a handful of people were running around doing everything. I didn't know what to do, so I increased the programs and activities, leading the church at a breathless pace that soon began to take its toll on the little handful of helpers who did all the work.

I was invited to do a week of prayer at Andrews University. While there, the Lord drew my attention to Ezekiel 37, the story of the prophet's vision of the valley of dry bones. As I studied the passage, the Lord revealed to me the single, most significant truth about my ministry and the church at that time. When Ezekiel first prophesied and preached as he was commanded, there was a "noise, and behold, a rattling; and the bones came together . . . sinews were on them, and flesh grew, and skin covered them; but there was no breath in them" (verses 7 and 8, NASB).

The Lord showed me that the dramatic increase in attendance was not real growth, but rather a bandwagoning response to the excitement of the "miracle Temple." The Holy Spirit impressed upon me that the sounds of success that attracted the attention of many in those early days of our restoration was no more than the bones rattling loudly as they came together. If I treated the situation as real growth it would eventually die out as the bones withered and dried up again, this time beyond resurrection.

Through the words of Ezekiel, the Lord commanded me to return to Boston, cancel all the programs, projects, and personalities, and preach again to my people. So I did, and since no one, including me, really knew what to expect of my ministry, I dared to be different and obey the divine instructions. It paid off tremendously as the directives to Ezekiel became my mandate.

The week I returned, and every week thereafter for months, I shared this revelation in my sermon, joining in my congregation's excitement as we witnessed how the "breath [of life] came into them, and they came to life, and stood [and are standing] on their feet, an exceedingly great army" (verse 10).

I was so busy with fixing up the Boston Temple and reclaiming former members who had been disenfranchised from the Adventist community (some for 10 years or more, and who now form 60 percent of our membership) that I totally ignored my own brokenness and desperate need for healing. Things came to a head a few weeks after the miracle rededication service by way of a simple mistake that almost no one noticed, but that threw me into a deep depression.

I had invited the Epic Brass, a horn quintet, to provide a musical Sabbath. The plan was that I would not preach; however, at a given signal, I would conclude the service with prayer. Everything was going perfectly when, only 15 minutes into their presentation, I misunderstood the leader's intention at a pause in the musical piece. I stood, prayed, and dismissed the congregation. The quintet was surprised, but followed my lead, concluding what must have been their shortest-ever concert. I was too embarrassed for words.

I still have no idea what happened. Perhaps I was burned out, having not taken even a day off since we started the renovations the previous November. I immediately turned my embarrassment into shame, then guilt, then despair. Whenever I'm totally drained of emotion and energy, I become physically sick, and this time it exhibited itself as a searing chest pain that caused me to cough uncontrollably. Several physicians in my congregation examined me, but no one could find the cause of this problem that became progressively worse until I became bedridden.

After two weeks in this state, I remembered a brochure that had been sent to our office from Gonzaga, a retreat center run by Jesuit priests, announcing an upcoming "silent retreat." I had never been to anything of this sort, but I sensed that the Spirit was directing me to go. Wendy made the reservations, and one cold Friday afternoon I drove to Gloucester, Massachusetts.

Gonzaga is an old castle built so close to the water's edge that sometimes the tide lashes against the outside walls of the dining room. The rooms were small and sparsely furnished with a monk's cot and a table hewn out of rough wood, and we all shared a common bathroom. The lights were always dim, making us feel as cloistered as the monks who once lived there. One could almost hear their chanting echoing through the silent halls. Because it was a silent retreat, I saw only a few of the other participants at mealtime, and we didn't speak to each other, obeying the code of silence.

At sunset I decided to take a walk along the beach. I sat down on one of the huge rocks that jutted high above the water. The sound of waves crashing against them echoed loudly in the dark lagoon below. The sun sank into the ocean, turning the blue water into a gray magnet that seemed to be drawing me into its agitated waves below. I felt overwhelmed with the pain of my early childhood and teenage years. I had been sexually violated by various relatives and often molested by some of the strangers who sat on the veranda of our little grocery store, quenching their thirst from its meager stock of soda. Now those memories threatened to overwhelm me. I was broken by the abuse in my childhood and the promiscuity of my youth, filled with guilt and shame that I hugged tightly, secretly, to my bosom, even though it was squeezing the life out of me. I was so despairing over the lost opportunities and the enormous mistakes I had made in life that not even my intellectual assent to Christ's salvation brought me even a semblance of peace. I have no words to describe my hurt. I threw myself facedown on that rock and cried out to the Great Rock of Ages, confessing every known sin and seeking forgiveness, pleading for healing. Day became night, and my warm tears began to freeze on my face in the icy night air.

Hours later I returned to my room, feeling as heavy as when I had left. On top of the despair, I now had to deal with the memories I had stirred up. I could find no peace in the silence that only mocked me, as self-messages swirled in my head, taking on a life of their own. By Sabbath afternoon I felt there was no help to be found in God. While I had been preaching to others about the value of being naked and vulnerable before God, I remained an emotional cripple and a dysfunctional derelict who had learned to wear fig leaves to cover up life's great hurts. I was so distressed by my situation that even though the snow was falling heavily that night, I stole away from the retreat and drove the treacherous 30 miles back to my home.

I began to feel better the next day. The coughing and chest pains stopped, but the emotional burden still lay heavily on my heart. Nothing inside seemed to have changed as I returned to work. The following weekend I had to return to California for another session of my ninth quarter Master of Divinity degree requirement for field school. I stayed in a motel nearby where I shared a room with my friend from seminary days, Sali Jo Hand.

This particular session began with a lecture by a psychologist. No one had said anything to me, but as the questions were asked during the session, I soon realized I had been targeted as the cause, or one of the causes, of a perceived conflict that had been created at the previous session. Normally, when I am under the gun like this, I do one of two things: act defensively and mouth off, or become depressed and suicidal. But when the day ended, I discovered that I had neither of those feelings. What's more, I invited some friends to a restaurant for dinner.

At the end of the meal, I gave the waitress my American Express card. She returned shortly with my card—and a pair of scissors—and proceeded to cut the card into small pieces, according to instructions she had received over the phone. Later, I learned that someone at my bank had forgotten to record my payment and kept my check in his desk drawer for more than two months. Since I hadn't used the card in some time, I was not aware of the situation. It was later replaced and I received a letter of apology from the bank, but my friends, nor I, could not know this that night. It was one of those embarrassing moments we all hope we will never experience. But I walked away unscathed. I began to think something must be wrong. My old despair button must be out of order.

After my devotional one morning I stepped out on the balcony of our motel that overlooked a mountain not yet browned by the California sun. As I admired its beauty and strength, the Spirit of God began to speak to me. He showed me how I had been healed at the Gonzaga retreat, but I had been so deep in self-recrimination He couldn't begin to work out the healing effects in my life.

The changes that progressively manifested themselves were tremendous, but I walked around waiting for the other shoe to drop. It never did. I have none of the old pain. That little girl in me who had been crying out for acceptance and recognition had been integrated into the adult me. I was no longer fragmented; I was a whole, healed child of God. In the years since this healing, I have learned to treat my body as a temple of the living God, to take vacations and days off for needed rest. It has been a difficult discipline, but I'm holding strong, exercising, and even eating right!

By the end of 1990 our congregation had grown so much that we had to hire our first associate pastor, Mark Chaffin. We asked our members not to share their faith at home, work, or anywhere else until we could see the fruits of the Spirit, as enumerated in Galatians 5, reproduced in our own lives. We set about accomplishing this through intensive Bible study and worship. I developed a strategy called "The Vine and the Branches," based on John 15. Every Friday night I invited 12 people to my home for vespers and served a light supper. Then we studied John 15. After completing this study, each participant was to start his or her own group of 12. Soon Pastor Chaffin and I became facilitators to several Friday-evening vespers at the church and in various homes. Several baptisms resulted from this ministry and church attendance continued to increase. During this process, we became aware of an incredible phenomenon that continues to be the major source of growth and new Bible studies. Janet's story is a good example. (All names have been changed.)

I knew I was in trouble the moment she walked into my office. Her stern look of disapproval and rigid body as she sat holding her purse on her knees all were telltale signs this was not a friendly call to affirm her pastor.

"There's a woman who's a disgrace to the Adventist Church," began

Mrs. Snipe, her words knifing through the tension between us. "She sits on the front pew every week," she added, as if I didn't know immediately whom she meant. "She looks like a prostitute, and my husband and I want to know what you plan to do about it."

Before I could answer, Mrs. Snipe sprang to her feet, demanding that I "tell that woman to take off the makeup and fake pearls before she comes to church again!"

I tried to say something, but she moved to the door with the speed of an agitated asp, pausing only long enough to hiss, "If you don't do something *immediately*, my husband and I will transfer our membership to another church!" She flung her head back so hard I thought her neck had snapped, but it was only the sound of the door slamming shut as she stormed out of my office.

Janet was indeed a prostitute. A Catholic native of Boston, she was a nominal practitioner of her family's faith when she became a promiscuous teenager and, eventually, an alcohol and drug abuser who traded her flesh to support her habit. After many unsuccessful attempts to leave that shameful lifestyle, Janet decided that her only way out would be to commit suicide before she was brutally murdered, as had been happening to some prostitutes, victims of a serial killer in Massachusetts who was still at large.

On the day of her planned demise a stranger visited her massage parlor, insisting that he was not interested in sex, but wanted to save her so that he could marry her someday. He told her to find the church that keeps the Sabbath, because those were the only people he knew who could help break the chain that kept her in her predicament. She was angry about his arrogant intrusion, but when he left and she began to think about what he'd said, she became very curious.

Since she had nothing to lose, she searched the Yellow Pages, under "churches," calling each in turn to find out which ones "kept the Sabbath." She hadn't a clue what that meant and had called several Protestant churches before an irate minister, put off by her questions, told her to "talk to the Adventists." That's when she called the Boston Temple Seventh-day Adventist Church.

I remember her call. I thought it was a crank call, and when she asked how much we charged for Bible studies, I was sure it was. When I insisted that we meet and talk, she hung up. I did not expect to hear from her again, but 30 minutes later I was very glad it wasn't Pastor Chaffin who answered the door.

The taxi driver seemed to be deliberately delaying his departure, leaning over to look out the passenger's window to see who had ordered this prostitute, whom he had delivered like a pizza to a church. As I loudly welcomed Janet to her first Bible study (for the benefit of the nosy cab driver), I thought that there are some definite advantages to being a female pastor.

Janet was a sight to behold. Her thick, long, blond hair, worn in frizzy curls, cascaded down her shoulders and back. Her lips, painted a shocking blood-red, matched her clawlike fingernails. Her eyes, rimmed with wide, black lines and highlighted by bright-green eye shadow, darted back and forth nervously. The hallway lights bounced like a prism from the dangling, lantern-shaped earrings that made clicking sounds every time she moved her head. And her skirt! Black leather, no larger than an oversized belt, wrapped around endless legs encased in black stockings that disappeared into six-inch, pencil-heeled shoes.

"You the person I spoke to a few minutes ago?" she asked cautiously.

"Yes," I said, inviting her quickly into the office, being careful not to stare.

"I'd like to speak to the priest."

"I'm the pastor," I said.

"But you're a woman!" she exclaimed, then clapped her hand across her mouth as if to force the words back down her throat.

Several hours later, after she had poured out the details of a promising life derailed by such sin and sorrow that she was contemplating killing herself that very day, Pastor Chaffin and I shared the gospel of God's favor with Janet and had the privilege of leading her to accept Christ as her personal Saviour. I gave Janet her first Bible, showed her how to read her name into such chapters as Romans 5 and 8, and to learn the disciples' prayer in Matthew 5.

Janet began to attend church the very next week and didn't miss a Bible study or Sabbath service throughout the entire time she lived in Boston. I didn't tell her how to dress, but that first time she showed up in church she wore a knee-length dress and considerably less makeup and jewelry than when we first met. She sat on the front pew so that she "wouldn't miss a single thing."

Under my administration, the philosophy of the Boston Temple is that our members and pastors are not to function as clothes police. The objectives of our mission statement, "to inspire discipleship in Christ, to function as an extended family, to minister in our neighborhood, and to nurture all God's people," demands that we function as the scarlet cord in the window (Joshua 2:15-21), accepting everyone just as they come to Jesus.

So you can imagine my surprise when Mrs. Snipe, one of our church leaders, paid me that infamous visit. How sad she couldn't rejoice with the angels in heaven over the restoration of her prodigal sister. Perhaps she had never read Ellen White's comments in *Evangelism*, page 272:

"There are many who try to correct the life of others by attacking what they consider wrong habits. They go to those whom they think are in error and point out their defects. They say, 'You don't dress as you should.' They try to pick off the ornaments, or whatever seems offensive, but they do not seek to fasten the mind to the truth. Those who seek to correct others should present the attractions of Jesus. They should talk of His love and compassion, present His example and sacrifice, reveal His Spirit, and they need not touch the subject of dress at all."

In her haste to "correct" Janet, she lost the opportunity of presenting "the attractions of Jesus," the salvation of God in progress, and being a part of the "something new" (Isaiah 43:19) springing forth in our church.

A few months later, long after the departure of Mrs. Snipe and her family who made good on their threat to leave, Janet shocked our congregation again. When she came to church that day, we failed to recognize her right away. Gone were the long tresses, the dangling jewelry, the finger rings, and heavy makeup. Even the defiant curl of her lips and the cheap perfume of the streets had been replaced by the soft smile of grace and the sweet scent of salvation. She was also rejoicing in her love for the handsome stranger who had kept his promise to her. I had the privilege of baptizing her in the presence of a congregation who rejoiced in her miraculous transformation.

Janet has since moved to another state where she serves as Sabbath school superintendent, teacher, and preacher. She returned to school to pursue an undergraduate degree in education, but often returned to Boston to "walk the streets again," she says, teasing. But now she's sharing her new-found freedom in Christ with her former friends. Sometimes she spends hours holding a drug-addicted woman who is dying with AIDS. She sings songs of praise, praying and reciting promises from Scripture about the unconditional love of God and the assurance of a place for them in God's kingdom in exchange for their hearts.

One Christmas, as we hugged in the foyer after church, Janet whispered,

"Pastor, I believe the Lord is calling me into the ministry. Do you think the seminary is ready for Rahab's resurrection?"

"Yes!" I shouted confidently, "I know they are, because I'm one of their graduates!"

The news that the "nets were breaking" and that we needed help to prepare the walk-in candidates who came through our doors reached the Religion Department at Atlantic Union College. Brian Burges, now a youth pastor, brought in a group of students to help us. One of the names the students were given for follow-up was Beth (not her real name).

Beth, a 20-year-old Jew, had come to Boston to study medicine. She had accepted Christ and was now on a quest to find a community where she could learn more about Him. She was walking past our church one day and noticed the sign over the front door. Wondering what kind of church it might be, she jogged over to the Star Market nearby and spoke to a shopper—who just happened to be an Adventist. She asked what kind of church we were. She was so excited to discover there was a Christian church that kept the Sabbath that she went straight home, called our office, and asked for Bible studies.

After several months of studies with the AUC group, I baptized Beth. To her parents' chagrin, she applied to one of our universities to pursue her postgraduate education. They were totally against her becoming a Christian. The week of her appointment with the university admissions director, she told her family about her decision and her educational plans. They were outraged. Their only daughter and sister had joined "a cult"!

Her mother flew to the university to be with her daughter when she met with the admissions director. She became physically and verbally abusive in her attempts to dissuade Beth from her determination to attend that university. Beth called me that evening, very distraught over the day's events. What could she do? She was being forcibly returned to her home by her very angry mother. Just as Beth tearfully appealed for help, the irate mother yanked the phone out of the wall, abruptly ending our conversation. Not knowing the location of her hotel, I was unable to do anything but pray. I called on the prayer warriors in our church to intercede on Beth's behalf as we anxiously awaited word from our sequestered sister.

Beth was taken home and locked in her room for nearly a month. Her only visitor was the rabbi, who tried to deprogram her. But as the days slipped into weeks, she became more committed to Christ and our church.

In exasperation, the rabbi recommended that her mother speak to me personally. Perhaps in this way she could secure enough information to convince her daughter to leave this "cult."

I agreed to meet with her and Beth in a restaurant of the mother's choosing. She wanted a neutral, public place for our discussion. She turned out to be a refined, cosmopolitan Jewish lady, but she became immediately antagonistic. She was initially shocked that I was Black and disturbed by my apparent youthfulness. She launched into a tirade against the Adventist "cult" that had captured her vulnerable, young daughter, turning her against her family.

I gave her room to vent her fears and anger without becoming defensive, while assuring her that our church, unlike others, was not afraid to admit its failures while promoting its accomplishments. And one of our big failures has been inadequate propaganda to inform the general public that we are a mainline Protestant church whose only rule of faith is the Bible, and the Bible only. I expressed my conviction that truth is never afraid of scrutiny, answered her questions honestly, no matter how penetrating and uncomfortable they were, then invited her to check into our beliefs and background before making her final judgment.

She began to lower her voice, and a great deal of the original tension slowly evaporated as she asked more questions. How had I come to be part of this church? What about my relationship with God? Where does Jesus fit into all of this? By the end of the conversation, I had given a great deal of my personal testimony, interlaced with the Gospel presentation. As we walked out of the restaurant, she spontaneously put her hand on my shoulder, the very first touch since our meeting. And I said to myself, "Gotcha!"

The next morning was the first Sabbath of the Southern New England camp meeting. Unknown to me, she and her daughter arrived on the campgrounds early that morning and stayed until late afternoon. They ate our food and met our people, a rich multiracial, multicultural community. The following Monday morning she called the admissions director to apologize for her behavior and tell him she would be proud to have her daughter attend his school and be a part of the Adventist Church.

When our associate pastor, Mark Chaffin, resigned to pursue his master's degree in chaplaincy, we hired Matthew Lombard, a teacher from the Berkshires. He served our church during 1992 and 1993, the most difficult period of my pastorate. Many wonderful people became the beneficiaries of his ministry. I remember Dan and Barbara Kelsey, who now direct the Helping Hands ministry, an effective outreach to the homeless.

Dan and Barbara visited the Boston Vegetarian Restaurant in downtown Boston and picked up a tract and a copy of *The Great Controversy.* One Saturday, while walking near Fenway Park, they saw our church sign and, even though they were not dressed for it, came in and sat down. I saw them when I stood up to preach and welcomed them. After the service I visited with them and asked for their phone number. They were so impressed when I called them a few days later that they visited us again. I turned them over to Pastor Matt, who began Bible studies with them.

One Sabbath, Dan, a man of imposing size and stature, brought one of his friends to church. From the telltale bandanna and fingerless leather gloves, I determined that the friend was obviously a biker. As they passed by the door where I was greeting the congregation leaving the sanctuary, Dan stuck out his chest to proudly introduce his friend to his new pastor.

"Eric, man," he said, pulling him closer so he could shake my hand, "this is the best g—d—preacher I have ever heard!"

But Jesus was working with Dan, transforming him inside and out. Several months later, Matt and I had the privilege of officiating at two ceremonies for Dan and Barbara. On the same day they were married, they were baptized. Now they minister to a host of homeless men and women each Sabbath on the Boston Commons.

~

During this same period, the Southern New England Conference was going through a time of economic difficulty. Tithe had decreased significantly, and to accommodate the financial shortfall in 1992, several pastors were let go and the conference was redistricted. I inherited the Swampscott congregation, located on the north shore, overlooking the ocean. The congregation had dwindled from 220 members to about 20, who could scarcely afford to keep the building heated.

One morning I received a two-minute telephone call that disrupted my life. The outgoing pastor of the Swampscott church, who had previously told me he was against women in ministry, called to announce that as of that moment the Swampscott congregation was mine. I was stunned! I knew this church was to be added to my responsibilities, but our conference president had indicated that the redistricting plan would not go into effect until after the first of the year.

The church keys had been left with the church elder, the pastor said, and I was responsible for prayer meeting that night. Just like that! There would be no official introduction to the congregation and no farewell or explanation about the change. I couldn't believe what was happening.

I called the Swampscott head elder and arranged for him to come to a strategy session with Matt and me. Though I didn't know it, this man was not the officially elected head elder, but one who had usurped the leadership since the head elder was usually late or absent. I realized the complexity of my problem when the real head elder called to register his complaint and inform me that the men in the small congregation would boycott the Sabbath service if the conference did not withdraw my appointment.

I called Chuck Klatt, the conference ministerial secretary, who immediately agreed that I shouldn't go to Swampscott that Sabbath. He called an emergency board meeting with the Swampscott church to explain the redistricting plan and how I was to be assigned there. The leaders protested that the Bible said women shouldn't be ministers and told Elder Klatt that both the conference and the denomination had lowered its standards by hiring women. They wouldn't be party to that. They declared that the growth of the Boston Temple from 27 to 250 was the work of Satan, because God was working very effectively to "shake and sift out" all the other churches. They gave me the title of "queen of apostates" and warned that if I stayed, they'd leave.

The following weeks were filled with meetings, rife with appalling accusations and derogatory remarks about women. It was frustrating and depressing, especially when I visited their homes and found that some of these men were not in total control there. Their women ruled the roost, so that the men talked like little lambs at home. But when they came to church, watch out! They turned into roaring lions stalking their prey.

Because these men were not satisfied with the decision of the conference, they began systematic harassment. First, some of their friends called at all hours of the day and night to urge me to do the Christian thing and resign as pastor of the Swampscott church. Then those men, Bible-quoting elders and deacons all, attended church when I was scheduled to preach, but only to conduct loud Bible studies on Paul's writings on the issue of women.

One Sabbath they stood up and interrupted the worship service, demanding to know by what biblical authority I was preaching and teaching in their church. One even declared that it was Eve who had brought sin into the world, and "I will not sit back and allow you to bring sin into this church!" They refused to vote me in as an elder so that I could perform all of my pastoral duties. They disrupted board meetings with loud arguments, angry outbursts, and petulant walkouts. But they never told me by what authority they behaved in such a despicable manner.

For nearly six weeks, as this controversy raged, the Spirit of God kept insisting that I, the mighty mouth of Massachusetts, must keep silent. It was very difficult. Sometimes I would tremble with restrained rage under a cool veneer of piety as I stood before the little congregation. At other times I was truly relaxed and unaffected, feeling affirmed and approved by the Holy Spirit, whose peace washed over me.

Near the end of the fifth week, during the long drive home after an even longer, emotionally exhausting meeting, I felt numb from the persistent rejection, paralyzed by the poisonous protests that caused me to call into question the validity of my ministry. I finally broke down and wept.

I wasn't ill, but I couldn't leave my bed. I was so discouraged I couldn't even pray. I wanted to run away, yet I knew I had to stay to the bitter conclusion. It was then that the Lord brought the story in John 20 to my attention, especially the question "Woman, why are you weeping?" Somehow, as I reflected on those words I became even more determined that I would not give in to the pressures. Somebody must have been praying for me, because after Elder Klatt gave the men an ultimatum to either cooperate with me or find another congregation to worship with, they left.

By July 1993 I was extremely stressed out. I had been asked to perform a wedding, but when I discovered that the couple needed extensive counseling and suggested they seek it, they refused. I will not perform a wedding when I have grave doubts about the situation. I explained my position and offered to fly to their location at my own expense if they would accept counseling, but they refused. Backed by my board, I decided not to perform the wedding.

The reaction of some of the family was so harsh an old "ulcer" problem flared up, and I collapsed while at a meeting at the New England Memorial Hospital church. I was taken to the emergency room, writhing in pain from severe stomach cramps. I was treated and sent home, but in September when I returned from speaking at a camp meeting in Canada, I collapsed again. The doctor described my internal bleeding as stress-induced ulcerated colitis.

In spite of these incidents, I left on a five-week tour of Australia, New

Zealand, and Hong Kong. The Longburn College in New Zealand was saved from being closed as a result of the blessings the Lord poured out on my ministry. In Australia, hundreds committed and recommitted their lives to the Lord as I spoke to thousands in the sports arena in Sydney. In Hong Kong I enjoyed a few days of much-needed rest and relaxation as I shopped for silk and enjoyed the holiday resorts with Dr. Doris Foo, principal of the academy in Kowloon, and mother of Grace Foo, a Boston Temple member.

Before I left the United States, several of my friends reminded me of how prejudiced the people were in Australia. I was met at the airport by Elder Ron Craig, a charming man who allayed my fears. I saw public posters inviting people to a Reggae party, so I knew there must be other people like me living in Sydney. When I arrived at the hospital cafeteria, though, I didn't see a single Black person anywhere. As I picked up my supper I noticed that people were staring and whispering. I was sure they were making racist remarks about me. As more and more people began to come in, the whispering became a buzz. I was in a panic. I left my meal unfinished and literally ran out of the cafeteria.

As I walked briskly down the hallway toward the front entrance, a little girl ran after me, pointing and shouting, "Look, Daddy, there she is! I seen her, Daddy!"

When I looked back, about four or five people were running toward me. I picked up my heels and ran.

The little girl's father was the first to catch up with me. Placing a gentle hand on my arm, he said, "Sorry my little girl frightened you, but your picture is posted all over Sydney. She just wanted an autograph!"

I relaxed and had a great time for the rest of my stay in Australia.

I returned to Boston and began a Revelation seminar in October to build up the Swampscott church. I had two car accidents that month, which should have signaled that I was on the brink of collapse, but I was in total denial about my human limitations. It wasn't until December as I was lunching with my friend Karen Lumb and collapsed in the restaurant that I realized I had finally run out. The ambulance was called and I was rushed to the hospital and treated for colitis.

Unfortunately, my problem turned out not to be ulcers or colitis. I had adhesions from an operation some 20 years before. My intestines had become wrapped in extra tissue that, over time, pulled them out of place. Because the condition had never been treated, only emergency surgery saved my life. I was not able to return to work for three months. I couldn't even attend the convocation in Denver, Colorado, to receive the North American Division Distinguished Service in Pastoral Ministry Award. My conference president accepted it on my behalf.

As a result of my three-month absence from my pastorate and one of the worst winters ever, by the time I returned to work in April, the Boston Temple church attendance had dwindled to well below 100. We faced severe financial problems and a $45,000 deficit. There was no alternative but to lay off our associate pastor, Matthew Lombard. Fortunately, he was immediately hired as chaplain of Greater Boston Academy. Before he left, we closed the Swampscott church and transferred the membership to the Boston Temple.

By August 1993 the conference had instituted a pilot program to help graduates with potential by providing half their salary. Also, by then our congregation had experienced another growth spurt, and we made a faith decision to hire an intern under this program.

In came Pastor Amado Luzbet, a new graduate of Atlantic Union College, to whom we assigned young adult ministry. In 1990 the conference designated me as the chaplain for the non-Adventist college/university campuses in the Boston area. Under this authorization, Pastor Amado created T.E.A.M. (Together Experiencing A Ministry) for the young adults, young professionals, and college and university students. Within a year he had baptized seven students, and more than 60 others were actively involved in the life of the church. He had developed leadership among the young adults to the extent that even in his absence the organization continues to grow. Our head deacon, Al Teixeira; the associate head elder, Sandra Smith; and most of our deacons are young adults. Boston University approved campus meetings and vespers conducted by our church, and agreed to recognize us as a denomination on its registration form, rather than our having to be identified as "other." Further, the university designated our church as a field school to train Master of Divinity students in the practical aspects of ministry.

Harvard University also gave us permission, and a place, to hold campus fellowships. One day a staff member called from the registrar's office to inform us of a policy change that would no longer require Adventists to take exams on Sabbaths.

Amado's ministry was so effective that at the end of two years the conference assigned him to a three-church district in the Berkshires. Our new associate pastor, Ken Baumgarten, had served as head elder from the time he was transferred from the Swampscott church. Among his many other duties, he is responsible for developing family life and prayer ministries. He is also a full-time student at Atlantic Union College, graduating in June 1996. He's already been hired by Northern New England Conference. Some on our board now joke that we are running a miniseminary. We're blessed to be so used by God.

# Chapter Eight

# The First, the Only?

know from personal experience that being "the first" or "the only" has been grossly overrated. Nevertheless, it was something I sought after all my life, and when it finally happened I was overwhelmed by the accompanying responsibility. I became the first Black female to be hired as a pastor in our denomination, the first and only woman of any race to be hired in my conference and union.

Perhaps because of their history of hiring women, life in the Potomac Conference was a pleasant experience. At camp meeting I worked with the men, hauling chairs to and from the big tent. No one pampered or disrespected me. I rode on the back of the truck and enjoyed a pizza treat with my male colleagues. It was my privilege to work with the youth beside such pastors as Maurice Battle, Jr., and Tim Evans, whose playful energy made light of the hard work involved in camp pitch and strike. There was never a day that I was made to feel like a "female" pastor at Sligo church, either. I was judged by my performance, not my gender. So I was totally unprepared for New England.

In going to the Boston Temple, I accepted a call to a church that no other pastor in the local conference, the union, or the North American Division wanted. I had been told repeatedly of a good lay brother who ran the Boston Temple with an iron fist. When he learned I was being considered for the position of pastor he banged his cane onto the floor and declared, "Over my dead body!" He passed away the week I finalized the arrangements to accept the call. I can only guess at the surprise of some of those who heard him make his declaration when they were informed that he would be laid to rest the day after I was introduced to the congregation. Sometimes some of us who are dedicated to the Lord become so zealous that we stand in the way of His doing that "new thing" spoken of in Isaiah 43:19. And so did many others who made those early years literally filled with blood, sweat, and tears.

There are those who say that pastors, and especially pastors' wives, should not make a special friend of anyone in their congregation. I'm glad I did not follow that old standard, because I would have missed one of the most refreshing experiences any Christian can enjoy while on this earth.

I first met Ella during a brief interview she and Sandi Robb Gilbert conducted with me at the prayer breakfast my first Sabbath at the Boston Temple. I noticed that she hung back in the big shadow of her husband, an important man in the community, but it was about three months later that I walked into the parking lot and saw her leaning against her car, crying, overburdened with trying to hide her pain at the failure of her marriage. Like the woman in Luke 8 who had the issue of blood and had spent all her living on physicians who were unable to cure her malady, Ella had consulted several pastors. The general advice was "Go home, give more, love more, cook better, heighten the romance. It's your job to keep your husband happy."

She was nervous as she spoke. "Pastor, it's a sin to be divorced, right?"

I wasn't sure if she was asking or telling me, because the statement had both implications. So I waited for her to continue.

Haltingly, she shared the heartbreaking details and her fear of divorce. When she finished, I explained to her the biblical basis for divorce and watched her shoulders sag. She looked like a trapped animal.

I knew that look. I, too, had experienced those feelings. The only difference was that I did not know the Lord during my awful ordeal . . .

By 1974 I realized that I would never be reconciled with my husband, a desperate alcoholic who had lost all gusto for life and all ambition to live. "No fault" divorce had just become a popular national phenomenon, and my lawyer confidently assured me that it would be "a piece of cake." I had never been to court before the day I sat waiting for my divorce. I had fulfilled all the pre-trial requirements, and since my husband did not respond to the notices of the hearing or show up to contest, I nervously waited for what my lawyer told me would be a mere formality. He didn't even think I would have to take the stand. At that time, I was at the peak of my popularity in

Hartford and certainly didn't want the news media to get hold of this story.

At least 30 people packed into the small room that reeked of body odor and cheap perfume. When my name was called, my lawyer stood up and advised the court that my husband was absent. Normally, the court would ask him a few questions and, since we had no assets or property to split, it would be a simple matter of the judge signing the papers and telling me when the divorce papers would be available at the justice department. Therefore, I was stunned when the judge asked me to take the stand. I turned tear-filled eyes toward my lawyer in a mute appeal for help.

As the judge began to question me, I soon recognized that under his black robe of authority was a pornographic voyeur who homed in on the intimate details of my life with a relentless interrogation. He demanded that I give graphic, detailed descriptions of marital intimacies. At times, when I saw he was dissatisfied with my response, I created some. He was indescribably repulsive when he leaned back in his chair, wiped his sweaty brow, and salaciously circled his thin lips with a large, pink tongue. I wasn't a Christian then, but even my unconverted heart rebelled against this shameful treatment.

When I finally gave my life to the Lord I became a passionate advocate against divorce. Even though I understand there are cases where it is necessary and I will compassionately support the parties involved, I still believe that God hates divorce because of the profound pain it causes in the lives of those involved.

I shared all this with Ella that day, and later preached a sermon entitled "The Shocking Truth About God: He Was Divorced" (based on Jeremiah 3:8). My own shameful secret of that court experience, which I had not yet released to God, plus Ella's pain, were used by the Holy Spirit to influence me to make an appeal at the end of the sermon and pray for the healing of all the broken emotions. When I called for all who had been divorced, or had loved ones who were divorced, everyone, except small children who didn't understand the invitation, literally ran from the pews to the front of the church, as if they had been eagerly anticipating the day when they would be liberated from the guilt and shame of divorce by the power of the Holy Spirit.

In the weeks and months that followed, Ella and I studied the Bible and *The Desire of Ages* and our friendship grew on the foundation of a common desire to know nothing more than Jesus Christ, and Him crucified. The Lord knew that I needed a stable, phlegmatic friend to balance my high-octane personality, and Ella was always there.

Words will never adequately describe the tremendous prejudice under which I lived in those early years in the Southern New England Conference. One of my first, most important discoveries was that the people in New England did not make friends easily. I was definitely not prepared for the cold shoulder I received when I was introduced at my first workers' meeting.

At the end of that meeting not all of the pastors who came to shake my hand did so to welcome me. Some seized the opportunity to tell me that they did not support women in ministry. Life was going to be very difficult. I learned to sit alone, to eat by myself in the cafeteria, and eventually built up quite a defense against pain caused by the not-so-subtle rejection. It didn't help me that my conference president was initially nonsupportive. Unfortunately, by the time he had changed his attitude, the damage had been done. I early decided that no matter how badly I felt about the attitudes and isolation, I was never going to let them see me sweat. I am so grateful for the unconditional love that many in my Boston Temple congregation provided to nurture me through those difficult months as I painstakingly tried to educate and love my fellow pastors unconditionally. Many times, though, I returned from these meetings with my colleagues absolutely shattered.

The camp meeting before the 1990 General Conference session in Indianapolis was a typical example. It was my first camp meeting in Southern New England, and it was also the worst I had experienced since becoming an Adventist.

I was informed that a group of pastors were convening a meeting to sign a letter to the General Conference president, Elder Neal Wilson, urging him not to allow the passage of the resolution regarding the ordination of women. Though uninvited, I decided to attend. My presence made some of the pastors hostile, and many refused to sign the letter unless I left the meeting. One of them tried to convince me that the meeting wasn't really about me, they were just following their convictions. These comments were as insulting as when some racists express their bigotry in my presence, then feel compelled to convince me that they have nothing against me personally, because "you're not like other Blacks."

I said nothing, just sat and listened to speaker after speaker.

The meeting turned out to be a dismal failure because very few wanted to sign the letter in my presence. As they began to leave, the chief spokesperson asked me to remain so he could speak to me.

"I know who you are," he began. "I was on the executive committee and heard that you are a feminist. The only reason you are here today is because you threatened to sue the conference if they didn't hire you."

Well, that was news to me.

"You are holding the leaders of this conference hostage, demanding that you be ordained or you will take legal action, and I'm not going to let you get away with it!"

"Now listen here," I said, my voice as cold as steel. "I don't know where you got your information, and at this point I don't care, because I'm not even going to try to prove that it's not true. You wouldn't accept anything I said, anyway. So listen up, because I'm going to say this only one time for as long as I'm here: You and your cronies do not intimidate me. You may not like it, but I'm here to stay, so you'd better learn to live with me." I picked up a copy of the letter they'd passed around and stormed out. I paused at the door and glanced at the stunned look on his face. "And one more thing," I said, "get off my back!"

I walked out of the cold, dark dungeon into the bright, warm sunshine. Almost blinded by rage, it was one of those moments when I wished I had a husband to hold me and comfort me. I was shaking like a leaf as I realized that this gossip had spread among the ministers, perhaps causing the backlash I was experiencing. I walked over to the water fountain near the entrance and ran the water over my hot face. As I leaned against a tree, trying to compose myself, the pastor with whom I had just finished the volatile encounter came up to me and handed me the book *In Search of the Cross,* by Robert J. Wieland.

"Read this, it might help you—"

I didn't even let him finish. I grabbed the book and ran from the campground. Years later (that's how long it took me to open that book, I was that angry), I found this message written on the flyleaf: *Hyveth, I hope this little book will prove to be the rich blessing to you as it has been to me.*

My eyes filled with tears. In the intervening years my colleague has since undergone a dramatic change in his attitude about women in ministry, and those words had a significantly different meaning than on the day he gave me the book.

Some of the pastors also expressed resentment about my travel schedule, especially when I was released from camp meeting responsibilities to speak elsewhere. I must admit that if the shoe had been on the other foot, perhaps I would have felt as they did. In fact, I sometimes did. Before God healed me emotionally, I bristled with jealousy if the spotlight focused on other women in ministry, in spite of the rich rewards I enjoyed. It took a lot of heart searching, fasting, and prayer to overcome this flaw, but it eventually helped me to be more patient and forgiving of my brothers who behaved unkindly toward me.

It was through the ministry of pastors like David Thomas that I was able to survive the stings of prejudice. I will always appreciate and admire him as one of the most principled men I have ever met. Until I got to know David, I was always suspicious of South Africans because I believed they were tainted by racism, whether they wanted to be or not. But David allowed Jesus Christ to give him a new heart, and he is truly free of gender and racial prejudice. Again and again, he would place my name on the list for ordination, arguing on my behalf at several executive committee meetings.

When Pastor John Nixon arrived at Atlantic Union College church several years ago, I found in him not only an ally, but a personal friend and staunch supporter of women in ministry. He is intellectually and spiritually stimulating, a man who stands for the principles of God, though the heavens fall.

I can finally say that I have earned the respect of most of my colleagues in ministry and am treated as a part of the team. At a recent pastoral retreat I delivered three sermons at the request of my conference president. The Spirit of the Lord blessed in such a mighty way that even some of those pastors who had argued against women in ministry and acted out their prejudices toward me, shared the tremendous heart and mind transformations that led them to apologize for their past behavior. I believe we are finally reconciled with each other, not by *my* might or *their* power, but by the presence of the Spirit of God in all our lives. It took this experience to knock the chip I wore like a block off my shoulder so that I could function as a truly called woman of spirit. I'm so glad that I did not leave the Southern New England Conference before this cycle was completed. Had I done so, I would remember only the wall of prejudice by which some kept me out of the collegiality of Christian ministry.

I almost did leave once. I received a call to be the senior pastor of a church in California. I fell in love with the church and the people, especially when one young man, who was representing the youth, looked at me with big, pleading eyes. I knew I was going to take the call. So why didn't I?

I once didn't marry a man I was in love with because his parents were too aggressive in expressing their acceptance for me. I thought that something had to be wrong for in-laws to love a woman of another race who was older than their son. So I backed out of the relationship and ran for my life. Well, that's how I felt about this church. I had met with only the church board and the conference president, and immediately after that meeting I was offered the church. Having had no contact with the conference personnel committee, I felt there was a missing link. When I got home, there were dozens of messages on my machine, urging me to come. The final stroke came, though, when they publicly announced that I had accepted the call and it leaked back to my church.

There was another consideration that factored into this situation. After Mabel Arrington and I had become good friends, she elicited a promise from me that I wouldn't leave the Boston Temple until after she passed away. One of the former leaders of our church, who was no longer attending but who seized every opportunity to undermine me, heard that I was moving to California and called Mabel. I will never forget her disappointment and the tremendous sense of betrayal she expressed. It was no small job to convince her that I wasn't going anywhere, and in the process I convinced myself.

There have been other calls. An administrator might say, "Hyveth, you'll be the first this or the only that if you accept this call." I'm no longer enticed by these possibilities because I have been all those things. I've already paid my dues, and now I want to enjoy a normal life, if there is such a thing, until Jesus comes. As one Christian writer put it, once you have risen from the dead, there's really nothing you can do for an encore!

There are some definite joys and sorrows in ministry that shape who I am today. Some years ago, with the approval of the conference, and by vote of the constituency, we closed the Swampscott church because the congregation was too small and the neighbors too antagonistic to continue operating successfully. The dream was to sell the church and relocate it in the town of Lynn, closer to where most of the members live. This took a great deal of persuasion, and we lost some members, including the former head elder. He actually left the denomination in anger to start his own church because he would not work with a female pastor. By the many doors that have been closed in my attempts to reestablish this congregation, I have reluctantly come to the conclusion that in the same way God denied David his desire to build Him a sanctuary, so He has thwarted my plans for a church in Lynn, Massachusetts.

But the joys are numberless! Our church in Boston has become a community church. The Vacation Bible School we conduct every year has resulted in a children's choir, 75 percent of whom are nonmember neighborhood children from a variety of religious and cultural backgrounds. I once mentioned Jesus to a little Muslim child. He looked up at me and asked, "Who's Jesus?" Now they come asking for Bible studies. Most of these children have never been outside of Boston, so in 1995 I took our children's choir to Washington, D.C., where they sang at the Metropolitan Adventist Church. Then we toured the Capitol and posed for photos in front of the White House.

When one of our 12-year-old choir members was accidentally shot by her playmate and the bullet lodged in her brain, the family turned to me for help and comfort. When I arrived at the hospital, the lobby was filled with police and people from the news media. The press even came to our church that first Sabbath after the accident. Even though her mother never attended, we were recognized as Nikki's church. As we prayed for her life to be spared, a little fellow, who less than a year before had never heard of Jesus, wrapped his arms around my waist and looking into my face with his big brown eyes said, "Pastor, Nikki is going to be all right."

"How do you know?" I asked with the healthy skepticism of an old soldier.

"I asked Jesus," he answered simply, "and you told us He answers our prayers."

Today, Nikki is nearly fully recovered, thanks to the faith of a group of little children who, not so long ago, didn't even know Jesus. We receive many compliments from our church neighbors for the work we do with the children, especially in providing them with a safe haven off the streets.

Our music ministry, directed by our head organist, Kevin Budd, attracts many worshipers. Our incredible adult choir is directed by Rodney Abriol, who is completing his master's degree at the New England Conservatory of Music. Our annual Christmas concert, started by Marcia Davitt, has gained wide appreciation in the community over the past few years. And of course T.E.A.M., our family life ministry, and the Helping Hands program that feeds scores of homeless people every Sabbath afternoon and provides clothing and blankets for them and other needy families.

My personal life is also filled with great joy. Some of the wounds my son bore that strained our relationship and estranged him from me and God are being healed. I can say this with confidence because when I asked his permission to share this story, he agreed, saying he hopes it will help another son or mother whose relationship is as broken as ours was, due to the dark, deep secret that almost destroyed him. I later had second thoughts about telling his story and tried to talk him out of it. What if his boss and friends from the churches and schools he had attended read this book? His life would no longer be a secret.

My delightful son looked at me and said, "It was because of secrets that I suffered so long, trying to make sure no one knew such a horrible thing had happened to me." He shrugged. "If they judge me, they will never be able to be as harsh as I've been on myself. If my story makes a difference to only one person, it is worth it. Go ahead, Ma. I'm a free man today. The scars are gone." He hugged me hard.

The healing of our relationship began more than two years ago, while Steven was still living in Maryland. He was having a very difficult time adjusting to life. He had joined the U.S. Marines immediately after high school. During his tour of duty he abused alcohol and was so suicidal that it's solely by the grace of God he's still alive. I tried everything to bring some peace to the emotions that were driving him to such destructive behavior. When nothing worked, I knelt before God and poured out my heart. He promised me that one day my son would be His, even preaching the gospel I so love. I'm still waiting, patiently.

Recently I baptized a young lady who tried to encourage parents whose children have left the church. "If I could find God and return to the fellowship of believers, so will your children," she said.

Her testimony moved me to the depths of my being. I have dreamed of a similar scene of my son confessing his love for Christ. As I stood in the baptistry with her, I asked God, in the hearing of my congregation, why He allowed my ministry to be effective with so many young people, but not with my own son. I then appealed to them to pray for his conversion. I'll have to write another book to chronicle the tremendous difference their prayers are making in his life.

It was impossible to figure out why Steven was such a troubled young man. He was almost killed when he drove his motorcycle into the back of a truck, leaving him with a foot-long steel plate in one thigh, and a painful limp when the weather gets damp. I took him to psychologists and counselors. I prayed with him, talked with him, got angry with him, but could not get through to him.

Then came a frantic call from his girlfriend, reciting a litany of destructive behavior that was increasing with every passing day. By the grace of God, I was able to convince him to come to Boston for a brief visit.

"Steven," I began, "I want to help you, but you must want to help yourself."

He became belligerent. "Why don't you leave me alone?" he barked angrily. "It's my life, and if I want to trash it, I will!" He paced around the room.

As I watched him, the Lord gave me a discerning spirit and I realized that his words belied his body language. He wasn't seeking to die; he was crying for help. I heard myself say, "You know, son, you are acting like someone who was molested as a child."

He stood perfectly still. As I watched, the veneer of wrath peeled away and my child crumpled over the dining table in a heap, sobbing uncontrollably.

"Oh, God, no!" I screamed. "This can't be happening! This is not the key I wanted to unlock the pain!" I reached out to embrace him, but he pushed me away. He wanted to talk, but the emotions fueling his guilt and shame made him not want to be touched by his mother.

When he spoke again, he was a little child. "I was 5 years old when we lived at Colt Gardens apartments in Hartford. There was a man from Argentina, a Vietnam vet. He used to have the biggest collection of miniature army toys, and sometimes he let me play with them."

Between sobs, the words I didn't want to hear spilled out. "One day he invited me into his apartment to play with his toys, and that's when it happened."

Even though I knew what he was going to say, a voice I didn't recognize as my own demanded, "What happened?"

Steven whirled to face me with a look of such naked rage I trembled. "He raped me, Ma!" he screamed. "That animal raped me!" He turned away from me and began sobbing again. "I feel so dirty. It's my fault. I shouldn't have gone to his house. I should have fought him off. I should have—I should have—"

I pulled my boy to me, forcing him into my arms where I held him for a long time, telling him again and again how I loved him, that it wasn't his fault. He had been such a tiny baby, only four pounds and four ounces at birth . . . He was only a small boy . . . He was only 5 years old . . . Now I understood his reluctance to return to America years before.

"Why didn't you tell me?" I whispered.

"He said he'd kill you if I told." He started sobbing again. "I had to save your life, Ma!"

"Oh, God, no!" I cried. "It's true. This evil does pass from generation to generation." Taking my son's face in my hands I said, "I used to say that every man in my life had abandoned me. But now I know I'm the luckiest woman in the world—two men have given their lives for me—my son, and God's Son. I'll be eternally grateful."

Months would go by, filled with assurances that it wasn't his fault, working through layer after layer of guilt and shame, before Steven could laugh again. He's now married and has been at the same job for two years, the longest he's ever stayed in a job. He's becoming a mature, responsible young man, attempting to reestablish himself with God and man. We have a great relationship, he and I—honest, affectionate, and love-filled—making up for all those lost years. He knows now that the circumstances of our lives do not have to make us operate as chickens when we were created by God to be eagles. He's learning to soar again.

I cannot tell you the number of men and women I have met in our church who were sexually violated as helpless children, and who are struggling to keep that horrible secret while trying to adjust to the demands of life in this sinful, violent world. Some of our children who abuse drugs and alcohol, or are promiscuous and rebellious, are trying to numb the pain of a horrible secret such as this. We must begin to be a more discerning and protective community. I urge parents to be vigilant. We can never know what evil lurks, even under the kindly smile of our neighbors.

If you are the victim, or the parent of a victim, please hear this mother who has been through this experience herself and can attest there is no sorrow that God cannot heal. One day soon our Saviour will rescue us from this evil age, and we will have victory over death and liberation from every exploitation the devil uses to steal our joy and rob our children of their dignity.

And as for me? I'm still single, contented, with time to serve the Lord in ways my married colleagues cannot. While I still encounter people who are concerned about my singleness, I'm now much more tender and forgiving with those who try to be matchmakers. These days I don't argue with them, but simply humor them as I trust that God will "fix me up," if He so desires.

I've had the opportunity to travel and speak in places I only dreamed of—Australia, New Zealand, England—and soon, I'll be going to Finland and Africa.

Several years ago I began classes at Boston University, working toward a Doctor of Ministry degree. I am completing the last classes before writing a thesis. My project will be developing a preaching model for women that will also help men teach women how to preach. There are feminist (White) and womanist (Black) models of preaching, plus many books by, and about, preaching women that include great sermons, but nothing like that which I am proposing to develop to augment those already written by, and for, men. So here I go again with that old "first and only" thing!

Earlier this year Abraham and DeLois Weekes, a couple who joined our church from San Francisco, invited me to their home for dinner where I was introduced to their friend, Dr. William Rankin, dean of the Episcopal Seminary in Boston. I shared with him a brief outline of my doctoral project. A few weeks later I received a letter from the Episcopal College of Preachers at the National Cathedral in Washington, D.C. Dr. Rankin had nominated me for a fellowship, given to only four people each year, and usually only to Episcopalians. Since all the fellowships had already been awarded, they suggested that I submit a proposal for future consideration. I did, and on January 2, 1996, began a six-week fellowship, becoming, to my knowledge, the first non-Episcopalian to be so honored. Graduation from Boston University will follow in September 1996.

So here I am, finally poised to accomplish my dream. God has taught me that if I dare to dream He is able to fulfill it, as long as I trust and obey Him. My greatest desire is to see Jesus and be welcomed to the marriage of the Lamb.

So what have I learned? That no matter how dark or how brilliant our past, no matter how great or how humble our present, we have this hope: To be eternally united in Christ in heavenly places, if only we will trust and obey! Maranatha!

*The following sermon has been special to the Boston Temple congregation since I first preached it there in 1989. I now dedicate it to my son, Steve, and to all who are learning to become eagles again.*

~

# Where Eagles Fly

**M**orning had broken, yet the mist hugged the earth in a passionate embrace, defying the early sun's power to break its bewitching spell upon the land. The farmer, long acquainted with nature's ritual, seemed unaffected by the scenery as he trudged through the dew-sprinkled meadow toward the hills near his home. As he hiked along the path, he came upon a rather strange-looking egg in a nest that had evidently been dislodged from the limbs of the very tall tree under which it lay. Since he was in the business of raising chickens, the farmer was immediately intrigued by the size and shape of the egg, which he took home and placed in the incubator to be hatched with the other eggs.

It wasn't long before this strange-looking egg produced an even stranger-looking chick. Larger than the others, with a broad, white tail band, white wing patches, and feathers on its legs clear down to its toes, the chick had a peculiar air about it. Though obviously a bird like the others, it took long strides and made peeping noises instead of walking and clucking like the other chickens. Yes, it was undeniably different as it grew bigger and bigger, and more and more out of place among the other barnyard birds.

But the farmer decided to raise it like a chicken anyway. He fed that strange bird like a chicken, he treated it like a chicken, and he even called it a chicken. And since that was the only name the big bird ever knew, it began to think and act like a chicken. It moved its oversized feet awkwardly as it struggled to scratch the ground like a chicken. Although its beak was too big and clumsy to peck at the feed on the ground, that giant bird lowered its head with great determination to learn this skill. Sometimes it longed to preen its feathers like the other chickens, but soon discovered this was only one of many chicken things it would never master. Still, not wanting to be different from the others, that poor bird tried so hard to be like the chickens that by and by it no longer felt so out of place in the barnyard.

One day a visitor came to the farm, and while walking through the barnyard he saw this strange-looking bird. Surprised, the visitor asked the farmer why he had an eagle living among his chickens. Well, the farmer replied, the bird may be an eagle, but it had learned to live, eat, and think like a chicken, and since that was all the life it knew, that's all it ever would be.

The visitor argued with the farmer. No creature created by God to fly in lofty places was beyond redemption, no matter how long it had been confined to a barnyard. He said, "This bird may have the habits of a chicken, it may walk and squawk like a chicken, but deep inside it has the heart of an eagle." Determined to prove his point, he picked up the eagle, held it aloft, and said, "You're an eagle—spread your wings and fly!"

The eagle flapped its large, graceful wings, stretching those majestic pinions that lifted him, soaring toward the sky. The farmer began making clucking sounds and threw some chicken feed on the ground. When the eagle saw this, he flew right back to the ground and started to eat. Though the farmer gloated over his success, the visitor never gave up on the eagle.

Early the next morning he once more attempted to give the eagle a vision of its high calling. Taking it to the top of the barn, he pointed out the vast expanse of the beautiful countryside that was the bird's to explore as it discovered that a world existed far beyond the small barnyard. Again the visitor told the eagle that it was not a chicken, but a magnificent bird created by God to fly above the clouds. And again the eagle, now eager to discover its authentic identity, spread its wings and took off. Alas, as the bird ascended toward the sun, the farmer clucked like a chicken and threw some of its favorite chicken feed on the ground. But just as the eagle began to dive toward the feed, it heard the sound of another eagle calling in the distant sky.

The eagle's body trembled, pulsating with powerful energy as it hung almost suspended in midair, mesmerized by that haunting cry. With one great swoop, that majestic bird stretched its wings and soared toward the vast expanses of the great blue yonder. It flew up, up, up and away, slicing the air as it rose toward the dawning of a new experience. Not once did that eagle take a backward glance; not once did it look down as it soared effortlessly higher and higher toward the call of the other eagle, never to be a chicken again, but to live out its destiny where eagles fly!

Ephesians 2:1-5 presents a good description of chickens (which we all were at one time or another) before Christ came to our rescue. Even though God found us in desperate straits, He lifted us up to the level of His only begotten Son, whom He sent as the Visitor to redeem us from the barnyard of sin and deliver us to the safety of His kingdom to live with God now and forevermore as the eagles He created us to be.

Satan is like the farmer, and most of the time he captures Christians and brainwashes us into thinking we are chickens instead of eagles. In fact, we owe an entire generation of Adventist young people an apology for our gross neglect of their spiritual needs, and for our persistence on treating them more like chickens than the eagles God intended them to be. Recent statistics support the extent of the alarming dropout rate of this segment of our community. A quick trip to any local congregation will also provide enough evidence to indicate that the church is losing one of its most valuable resources at breathtaking speed. The problem has no ethnic or national boundaries. Young people from families of both church leaders and laymen, rich and poor, join the swelling ranks of disenchanted, nonparticipating church members.

How did this happen? Let me suggest the following:

First, we failed to instill in our young adults a positive vision of the hope and history out of which the Seventh-day Adventist Church was born. Many young people have little or no knowledge of our Adventist history and are genuinely frustrated with some of our tendencies to either tenaciously cling to traditions that isolate us from reality, or to water down our original beliefs and message until they become irrelevant and meaningless.

Second, the oft-repeated dictum "The youth are the church of tomorrow," a clearly unbiblical statement, has come back to haunt us in a self-fulling prophecy. The constant repetition of this statement by leaders who are reluctant to relinquish positions and open every aspect of church life to young people has diminished their interest in the Advent message and movement. Young people have heard that they are the church of tomorrow and have patiently waited to become that church. But as time passes, "tomorrow" never comes, so they leave. Of course, tomorrow never comes because the Bible teaches that tomorrow is promised to no one. The fact is, we're learning that if this generation is not made a part of the church today, they will not be a part of the church at all!

Third, and perhaps more than any other factor, the institutional and individual inconsistencies in practice and preaching of the doctrinal beliefs and lifestyle issues have contributed to young adult inactivity in our church. Some of these have their roots in homes where parents carry a double standard. Others stem from the local congregation where many young people have to contend with the hypocrisy of members who gossip about other church members six days a week, then pose as pious protectors of the faith on Sabbath.

Fourth, it should be obvious to us by now that many of the programs and projects in which we invest huge sums of money seldom, if ever, attract or appeal to young people. It ought to be evident that large tents, multiple-media evangelism, and even Revelation seminars are not the keys to winning the loyalty of this productive, resourceful, highly educated generation of believers. Therefore, every energy should be channeled and every resource pooled to find creative solutions to this real dilemma. But we don't even discuss it openly, as though our silence will make the problem go away.

I am convinced that God wants to end this eerie parade of young adults walking out the door of His church. That's part of the reason He has allowed this church [the Boston Temple] to continue in its present location, in the heart of a community where thousands of students and young professionals live and search for their purpose in being. We have the awesome challenge before us to be the catalyst of change, drawing young people out of their obscure existence into a vibrant life with the Lord and His church. If you have been previously perceived as chickens, this is a warning to our observers that beginning today, we've begun to spread our wings and there's only one way to soar—up where we belong, where eagles fly!

The eagle is a familiar symbol in the Scriptures. Why does God single out this bird above all others to symbolize character traits He wants His people to embody? Perhaps because of its steadfastness, diligence, unswerving loyalty, and tender care for its young.

It is interesting to note that eagles are not as easily reproduced as chickens, and no matter how well-disguised, once an eagle, always an eagle. So it is with royalty. You may know the story of the prince and the pauper, in which the young prince swapped his royal throne and clothing for the rags of a street urchin. The prince sent him to take his place in the palace, while the young prince moved among the beggars and paupers to discover how he could better serve all the people in his kingdom. But no matter how hard he tried, or how tattered his dress, everyone who came in contact with him recognized that he did not belong among the beggars. He had a regal bearing, a peculiar air and speech that contradicted his shabby appearance. It was exactly that distinction that eventually revealed his secret and forced an end to his charade so that he had to return to his throne sooner than he planned.

According to Philippians 2:5-8, Prince Michael willingly chose to become Jesus Christ, the God-man, made lower than angels, a pauper, if you please, so that He could teach the poor in spirit and the slaves to sin how to live as princes in the kingdom of God. One of the most striking qualities that caused those who knew Jesus to be constantly amazed was His unique ability to present the familiar themes of God with authenticity and authority. People marveled because He did not speak like the scribes and Pharisees, but spoke with freshness and great wisdom, qualities that are quickly disappearing from among our people. Why? Perhaps because we've forgotten that we are princes and princesses of the royal household of God with all the rights and privileges to so live.

If anything marks us as chickens, it's our increasing inability to handle the great themes of the everlasting gospel with compassion and charity. We are content to sit on unique Adventist perches where we repeat meaningless mottos about having the truth and being the remnant, vain words that no longer have the power to convince ourselves, much less to convert those around us. We are fast becoming overpopulated with uniform birds of a feather who flock together once a week to pat our soft bellies, boast about our pointed beaks, and muse over our little heads that continue to hold fewer and fewer spiritual ideas and more and more philosophical ideologies. We've become chickens who are too chicken to take the risk for God and dare to be different. We desperately need keen-eyed, wide-winged creatures who are willing to soar where eagles fly, to explore the unlimited ranges of the kingdom of God. Jesus is asking us to be His eagles today. Will we?

Christian author Chuck Swindoll describes "eagle thinkers," who are very different from chicken people. Chicken people like to stay on the spiritual ground where it is safe, where they can feel the earth beneath their feet, earth carved out by the blood, sweat, and tears of risk-taking eagle pioneers. They like to pick over the same old feed and listen to the same old words, again and again, until they can follow the pattern by rote. They like to travel in groups, giving a little scratch here, or a little peck there from time to time, pulling up an occasional worm. They can stay in the same yard, in the same rut, year after year, and I bet you can't remember the last time you saw a chicken fly. Chicken people are predictable, secure, boring, and as long as they have someone to throw a little feed to them at regular intervals, they are content with their lot. Most of the time they would rather starve or swallow junk than go out and find fresh food for themselves. They are always threatened by young, eager eagles who dare to spread their wings and fly.

If you want to know who the chickens in a church are, just listen to their complaints. They're the ones who are always disgruntled and critical because they seldom take the time to do more than scratch the surface of the Word of God. But not so the eagles. There's not a predictable pinion in their majestic wings! They love to think. They are driven by an inner urge to search, to discover, to learn. They are courageous, spiritually vibrant, tough-minded, willing to ask hard questions and perform intense, objective self-examination, bypassing the routine in pursuit of fresh, vigorous truth. Unlike the intellectually impoverished chicken, eagles take risks getting their food because they hate overprocessed food that is boring, repetitious, dry, and out of context with their personal experience and needs. When they encounter a problem, they come up with creative solutions.

An eagle-minded congregation would consider innovative approaches to combat the tide of disenchanted members. They would require consistent preaching of the gospel of Jesus Christ and practicing of the fundamental doctrines in the Bible. They would create aggressive programs that clearly announce that the church not only loves its young people, but cannot survive without them. An eagle-minded congregation would urge members to become involved with young people, applying the warmth of compassion rather than the whip of criticism to nurture them back into respected, full-fledged fellowship, so that they can cease to feel like they are chickens and dare to be eagles.

In every culture the eagle is recognized as a rare bird, a king of birds, a prized national emblem. Although the dictionary classifies the eagle as a large bird of prey, related to hawks, experts on birds identify the existence of only two species of eagles in North America—the golden and bald eagles. All other species of eagles are said to be extinct. Chickens are so common they've never made the endangered species list. No matter how many chickens are killed for food or fun, they just keep on multiplying, while the eagle remains one of the most protected species in the animal kingdom. It is as uncommon and irreplaceable in its kingdom as you and I are in the kingdom of God. Perhaps that's why God so often uses the eagle as a symbol of His people, while the chicken, which represents those who rebel against Him, seems to multiply faster than we can count them. Furthermore, it is more likely for an eagle to think it is a chicken, and learn to live like one, than for a chicken to pass itself off as an eagle. And in spite of all its outstanding characteristics, it's much easier to shoot down an eagle than a chicken. That is why we need fewer chickens and more eagles on our religious skyline.

Another eagle quality to be emulated by God's people is its unlimited strength. Hans K. LaRondelle has written an impressive book entitled *Deliverance in the Psalms.* When he discusses Psalm 103:5, he points out that an eagle, unlike other birds, can live as long as 100 years and retain its vitality, youthfulness, and strength and be as fresh and vigorous on the day it dies as the day it winged its way from its mother's nest. Perhaps that's why Isaiah uses it as a symbol in chapter 40:28-31. No matter how wild the weather, an eagle can fly in the eye of the storm and is never smashed by the fierce winds against the rocks. It uses its great strength to rise high above the storm into clear, calm skies.

To be an eagle person means that you, too, possess the power to face the storms of life and rise above them. Storm clouds will always appear, and we cannot run from them. We must confront them in the strength of the Lord as we soar in the calm air of His presence. Eagle people take advantage of the rising air and the strong currents of opportunity that come with storms. They may be buffeted and beaten from all sides by raging winds, but still they can spread their gracious wings and glide above the torrents to find rest and peace in God. Being an eagle person may be a lonely experience. Not everybody understands eagle people. And what we humans don't understand, we fear. What we fear we attack, reject, or attempt to destroy.

In spite of all the threats, we are no longer chickens. Young people, you are no longer chickens. Little children, you are certainly not chickens. All of us are eagles, created to spread our majestic wings and fly away from the common things into the sacred bosom of our loving Lord and be at rest. Not tomorrow, not soon, but now, today, while it is yet today! Now listen well, because I want you to hear what I am about to say. No amount of church going, hymn singing, long praying, religious talking, pious walking, or working for our salvation will put power into our wings so that we can fly away from the dark, deadly barnyard of this world where we are held captive. Only the call of God, heard through the preaching and teaching of His Word and relived in personal testimonies, individual devotions, and corporate Bible studies, can lift us up where we belong, where the eagles fly.

I once attended a boarding school in Jamaica. It was a Christian school, administered by a family from Scotland for the children of the rich and famous from around the world. Eventually the Jamaican government decided that some of its poor children should have an opportunity to enjoy the benefits and resources which, until then, had been exclusively reserved for wealthy foreigners. To gain entrance into this school, one had to pass a tough exam and win a scholarship. I was fortunate to be among the first 12 students to receive this prestigious opportunity.

I had the reputation even then of being very different from the rest of the crowd, someone who was not afraid to take risks, even if such risks resulted in the harshest punishment. One rule forbade those of us who didn't have straight hair to use hot combs to straighten our hair, forcing us to wear it natural in an "Afro." There's nothing wrong with wearing one's hair natural, but this was long before the early 1960s when Afros became the symbol of what's Black and beautiful. So it was always embarrassing for me to have this huge, uncontrollable bush on my head while nearly everyone else had neat braids and bows.

At the beginning of each term our suitcases were thoroughly searched at registration time, and all our silk underwear and straightening combs were confiscated as tools of the devil. I figured that if I took a dinner fork and heated it over one of the kerosene lamps in our dorm (we didn't have electricity yet), I could do a reasonable job of straightening my hair. One day while I was busily burning myself to death with one of these hot forks, the girls' dean caught me red-handed. I was sent to sleep in the basement for two weeks. What was so horrible about this punishment was that no one in their right mind ever ventured to walk alone in the basement at night because it was rumored that vicious ghosts and hostile spirits roamed the place, seeking living souls on whom to vent their pent-up rage.

I was sent to sleep in that basement for two weeks, and I lived to talk about it! I didn't encounter a single ghost, hostile or friendly, during that time. At the end of my punishment everyone was eager to hear every detail of my "dungeon" experience. Of course, I was happy to oblige with spine-chilling tales of encounters with horrible spirits. One afternoon just as the sun was setting, I stood before a large group of girls seated on the steps of the girls' dorm, painting vivid word pictures of my struggles with the different spirits I'd met in the basement. The girls were hanging on my every word, every now and then screeching in fright, when the dean walked by.

"Hyveth, you will never amount to anything," she said. "You'll always have one sordid story or another to tell. Today it's about your experience in the basement. Maybe when you grow up it'll be about your exploits in prison. In any case, young lady, you'll never amount to anything!"

I was already striving for acceptance by lying, but when she said those words I was transformed from a young eagle, eager to soar among the possibilities of life, into a chicken who spent the following years barely scratching the surface of my true potential. Those words became a branding iron that seared into my subconscious mind to haunt me until Jesus rescued me. (As it turned out, I was told later that the dean was the one who spent time in prison for helping her family defraud the government out of thousands of dollars of scholarship funds.) I was driven to despair. I determined I would prove her wrong and win her approval by becoming somebody. But no matter how hard I worked, no matter how much I attained, I still heard the dean's voice saying that I'd never amount to anything. I drove myself harder every day, sometimes to the point of burnout, to make sure those words would never come true in my life. And after all that was done, I still ended up being afraid I would never amount to anything.

Perhaps some of you are broken images of who you truly are and are haunted by negative self-messages echoing in the halls of your minds. No matter how well-dressed or well-educated we are, we've come with misgivings about ourselves, painfully aware of our inadequacies, bowed low by the storms of life, hostages of childhood experiences, broken by failed relationships, and disappointments in life. All seem to confirm that we were raised like chickens and that's what we'll always be. Some of you have been told on too many occasions, by parents and peers, teachers and preachers, that you are chickens until, unfortunately, you've come to believe and accept it.

But listen to what the Word of God says in Ephesians 2, verses 4 and 5: *"But God,* [emphasis supplied] being rich in mercy, because of His great love with which He loved us, even when we were dead in our transgressions, made us alive together with Christ (by grace you have been saved)," and called you eagles, made to reign with God in majesty, like princes and princesses. You must not settle for anything less. You must not allow the meanness, the jealousy, others' lack of vision to make you chickens. You are eagles! Get off your proverbial perch of self-pity and exchange the safety and comfort of your barnyard existence to soar, to explore the wide horizon of God's Word and will. As Pastor Swindoll says, eagles are awkward in barn-yards and are awful misfits among chickens. They look pretty silly trying to pick over tasteless, dry feed on the ground when their beaks were made to tear into the living Word made flesh.

Let us, like the eagle, make our majestic flight above the clouds of spiri-tual mediocrity into the pure air of the Word of God. Let us soar with the spir-itual eagles whom God has strategically placed around us to call us to higher planes where eagles fly. Let us soar up where we belong, where eagles fly!

# On Wings of Praise

## by Kay D. Rizzo

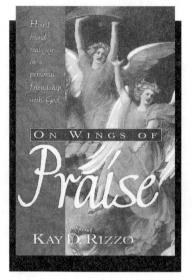

K ay Rizzo shares how praise to God lifted her from her "spiritual winter" and filled her life with a joy and power she had never known. "I discovered that praise was a *choice*, not a response," Rizzo writes. And her conscious decision to praise God in all things had a profound effect on both her personal and spiritual life. "Prayer combined with praise changed my heart," Rizzo says. "It will change yours, too." In this upbeat book she shows you how.

Paper, 171 pages.
US$12.99, Cdn$18.99.

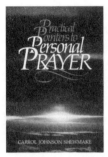
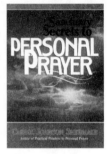

# The Incredible Answers to Prayer Series

## by Roger Morneau

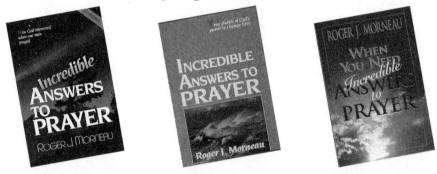

ROGER MORNEAU is a man of incredible faith. When he prays, things happen. And it's exciting! As a result, he's received thousands of letters and telephone calls from people requesting intercessory prayer. He shares many of those requests in this series along with God's thrilling answers.

He also shows how you can walk more closely with God, share His power and love with others, and receive incredible answers to prayer. Titles include *Incredible Answers to Prayer, More Incredible Answers to Prayer*, and *When You Need Incredible Answers to Prayer*.

Paper, US$7.99, Cdn$11.49 each.
Also available on video. US$34.95, Cdn$50.45 two-volume set.